DATE DUE

PREPARING
FOR THE WORKPLACE

✳

CHARTING A COURSE FOR FEDERAL
POSTSECONDARY TRAINING POLICY

Janet S. Hansen, *Editor*

Committee on Postsecondary Education
and Training for the Workplace

Richard P. Nathan, *Chair*

Commission on the Behavioral and Social Sciences and Education

National Research Council

NATIONAL ACADEMY PRESS
Washington, D.C.   1994

NATIONAL ACADEMY PRESS • 2101 Constitution Ave., N.W. • Washington, D.C. 20418

NOTICE: The project that is the subject of this report was approved by the Governing Board of the National Research Council, whose members are drawn from the councils of the National Academy of Sciences, the National Academy of Engineering, and the Institute of Medicine. The members of the committee responsible for the report were chosen for their special competences and with regard for appropriate balance.

This report has been reviewed by a group other than the authors according to procedures approved by a Report Review Committee consisting of members of the National Academy of Sciences, the National Academy of Engineering, and the Institute of Medicine.

This project was supported by the U.S. Department of Education.

Library of Congress Cataloging-in-Publication Data

Preparing for the workplace : charting a course for federal
  postsecondary training policy / Janet S. Hansen, editor ; Committee
  on Postsecondary Education and Training for the Workplace ;
  Commission on the Behavioral and Social Sciences and Education,
  National Research Council.
      p.   cm
    Includes bibliographical references and index.
    ISBN 0-309-04935-0
    1. Career education—Government policy—United States.
  2. Postsecondary education—United States. 3. Federal aid to higher
  education—United States. 4. Labor supply—Effect of education on.
  I. Hansen, Janet S. II. National Research Council (U.S.). Committee
  on Postsecondary Education and Training for the Workplace.
  III. National Research Council (U.S.). Commission on Behavioral and
  Social Sciences and Education. IV. Title : Federal postsecondary
  training policy.
  LC1037.5.P72   1993
  378'.013—dc20   93-37934
                                                                    CIP

Printed in the United States of America

The National Academy of Sciences is a private, nonprofit, self-perpetuating society of distinguished scholars engaged in scientific and engineering research, dedicated to the furtherance of science and technology and to their use for the general welfare. Upon the authority of the charter granted to it by the Congress in 1863, the Academy has a mandate that requires it to advise the federal government on scientific and technical matters. Dr. Bruce M. Alberts is president of the National Academy of Sciences.

The National Academy of Engineering was established in 1964, under the charter of the National Academy of Sciences, as a parallel organization of outstanding engineers. It is autonomous in its administration and in the selection of its members, sharing with the National Academy of Sciences the responsibility for advising the federal government. The National Academy of Engineering also sponsors engineering programs aimed at meeting national needs, encourages education and research, and recognizes the superior achievements of engineers. Dr. Robert M. White is president of the National Academy of Engineering.

The Institute of Medicine was established in 1970 by the National Academy of Sciences to secure the services of eminent members of appropriate professions in the examination of policy matters pertaining to the health of the public. The Institute acts under the responsibility given to the National Academy of Sciences by its congressional charter to be an adviser to the federal government and, upon its own initiative, to identify issues of medical care, research, and education. Dr. Kenneth I. Shine is president of the Institute of Medicine.

The National Research Council was organized by the National Academy of Sciences in 1916 to associate the broad community of science and technology with the Academy's purposes of furthering knowledge and advising the federal government. Functioning in accordance with general policies determined by the Academy, the Council has become the principal operating agency of both the National Academy of Sciences and the National Academy of Engineering in providing services to the government, the public, and the scientific and engineering communities. The Council is administered jointly by both Academies and the Institute of Medicine. Dr. Bruce M. Alberts and Dr. Robert M. White are chairman and vice chairman, respectively, of the National Research Council.

Contents

v

Preface

As of March 1991, 79 percent of U.S. men and women 25 years and older had not attended 4 or more years of college. How are these people prepared for work? This is a big question and a major concern in the country. The role of the federal government in the field of work force preparation is the subject of this report. At various times during the 2-1/2 years that our committee worked on this study, we talked about calling our report "The Other 79 Percent" as a way to dramatize the challenge of our inquiry.

Increasingly, opinion in the country has coalesced around the proposition that a high-skills, high-productivity work force is the key to the nation's ability to compete in an ever more interconnected global economy. Yet, as our report says right in the first sentence, "postsecondary training for the workplace is a troubled enterprise in the United States."

The National Research Council was asked by the U.S. Department of Education to establish our committee to address the question of what the federal government's role in postsecondary training ought to be. We had two first-order definitional questions to answer in our work: What do we mean by postsecondary training? What is the present federal role in this enterprise?

In answer to the first question, we defined our universe as including organized activities supplied by schools, employers, or other agencies and organizations that provide training, apprenticeship, and skills development for the workplace focused on individuals who have a high school diploma or who are older than the average high school student. This universe includes much of the work of community and technical colleges, proprietary schools, area vocational and adult schools, community-based organizations, apprenticeship programs, employer-sponsored training programs, and military training programs. We identified four types of training that individuals need at the post-high-school level: qualifying training to prepare for initial entry to the work force, skills improvement training for people on the job, retraining when economic changes make jobs obsolete, and second-chance training for those with low levels of education and skills that hamper their employability.

It is worth noting that arguably the single most dramatic development in all of American education in the last 30 years has been the growth of community colleges. Enrollment has grown nearly sevenfold since the early 1960s: it is now close to 5 million people in 1,000 community colleges in which occupational programs are a major component.

Our second question about the federal role in postsecondary preparation for the workplace is much more important than at first blush might seem to be the case. In a word, the federal role is *small*. Expenditures through federal postsecondary training programs amount to about $20 billion annually, but this is only a small fraction of what state and local governments, employers, and individuals spent on training activities. Postsecondary activities are also highly fragmented within the federal establishment. The largest programs (excluding those for military personnel) are found in the Departments of Education, Labor, and Health and Human Services, but several other cabinet departments are also involved.

Because the federal government shares responsibility for work force training with so many other actors, issues of federalism and governance were central to our analysis. State governments have the lead role among governments in postsecondary training. Local governments, private profit-making (proprietary) schools, nonprofit community-based groups, and private firms are also major actors. The biggest federal activity in support of postsecondary training comes not through direct aid to institutional providers, but through grants and loans to students. Many of these students attend proprietary schools, where new controversies have arisen about their practices.

As our deliberations proceeded, we constantly encountered—at every level of government—a lack of systematic thinking and action to provide individuals—and this is what counts—with ways to find and obtain the best preparation to be productive workers. Overcoming fragmentation and incoherence and improving the quality of postsecondary training are even bigger needs than making individual federal training programs work better, though it is obviously important to do the latter as well. Our final chapter discusses six functions we believe the federal government should undertake to help move the nation towards a coherent and high-quality postsecondary training system that meets the needs of both workers and employers for all the training that individuals will need over the course of their working lives.

Much of our attention was devoted to the key role of states in providing postsecondary training and to identifying ways the national government could stimulate and facilitate strong action at the state level to integrate and strengthen programs for workplace preparation. In our view, the federal government should act as a catalyst and agent of change on a basis that draws on and reinforces the best practices of the leading states that have taken a systemic approach to work force development.

In the usual way in a preface, we pay tribute to the people who helped us do our job. Most important of all, Janet S. Hansen served ably, patiently, and energetically as the study director for our committee. She moved over (or up) from being a member of the group at the outset of our work to the position of study director in December 1991. We thank her for agreeing to do this. Janet was a tiger in our meetings, pressing us all the time to be rigorous and to tell her (best of all in writing) exactly what we meant. We tried very hard to meet her standards.

The U.S. Department of Education sponsored this project. Many officials of the department and other federal agencies assisted us and our staff throughout our endeavors, and we thank them. We are especially grateful to our project monitor, David Goodwin, and to Maureen McLaughlin of the Department of Education and to Barry White and Cynthia Brown of the Office of Management and Budget. They met numerous times with the committee and provided a valuable perspective on the questions facing federal policy makers responsible for designing and implementing postsecondary training programs. We also want to acknowledge the contributions of the late Fred Fischer of the U.S. Office of Management and Budget, who was instrumental in identifying the need for this study.

At the National Research Council, Alexandra K. Wigdor, director of the Division of Education, Labor, and Human Performance, provided critical guidance on the study process. Daniel Levine served ably in helping to organize our committee. Research associate Laurel McFarland (on leave from the Brookings Institution) assisted in getting the study launched and in framing initial avenues for the committee to investigate; she also drafted several helpful background papers. Upon her return to Brookings, Barry Sugarman took up responsibility for many of the fact-finding and data-gathering tasks so important to a committee like ours. At a crucial period late in the study, Gerald Hauser, serving as an intern, picked up on the substance of the study amazingly quickly and was enormously helpful in filling in holes in the draft report. Throughout the study, Cindy Prince, our project assistant, attended to the myriad administrative needs of the study and to the care and feeding of the staff and committee members with skill

and good humor. She and Elaine McGarraugh also had the important responsibility of ensuring the accuracy of the manuscript as it wound its way
through the editorial process. Jeffrey Porro, editor, helped improve the
presentation of the committee's ideas. Eugenia Grohman supervised the
editing of the manuscript and shepherded it through publication. We thank
them all.

The committee also appreciates the assistance we received from a group
of scholars literally from around the world who prepared background papers
to inform our deliberations. We are grateful for the ideas offered by Larry
Bailis, Sara Connolly, Robert Gregory, Arthur Hauptman, Julia Lane, Sarah
Liebschutz, Lisa Lynch, Thomas Rauberger, James Rosenbaum, David Stern,
and Margaret Vickers. In particular, we note the contribution made to our
discussions by Richard Elmore, whose paper on improving the quality of
postsecondary training became the core of Chapter 6.

As the chair, I get a final word on the committee itself, the way it
congealed, and how we worked together to find our way in a field that is
broad-gauged and in many ways more institutional and policy-laden than
the usual territory of a National Research Council committee. As is often
the case, there were moments of excitement (to put it politely) as we compared notes and rubbed ideas together, first to learn, then to agree on findings, and finally to work out how we view the federal role in postsecondary
training for the workplace. One member of the group said at the final
meeting that he was happy to have us conclude our deliberations and hoped
never again to see us all at the same time. He was kidding, of course, but
the point is that any such group has to work hard at coming together. I
thank my colleagues for their help and support in doing this. I am proud of
the work we did and hope they are, too.

> Richard P. Nathan, *Chair*
> Committee on Postsecondary
> Education and Training

PREPARING FOR THE WORKPLACE

✳

CHARTING A COURSE FOR FEDERAL POSTSECONDARY TRAINING POLICY

Executive Summary

Postsecondary training for the workplace is a troubled enterprise in the United States. Although it is not in crisis, it suffers from a number of shortcomings that, if not addressed, can impede the nation's ability to provide a prosperous future for U.S. workers. The federal government is not the primary sponsor of postsecondary training, but it can be a critical catalyst in moving the enterprise toward the quality and coherence it currently lacks.

Improving the skills of American workers is not a panacea for the nation's economic problems, but it is important. Workers' inadequate skills can keep businesses from adopting advanced technologies and transforming themselves structurally in the ways that are necessary to use the technologies most effectively. Many analysts believe that the United States must follow a high-skill, high-wage path to remain economically competitive in a rapidly changing world. Even if this high-skill, high-wage future turns out to be overstated, better training will improve the economic well-being of those who are well trained.

Improving postsecondary training for the workplace has implications for a majority of the nation's workers. Fewer than one-quarter of Americans attend college for the 4 or more years needed to receive a baccalaureate degree. Many of the others, representing most present and future U.S. workers, do pursue some kind of formal or informal preparation for work after leaving high school. Yet public policy has tended to concentrate on the two ends of the training spectrum—high school and college—rather than on the middle ground in between.

1

Despite the lack of an explicit focus on postsecondary training, the federal government has over the years evolved an array of programs that provide support for job training. Several dozen programs in seven different cabinet departments provided $20 billion to state and local governments, training providers, and individuals seeking training in fiscal 1991. The largest of these expenditures are found, not in the programs typically regarded as the focal points of federal training policy—such as the Carl D. Perkins Vocational and Applied Technology Education Act and the Job Training Partnership Act—but in the grants and loans provided by the U.S. Department of Education to students in occupationally oriented postsecondary institutions.

Recent problems in the student aid programs (particularly in occupationally oriented schools), coupled with a more general concern about the existence of multiple federal programs aimed at job training, led the Department of Education to ask the National Academy of Sciences to establish a committee to look at postsecondary education and training for the workplace. The committee was asked (1) to help the federal government consider the implications of multiple federal approaches to the provision of postsecondary vocational education and job training; (2) to consider policy alternatives, ranging from increased coordination of existing programs through reallocation of resources to entirely new approaches; and (3) to make recommendations for a coherent and efficient federal policy on postsecondary preparation for work.

FINDINGS

A future of skilled jobs for well-trained workers requires attention to the economic and labor market environment in which training occurs, to employer needs and to patterns of developing technology, as well as to the training policies addressed in this volume. That both demand and supply affect outcomes, however, does not reduce the need to seriously assess weaknesses in the training of the work force and to try to improve the way U.S. workers are trained.

There are four kinds of work-related post-high-school training that modern economies usually believe it necessary to provide: (1) qualifying training, initially preparing people for work; (2) skills improvement training, for employed individuals who want further education and training to upgrade their skills and increase their job mobility; (3) retraining, for those who have been or are about to be displaced from their jobs and so need to prepare for a new line of work; and (4) "second-chance" training, for individuals who need some combination of basic education and job skills, perhaps in combination with other social services, to reach economic self-sufficiency through employment.

Although postsecondary training is not primarily a federal responsibility, the multibillion dollar expenditures of the federal government on postsecondary training can influence the direction and efficiency of that training in the country. At present, however, there is little attention given to how federal programs affect worker training and little understanding of whether the various parts accomplish what they are supposed to or of how the parts relate to each other.

In fact, the biggest problem is that the United States does not really have a training *system* at all. That is, postsecondary training in the United States is not coherent, readily accessible, closely connected to the world of work, with clearly visible and positive effects on those trained, and of acceptable and measurable quality. In an ideal system, individuals seeking to enter or advance in specific occupations would know what kind of training employers value and where to find it. Employers would know what skills and competencies have been developed as a result of training programs. Individuals would have the information they need to gauge their interest in and suitability for various jobs, as well as the likely demand for workers in various fields. Employers would have information about the existing and future supply of trained workers and the means to signal their needs to training institutions.

Instead of such a system, the committee found a variety of providers and programs that supply very good training to some people but less adequate or no training to many others. Although qualifying training is readily accessible to many people, the range of options is undoubtedly confusing to some. Qualifying training relies heavily on schools; workplaces are much less often used as formal learning sites. For different reasons, skills improvement training, retraining, and second-chance training are all less widely available.

Evidence about the results of training is less thorough than we would like, but on balance the results are positive, though sometimes modest. Some kinds of training, particularly for disadvantaged youth, do not appear to be working. The quality of training is mixed, and processes for quality assurance are underdeveloped. Linkages to employers are often weak.

At the crucial level of local labor markets, programs and providers sometimes work together in more harmony than the fragmented national picture would suggest, but the pieces seldom add up to anything that can be described as a system. The federal government, with its proliferation of programs and lack of a coherent overall approach, bears part of the blame for this situation. In recent years a number of states have begun to restructure their programs and processes to more systematically and effectively address work force development. The spread of such efforts is encouraging, though it is too early to evaluate their effect in any formal way.

CONCLUSIONS AND RECOMMENDATIONS

The committee concludes that the most important task facing the federal government is to help the nation focus its attention on linking the various pieces of and partners in postsecondary training in ways that will provide coherent and high-quality training opportunities for individuals at various stages in their working lives.

We believe that federal policy should have three major objectives:

(1) fostering high-quality training;
(2) improving existing federal programs; and
(3) encouraging systemic reform.

It is not enough to improve the existing array of categorical programs aimed at specific needs, although improvements must be made. More important is that the federal government must take the lead in promoting policies that encourage quality and coherence in the training system as a whole. We believe that the federal government must be a catalyst in encouraging postsecondary training to evolve in ways that better meet our criteria for a well-functioning system.

The term *postsecondary training system* as used in this report encompasses the notion of a variety of state and local systems, not a single national model. Coherence in postsecondary training is ultimately rooted at the local labor-market level. States are central to developing a training infrastructure that will meet local needs, because they are responsible for many of the training institutions and much of the public funding for training. Thus, a national system should, in fact, be composed of a variety of systems that differ somewhat among states and localities but that present potential trainees and employers with integrated training opportunities and information.

Principles to Guide Federal Action

In developing policies to address these objectives, the federal government should adhere to seven principles.

1. *The federal government should refocus its attention, emphasizing the importance of building a postsecondary training system rather than continuing the piecemeal approach that has characterized past efforts.*

The biggest needs in postsecondary training are for systemic approaches to training and for structures that can tie together the different parts of training and let individuals move easily among them.

There are no "one-size-fits-all" or "magic-bullet" solutions in a country in which the responsibility for training is highly decentralized and when the four types of training needed by workers are so different from one another that multiple approaches and programs are inevitable. Federal policies in the past have paid attention to the differences. All forms of training are related, however, as parts of the process of initially preparing and continuously improving the nation's work force. Good public policy now requires the federal government to give attention to linking the parts together in ways that are coherent to both workers and employers.

2. *While not reducing its commitment to fostering equity, the federal government should give special attention to the problem of ensuring quality, in response to the pervasive sense that the quality of American training is at best mixed and often poor.*

Too little is known about what is actually accomplished by training and what happens to those who are trained. Too little information about the outcomes and results of training is available to potential trainees and those who hire them. The problem of ensuring quality is admittedly complex in a decentralized system, but the federal government can encourage improvement in the quality of postsecondary training in ways compatible with American traditions and institutions.

Another way of improving the overall performance of the postsecondary training system is for the federal government to respond to the information that is available about what works and what does not and to make changes when there is evidence that public programs are not achieving their goals. Youth training programs are a good example. The nation should not abandon its concern for high-risk youth because current youth training does not appear to benefit participants. But decision makers should acknowledge forthrightly that current approaches are not working and should aggressively explore new avenues.

3. *The federal government should pursue changes in postsecondary training through policies that emphasize continuous improvement rather than radical reform.*

Much is unknown about what constitutes good practice in training for work and about the effects and outcomes of work-oriented training institutions and programs. At the same time, this is a vital period of innovation and analysis. At such a time, it is more appropriate for the federal government to encourage experimentation, evaluation, and policy evolution than to attempt a radical overhaul of its or the nation's approach to training activities. The approach we propose requires the federal government to think in new ways about how it manages public programs. Part of the federal role in continuously improving postsecondary training should be to evaluate the pace at which good practices are adopted and to determine what kinds of technical assistance and incentives might encourage faster diffusion.

One particular area in which the federal government can make an important contribution is in encouraging experimentation with and evaluation of promising training practices and structures that are used in other countries. One example of an approach more prevalent abroad is the use of workplaces rather than schools as training sites for qualifying training. Other countries also have connecting structures and standard-setting mechanisms that tie the training system together: these approaches may lend themselves to adaptation in the United States.

4. *The federal government should recognize the key roles that states play in the development of an effective training system.*

State governments are responsible for a wide range of domestic programs, making it logical for them to have the lead role in implementing training policy. The federal government should not micromanage programs of training for the workplace. States have demonstrated staying power and the ability to innovate effectively over the past decade in a number of related policy areas, including welfare reform, school reform, and economic development.

5. *The federal government should seek to enhance the involvement and stake of employers in training policies and systems.*

Linkages between employers and the world of training need to be stronger because the success of training ultimately depends on its usefulness in the workplace. Involving employers in systemic reform efforts is crucial to securing their attachment to the training system. But employers' interests are not the only interests that must be served by training; their needs must be balanced with the needs of those who require not only firm-specific training but also broader and more transferable skills.

6. *The federal government should resist the temptation to spread its resources so thinly that little or no effect is possible.*

With federal resources constrained by the budget deficit, it is more important than ever to focus available funds where they can do the most good. In addition, focusing resources on successful programs or programs likely to be successful can help create true partners in support of the programs; improve the reputation of training programs and thus reduce the stigmatization of participants, especially those in second-chance programs; and reduce the complexity created by the existence of dozens of (often very small) federal programs.

7. *"Do no harm": federal policy makers should recognize that it is possible for federal programs to hurt people and should be cautious about extending "help" in such circumstances.*

One way that federal programs can actually harm people can be seen in student loan programs. If individuals purchase training that offers little hope of giving them the capacity to pay back loans, they have a high chance of becoming defaulters. They risk often unpleasant pursuit by loan collectors, finding their credit records damaged, and losing future eligibility for student assistance for which they might otherwise have qualified. Those who design public policies should avoid creating situations in which individuals are likely to be harmed by participating in a public program.

Fostering High-Quality Training

The primary aim of postsecondary training policy should be the development of state and local systems of training that provide high-quality training to individuals throughout their working lives.

In thinking about how this goal could be accomplished, the committee gave a great deal of attention to the question of whether performance management and standard-setting, which are being increasingly adopted in federal training programs, are likely to be effective tools to improve the quality of postsecondary training. Our analysis led to three major conclusions.

1. *The impulse behind performance management and the spread of performance standards in federal programs is praiseworthy, but the complexities involved suggest that a cautious approach is warranted.*

Standards can be specifications of how well a person or entity is performing on a specific measure or indicator (as in the Job Training Partnership Act performance management system), or they can be statements embodying a coherent vision of what an individual should know or be able to do at a given stage in his or her educational development (as in the curriculum standards for mathematics and science being developed by various professional groups).

Standards can, in the right circumstances, produce a variety of benefits: providing clearer guidance and direction for education and training institutions; focusing providers primarily on outputs rather than inputs; encouraging greater coherence and coordination among services aimed at similar populations; improving accountability; improving evaluation and diagnosis; and certifying institutions and credentialing individuals. However, there are a number of complex problems involved in designing standard-setting systems, problems that become even more complex in the decentralized and fragmented world of postsecondary training.

Even when federal authority is clear, as in a program like the Job Training Partnership Act, the difficulty of distinguishing overall program outcomes from the value added (impact) of a program means that standard-setting is not an easy process. The possibility of perverse results from standard-setting efforts leads us to urge caution in tying performance standards to outcomes, care in the use of incentives and sanctions when they may lead program administrators to emphasize inappropriate objectives, and work to develop better ways of measuring effects and reflecting them in the standard-setting process. We also urge, along with improving outcome-oriented standards, that attention be given to so-called design standards that are process oriented (rather than emphasizing either inputs or outcomes) and that focus on spreading the adoption of validated best practices about how to conduct training programs.

2. *The federal interest in quality assurance must extend beyond federal programs if the entire postsecondary training system is to improve; this suggests an approach to standard-setting emphasizing changing institutions rather than regulating federally funded activities.*

Much of postsecondary training lies beyond the clear influence of the federal government. Performance management should go beyond its traditional focus on establishing measures and standards in specific federal programs, aiming instead for improvement in the entire postsecondary training system.

There are two general approaches available for the task of standard-setting. The first, currently found in federal performance management systems, assumes that any federal effort to set standards should be focused on the recipients of federal funds and that federal money is the federal government's main source of leverage. The second, which we prefer, assumes that the federal government's interest in improving the quality of training goes beyond just those providers and recipients directly affected by federal funds. In this view, the federal government has two main sources of leverage—its funding and its capacity to set a national agenda and mobilize key institutional interests behind that agenda.

We recommend that the federal government pursue a quality assurance approach to postsecondary training that reaches beyond the providers and recipients of federally funded training and that attempts to influence the entire training system through: fostering the development of voluntary, national, occupationally based skills standards; improving information systems; and building capacity for improved performance in the providers of postsecondary training.

3. *The federal government should emphasize continuous improvement*

rather than top-down management strategies that focus on regulatory compliance in its approach to quality assurance.

This approach is more compatible with the diffuse authority exercised by the federal government in many parts of the postsecondary training world. Emphasizing improvement rather than compliance also helps to avoid the danger that standard-setting for postsecondary training will degrade into a minimum-standards approach.

Improving Federal Programs

The committee believes that the federal government needs to make sure that its own postsecondary training programs work as well as possible. We recognize that the existing array of programs reflects different training needs as well as a diversity of financing mechanisms. We did not find strong arguments for such design changes as "voucherizing" all support for postsecondary training or converting all programs to contracts with service providers. We also found that little is known about the effects of many current efforts. For these reasons, we do not recommend a radical restructuring of federal postsecondary training programs. Rather, we argue for continuous improvement and propose a number of initial steps to enhance current federal activities:

1. Qualifying training
    a. Support and evaluate the institutional integrity provisions of the 1992 Higher Education Act amendments designed to increase state oversight over institutional eligibility for federal student aid programs.
    b. Augment the institutional integrity provisions by requiring states to use employment and wage records to monitor the posttraining performance of all vocational programs in which significant numbers of students borrow through federal student loan programs.
    c. Conduct a demonstration project allowing one or more states to determine the eligibility of training programs within postsecondary institutions for federal student aid funds based on criteria the state would propose.
    d. Conduct a limited number of large-scale demonstration projects to test the feasibility of expanding youth apprenticeship programs, while also working to integrate youth apprenticeship into a system of structured school-to-work pathways for youth that include other career-oriented approaches, such as Tech-Prep, career academies, and cooperative education.

2. Skills improvement training and worker retraining
   a. Promote the adoption of new forms of workplace organization, make firms aware of training options, and sponsor experiments and demonstration projects with new labor market structures that would enhance workplace restructuring.
   b. Consolidate federal programs for dislocated workers.

3. Second-chance training
   a. Increase the federal matching rate in the Job Opportunities and Basic Skills (JOBS) program to encourage full participation by states.
   b. Test innovative and far-reaching second-chance strategies for disadvantaged youth, in recognition that current approaches are not producing positive results for this important group.
   c. Extend the experimental approach to evaluation that has contributed significantly to the evolution of federal training and welfare programs to the field of adult basic education and the activities funded under the Adult Education Act.

Encouraging Systemic Reform

Although we have strong reservations about the federal government's trying to micromanage programs, we believe that it has an important new role to play as a catalyst or agent of change in encouraging systemic reform.

We find there are six functions through which the federal government could encourage the building of a postsecondary training system: (1) making grants (primarily to states) to help them build public and private capacity to act in system-like ways; (2) rationalizing conflicting federal requirements; (3) granting waivers upon application from states who need relief from federal rules to carry out systemic reforms; (4) creating the framework for the development of national skills standards; (5) conducting research and fostering the development of integrated information systems; and (6) reporting annually on the state of the American work force.

We reviewed a number of alternative vehicles through which the federal government could carry out those functions. Most of us concluded that existing arrangements are inadequate to the role we believe the federal government should play and that a new mechanism is needed if the federal government is to contribute meaningfully to the transformation of postsecondary training.

The option we analyzed most carefully involves creation of an Office of Work Force Development, modeled on the National Science Foundation. We envision an office with high visibility and significant powers to lead the federal effort to spark improvement and reform in postsecondary training by carrying out most or all of the functions just described. We think it is crucial to involve important nonfederal constituencies in the activities of the office and would do this in various ways, including careful composition of the office's governing board and a skills standards oversight board and the use of a peer review process to advise on the approval of grant applications and waiver requests. We would like to see this office "pick winners" quite consciously, rather than operating in an automatic and formulaic way.

All of the committee members agree on the need for the federal government to become an agent of change in the task of building a strong postsecondary training system in the United States. We differ somewhat on the best vehicle for carrying out this role. We all believe, however, that the federal government should take on the functions we have identified and, with them, a new and critically needed role as catalyst in encouraging the development of a training system equal to the world's best.

1

Introduction

Is the American system of work-related education and training strong enough to meet the challenges posed by an increasingly competitive world economy? How do federal programs, particularly those supporting postsecondary training, contribute to developing the skills of the nation's work force, and how can they be improved?

Historically, local decision makers have determined education and training activities in the United States. States and localities have been primarily responsible for funding and organizing school-based preparation for work. Employers have determined how much work-based training takes place and which of their employees have received it. Individuals have chosen their own training, with little guidance, in a wide variety of institutional settings. Only "second-chance" opportunities for the disadvantaged, including the unemployed and those on welfare, have been the special responsibility of the federal government. Nevertheless, the federal government has developed an array of programs supporting preparation for employment (see Chapter 2).

Among the largest of these programs are the grants and loans administered by the U.S. Department of Education under the Higher Education Act. These grants and loans provide over $20 billion annually in assistance to students in postsecondary programs (College Board, 1993).[1] Between one-fourth and one-third of this total goes to students in vocational programs that do not lead to baccalaureate degrees. These grants and loans are the largest single source of federal funding for postsecondary vocational training, although they were not designed with the needs of vocational students and schools in mind and were not originally envisioned as a major source of funds for work-related training. High default rates on student loans among vocational students brought not just the loan programs but all of student aid into disrepute in the 1980s.

Student aid problems and concern about the number of federal programs aimed at job training led the U.S. Department of Education to ask the National Academy of Sciences to establish a committee to look at postsecondary education and training for the workplace. The committee was asked to help the federal government assess the implications of multiple federal approaches to the provision of postsecondary vocational education and job training; to consider policy alternatives, ranging from increased coordination of existing programs through reallocation of resources to formulating entirely new approaches; and to make recommendations for a coherent and efficient federal policy on postsecondary preparation for work.

THE COMMITTEE'S CHARGE: POSTSECONDARY TRAINING

The charge to the committee to look at *postsecondary* preparation for work has directed our analysis toward those components of work-related education and training occurring after high school rather than focusing on high schools themselves, which have received so much national attention in recent years. While high schools are the building block for what comes after and cannot be neatly divorced from subsequent preparation for work, their operation lies largely beyond our purview. (We want to acknowledge, however, that there are important questions about how high schools should be involved in preparing young people for work that warrant more attention than we have given them. In addition, the apparent failure of secondary education to provide adequate preparation for large numbers of people has important consequences for postsecondary education and training, in particular focusing it more on remediation than we wish were the case. Thus, our failure to speak extensively about secondary school issues does not mean that we think our current system is operating as it should.)

In the education world, *postsecondary* has a fairly clear and limited meaning, but the definition becomes fuzzy when extended to the employment arena. The U.S. Department of Education, in its Institutions of Postsecondary Education Data Survey (IPEDS), defines postsecondary education as "the provision of formal instructional programs whose curriculum is designed primarily for students who have completed the requirements for a high school diploma or its equivalent. This is to include programs whose purpose is academic, vocational and continuing professional education, and to exclude avocational and adult basic education programs" (U.S. Department of Education, 1988:2-2).

Postsecondary education takes place in 2-year and 4-year public and private nonprofit colleges and universities, in proprietary profit-making trade schools whose programs may last from a few months to several years, and in public vocational-technical schools that offer post-high school programs of 2 years or less. Federal student aid programs use essentially the IPEDS definition to determine eligibility, with some restrictions as to the length of the program, its credit status, and the full-time or part-time enrollment status of the student. However, institutions that clearly fall within this definition of postsecondary, such as community colleges, also offer programs (such as adult basic education) that are excluded from the definition.

Postsecondary education can be academic or vocational. The Carl D. Perkins Vocational and Applied Technology Education Act of 1990, which provides federal funds to states for distribution to school districts, schools, community colleges, and technical institutes, defines vocational education as "organized educational programs offering a sequence of courses which are directly related to the preparation of individuals in paid or unpaid employment in current or emerging occupations requiring other than a baccalaureate or advanced degree." The term vocational education can apply to both high school and post-high school programs. This frequently leads to ambiguity in discussions of vocational education.

The closer one gets to education that is occupation oriented, the greater is the problem of distinguishing between *education* and *training*. *Education* has the connotation of being longer term in nature, and emphasizing the development of cognitive skills (although job- or occupation-specific preparation may be offered as well), leading to a credential such as an associate, bachelor's, or graduate degree. It is typically thought to take place in schools and colleges. Training connotes a shorter-term program that emphasizes the specific skills needed in a particular job or occupation (although these skills have cognitive as well as technical dimensions). Such programs may lead to a certificate, diploma, or technical associate's degree, but they do not necessarily carry with them any formal credential or academic credit. Training takes place not only in schools and colleges, but in many other settings as well; for example, community-based organizations and workplaces.

Accepting the distinction between education and training, this report focuses on training: preparation for work that takes place in programs other than those leading to transfer-oriented associate, baccalaureate, or advanced degrees. Persons who undergo job training can be broadly categorized into four groups: (1) those who seek initial preparation for employment, largely young people who have not yet been employed in full-time jobs and, to a lesser extent, women entering the work force for the first time; (2) employed individuals who desire continuing education and training to upgrade their skills and increase their job mobility; (3) those who have been or are about to be displaced from their jobs and who need to be retrained in preparation for entering a new line of work; (4) people who have "fall[en] out of a 'normal' developmental progression that should lead to eventual self-sufficiency through employment" and who need some combination of social skills and resources, basic academic skills, or job-related skills in order to obtain a job (Bailey, 1987:165). The latter group is the traditional target of the so-called second-chance employment and training programs designed to improve the fundamental workplace competencies of the unemployed. In this volume, we refer to the four kinds of training sought by these different groups as qualifying training, skills improvement training, retraining, and second-chance training.

Federal programs cover all four types of training, ranging from financial aid that subsidizes qualifying training and (to a much lesser degree) skills improvement training to the Job Training Partnership Act (JTPA) that offers retraining for dislocated workers and second-chance training for the disadvantaged. To carry out effectively the U.S. Department of Education's mandate to review the multiple programs supported by the federal government, only some of which are postsecondary programs in the narrow sense, and to make recommendations for a coherent and efficient federal policy on postsecondary preparation for work, the committee has adopted a broad definition of postsecondary training.

For the purpose of this study, therefore, *postsecondary training refers to organized activities, supplied by schools, employers, or other agencies and organizations, designed to prepare individuals with high school diplomas or who are older than the typical high school student so that they can obtain or advance in jobs that do not require a baccalaureate or advanced degree.*

Who Gets Postsecondary Training?

More than 50 percent of Americans obtain postsecondary training as we define it, which is, roughly, training after high school not leading to a 4-year degree. As of March 1991, only 21 percent of the U.S. population aged 25 and over had attended 4 or more years of college, and 22 percent had finished less than 12 years of schooling (Bureau of the Census, 1992a). In between these categories, 18 percent had completed 1-3 years of college and 39 percent had completed 4 years of high school. Since the "1-3 years of college" category includes only enrollment in what the Bureau of the Census calls "regular schools" (colleges and universities granting degrees), it excludes much of the proprietary trade school sector and thus underestimates the proportion of the population that should appropriately be counted in the post-high school, sub-baccalaureate group. It also excludes individuals whose highest formal educational credential is a high school diploma but who have received training for work in nonschool settings. As an upper bound, the group for whom postsecondary training is potentially important encompasses the three-fifths of the population sandwiched between the highly educated one-fifth at the top of the qualifications ladder and the high school dropouts at the bottom.

This is a heterogeneous group, composed of individuals who started but never finished baccalaureate degrees, those who earned formal postsecondary training credentials, and high school graduates who may or may not have participated in formal training that did not occur in "regular schools." When adults without high school diplomas are added in, about four-fifths of the adult population are included.

Despite rising levels of educational attainment, college completion remains the exception, even among young people. The proportion of high school graduates proceeding directly to work after high school fell throughout the 1980s; postsecondary schooling rates increased over the same period (Haggstrom et al, 1991:29). Nevertheless, the proportion of 25- to 29-year-olds who have completed 4 or more years of college has remained virtually unchanged, at 23 percent, since 1980 and is actually lower than it was in the mid-1970s (Bureau of the Census, 1992a:97).

Postsecondary Training for What Jobs?

The 1991 survey by the Bureau of Labor Statistics (BLS) (1992) of how workers were trained for their jobs provides data on the incidence of postsecondary training and identifies the occupations for which this training is especially important. At the same time, it illustrates the fluidity of occupational training in the United States, especially in middle-level positions where people enter similar jobs through different training routes.[2]

Table 1.1 indicates that, in 1991, 57 percent of workers aged 16 and over reported that they needed specific skills or training to obtain their current or last job. Schools were the single most-frequently cited source of this training (reported by one-third of workers), followed by informal, on-the-job training (27 percent of workers). Since workers could report more than one source of training, the proportion of people who reported needing training of some kind (57 percent) is less than the sum of the proportions who reported needing training of various specific types.

Schools providing postsecondary training were important sources of qualifying training for technicians and related personnel. Individuals who depended on school-based postsecondary training to qualify for their jobs were most apt to be working as inhalation therapists, stenographers, dental hygienists, licensed practical nurses, physicians' assistants, funeral directors, boilermakers, radiological technicians, electrical and electronic technicians, and administrators in protective services.

TABLE 1.1   Sources of Qualifying Training by Occupational Group for
Workers (in percent), 1991

Occupational Group	Workers Who Needed Training	School Training			
		High School Vocational Education	Post-high School Vocational Education	Junior College or Technical Institute	4-year or Longer Program
Total, all occupations	57	4	3	8	20
Executive, administrative, and managerial	72	3	2	9	36
Professional specialty	92	1	3	10	69
Technicians and related support	86	5	8	24	28
Sales occupations	43	1	1	4	11
Administrative support	55	11	3	10	9
Private household occupations	10	2	—	1	1
Service workers, except private household	37	2	4	6	3
Farming, forestry, and fishing	28	2	1	2	5
Precision production, craft, and repair	62	6	4	9	4
Machine operators, assemblers, and inspectors	38	3	1	3	1
Transportation and material moving	42	1	1	2	—
Handlers, equipment cleaners, and laborers	20	1	—	1	1

NOTES: — indicates value too small to display or data not available. Because some workers
took more than one type of training, individual items may not sum to totals.

SOURCE: Bureau of Labor of Statistics (1992).

Company training was cited most often by public transportation atten-
dants; structural metal workers; aircraft and aircraft engine mechanics; tool
and die makers; elevator installers and repairers; police, detectives, and
their supervisors; locomotive operators; insurance salespersons; supervisors
of guards; and electrical power installers and repairers.

Informal, on-the-job training was especially important for administrators of protective services; surveyors and mapping scientists; printing ma-
chine operators; camera, watch, and musical instrument repairers; supervisors in agricultural occupations; construction inspectors; data processing
equipment repairers; industrial engineers; statistical clerks; and personnel
and labor relations managers.

Formal Company Training	Informal On-the-Job	Armed Forces	Correspondence Course(s)	Friends, Relatives, or Other Nonwork-Related Training
12	27	2	1	7
17	37	3	2	9
11	25	2	1	8
17	31	5	1	8
13	26	1	1	7
10	30	1	1	4
1	3	—	—	4
9	18	2	—	7
2	17	1	—	12
19	36	5	2	12
8	25	1	—	5
11	24	1	—	10
3	14	—	0	4

The BLS survey asked workers if they had had any training to improve their skills since obtaining their present jobs. About 41 percent of workers received such training. Workers relied less on schools for this skills improvement training than for qualifying training. However, their use of formal company programs and informal, on-the-job training (16 percent and 15 percent, respectively) was only marginally higher than their use of schools for upgrading their skills (13 percent). These patterns vary by occupational type. Table 1.2 shows that workers most apt to participate in skills improvement training are found in the same occupations as those most likely to get qualifying training: executive, administrative, and managerial; professional specialty; and technicians and related support.

TABLE 1.2   Sources of Skills Improvement Training by Occupational Group for Workers (in percent), 1991

Occupational Group	Workers Who Took Training	School	Formal Company Program	Informal On-the-Job Training	Other
Total, all occupations	41	13	16	15	7
Executive, administrative, and managerial	53	18	25	18	12
Professional specialty	67	34	20	17	15
Technicians and related support	59	20	26	22	9
Sales occupations	35	7	16	15	6
Administrative support	40	12	16	16	4
Private household occupations	6	2	0	1	3
Service workers, except private household	29	7	9	13	5
Farming, forestry, and fishing	21	7	3	7	7
Precision production, craft, and repair	38	9	17	16	4
Machine operators, assemblers, and inspectors	25	4	8	15	2
Transportation and material moving	25	2	10	11	3
Handlers, equipment cleaners, and laborers	15	1	5	9	1

NOTE: Because some workers took more than one type of training, individual items may not sum to totals.

SOURCE: Bureau of Labor Statistics (1992).

Postsecondary Training and the Labor Market

The labor market environment in which individuals and firms operate conditions and influences their decisions to undertake or provide training.

Individuals elect to pursue training from a variety of training providers when they believe the training will benefit them. Their assessment depends on what is being offered; the costs to them of the training, net of scholarships or other subsidies; their ability to obtain loans to fund training; and the information they have about providers and opportunities. Their assessment of benefits and costs is also affected by other social and economic policies, such as the availability of and conditions of eligibility for welfare and income support benefits for the unemployed or underemployed.

An equally broad but different set of considerations influences the decisions of firms about whether and how much training to support, because employer-sponsored training represents a joint decision by employer and employee. Much of the value of employer-provided training hinges on the continuing relation between employer and employee. No employer wants to train a worker if that worker is likely to leave soon with skills that he or she can use elsewhere (unless the worker agrees to work at relatively low pay).[3] And no worker will willingly accept low wages for training if he or she has little or no job security.

The American labor market is distinguished among industrialized nations by a high degree of mobility among workers, particularly young workers, who switch employers frequently in their search for the right "fit" (Organisation for Economic Co-operation and Development, 1993:Chapter 4). This mobility is widely thought to discourage employers from providing training, since their investment in an employee can be lost if the worker takes the skills learned to another firm. There are, to be sure, important benefits from having a highly mobile work force. Among other things, there is much to be said in favor of young people moving around from employer to employer to find the job that most suits them, just as there is much to be said for consumers shifting their purchases until they find the right product. But the committee detected growing concern about the costs posed by a labor market that discourages firms from training in an increasingly competitive global economy, as our discussion in the next section and subsequent chapters indicates.

Any labor market system involves a host of structures and policies in addition to explicit training policies that impinge on individuals' and firms' training decisions. Training may be more prevalent in the presence, for example, of labor relations policies that encourage employee participation in firm decision-making or of high minimum wage requirements that make it difficult for firms to adopt low-wage, low-skill production strategies. Job mobility can be influenced by public policies and/or social mores that limit the wage gains from job-hopping or that impose costs on firms who hire employees trained by others. It is clear that the United States has a labor market system that differs in important respects from those overseas (see Chapter 4). What is not yet clear is whether the differences should be viewed as strengths or as weaknesses. Those who study labor markets are giving increasing attention to the impacts and implications of diverse institutional arrangements.[4] The tradeoffs from different approaches are complex, however, and there is no consensus that any particular set of institutional arrangements is best.

Whether and how to reform broader labor market institutions and policies in the United States was beyond the committee's scope. While we allude from time to time to these broader concerns, we focus primarily on a narrower question: given current labor market realities, how can the federal government improve its diverse set of postsecondary training programs? Thinking about how to rationalize and improve this one part of our labor market system proved to be a formidable undertaking by itself. We hope we have provided a foundation on which more extended investigations into the nation's employment and training policies can be built.

Postsecondary Training and the American Economy

Fears about the future of the American economy have become widespread in the 20 years since 1973, when productivity growth in the United States decelerated. Growth of labor productivity between 1973 and 1979 averaged only 0.9 percent per year, less than one-half of its previous, long-term level. The years 1980 to 1990 saw only a slight revival at 1.2 percent per year. Slow productivity growth meant a slow growth in earnings adjusted for inflation and threatened the hopes of many for a rising standard of living. Older workers do not have the same prospects for income growth as they would have had several decades ago: whereas a 40-year-old man working full time in 1948 saw his earnings nearly double in the succeeding 25 years, a 40-year-old man working full time in 1973 actually saw his earnings drop 4 percent by 1989. Younger workers fared worse: the earnings of young (25 to 34 years old), male, high school graduates working full time in 1989 were 15 percent lower than those of their counterparts 10 years earlier (Murnane and Levy, 1992). Total compensation (including fringe benefits) shows the same pattern of rapid pre-1973 growth and slow post-1973 growth seen in the data on earnings (U.S. President, 1992:95; Levy and Michel, 1991:8).

While the United States still has the highest level of labor productivity in the world, its advantage has narrowed as its rate of growth in output per employee has lagged behind that in such countries as Japan, Germany, France, Italy, and the United Kingdom. The nation has come to fear for its ability to compete economically. These fears have coincided with a rising concern about the quality of the nation's schools. The influential study, *A Nation at Risk*, was published by the Secretary of Education in 1983 (National Commission on Excellence in Education, 1983) and sparked a heated controversy over whether the nation would have an adequately trained work force to meet the global challenges of the twenty-first century.

The link between economic competitiveness and the quality of the work force has been controversial, however. Debate has raged over whether changes in the nature of work require more or less skill on the part of workers. Is the workplace being "upskilled" or "deskilled"? Does the nation need to increase its investment in its human resources, or might we improve education and training only to find that we have "too many smart workers for too many dumb jobs" (Carnevale, 1992:28)? Although the committee's focus is not on these questions per se, we are very aware that they do raise serious analytical and policy issues.

The upskilling-deskilling debate is largely an issue of "whether new technology, especially computer-based technology, has led to a reduction or an increase in skills required at the lower and middle levels of the employment hierarchy" (Bailey, 1989:2). After a quarter-century when the economy demanded increased skills, and a generation of workers trained with the help of the G.I. Bill enjoyed steadily increasing real earnings, pessimism set in during the mid-1970s. Case studies found evidence of deskilling in clerical occupations, computer programming, and manufacturing at the same time that an increasing proportion of the work force was employed as professionals or managers.

The fact that the wage premium paid by employers for college graduates fell seemed to bear out the hypothesis that the United States was increasing its supply of highly skilled workers more rapidly than employer demand. Researchers also proposed life-cycle theories of technological change to explain why a need for advanced skills could be found among people working with new technologies while skill levels fell as a technology matured. Occupational projections suggested that low-skilled occupations would add the largest number of new jobs to the economy and that low-skilled occupations would grow faster than high-skilled ones. But another turnaround began in the mid-1980s as the wage premium paid to more highly educated workers rose sharply. Case studies and occupational projections now suggested that there was not a "proliferation of powerless, low-skilled workers" and that, in many instances, skill demands were increasing.

Bailey attributes the changing perspectives on how technology affects skill requirements to a too narrow definition of jobs and tasks, a simplistic approach to the effects of technology, and an unwarranted tendency to assume that similar technological changes have similar effects no matter the historical context in which they are introduced. Defining jobs as a series of well-defined tasks caused researchers to underestimate the effects of technology. While certain tasks might be simplified by new technology, jobs could be reorganized in ways that, taken as a whole, result in a greater demand for skills as a result of technological change.

Some analysts allege that the strategies that firms must use to cope with the new global environment—more decentralized and flexible forms of organization; team approaches to work and other forms of workplace experimentation; new, closer, and more responsive relationships between suppliers and customers—can have major implications for the skills needs of their workers and thus their human resource strategies. Bailey's research on four industry sectors (apparel, textiles, business services, and financial services) and a review of recent occupational trends and projections suggest that the required level of skills in the workplace is increasing. Studies done by Kochan and Osterman (1991), Mishel and Teixeira (1991), and Murphy and

Welch (1993) confirm this picture of a generally rising demand for skills in the economy. The wage premium for educated workers has been growing; part of the explanation appears to be that new technologies are more complementary with skilled than unskilled labor. Berman et al. (1993) report that U.S. manufacturing firms that invest more in computer technologies and research and development also show larger increases in demand for educated workers. Immigration and imports have also played a role in the shifting demand toward educated workers. Apparently, immigrants and the low-skill labor embodied in import production are better substitutes for low-skill than high-skill workers.

Still, the increasing proportion of jobs at the bottom of the wage scale and the apparent ability of employers to adjust to the low skills of workers show that the economy can generate low-skill jobs without causing insurmountable problems for employers. Workers, however, cannot make a decent living in this manner.

Some argue that America's competitive position in the world and ability to provide a satisfactory standard of living to its citizens depend on shifting to "high-performance workplaces" that utilize skilled workers more extensively than in the past. The Commission on the Skills of the American Workforce (1990) identified (and titled its report) *America's Choice: High Skills or Low Wages!* and argued that "America is headed off an economic cliff" unless it develops a skilled work force for reorganized, high-performance workplaces (p. 8). Others use different descriptive terms to make essentially the same argument. Osterman (1988), for example, contrasts the "industrial" and "salaried" models of organizing work, observing that the industrial model "is under increasing attack and most of the innovations in human resource policy in the past decade can be read as efforts to move away from and transform this system" (p. 69). Porter (1990) argues that the United States is at a critical point, with important choices to be made about improving its human resources and a growing need for companies to "begin investing more in their employees and viewing them as assets" (p. 726). Kochan and Osterman (1991:2) summarize the argument for transforming work and the work force:

> Debates over the development of human resources have taken on added importance in recent years with the growing recognition that our competitiveness and standards of living depend so greatly on our ability to gain competitive advantage through high-quality human resources. In a world where firms in advanced industrial economies find it difficult to compete on the basis of low labor costs, United States firms must find other sources of sustainable competitive advantage such as technological superiority, product innovation, quality of goods and services, etc. All of these alternatives to cost competition are thought to depend on having a high-quality labor force and organizational policies that allow human potential to be fully

realized. This approach rests on the premise that higher skills and better utilization of human resources within the firm pay off in higher productivity, product quality, or other measures of economic performance.

The U.S. Office of Technology Assessment (OTA) (1990:115) shares a similar view of the changing organizational patterns in United States industry, which it captured in a series of contrasts between old and new models (see Table 1.3).

But, while many believe that it is desirable to move toward high-skilled, high-wage jobs and high-performance workplaces, it is not clear that American firms are moving rapidly in this direction. Osterman (1988) argues that both objective constraints and managerial ideology are more likely to lead most firms to a stalemate and little change rather than to a transformed workplace. Bailey (1989) finds some evidence of change in the four industries he examined, including a growing demand for workers with 2-year college degrees; but Mishel and Teixeira (1991) claim that Bailey's conclusions, based on a relatively small and selective sample, are too optimistic about the extent to which a substantial transformation of the content of jobs is taking place. Kochan and Osterman (1991:43) conducted eight case studies in a sample of United States plants in high-technology industries and found that "only two of the eight could be described as being deeply committed to human resource development." The authors of *America's Choice* (Commission on the Skills of the American Workforce, 1990) and the head of a major business group involved in studying training issues (Carnevale, 1992:30) assert that only 5 or 1 percent, respectively, of American workplaces have been transformed along lines of the high-skills model. A new national survey across a representative range of American industries (Osterman, 1993:5) found that "thirty-five percent of private sector establishments with fifty or more employees have achieved substantial use of flexible work organization."

The BLS training surveys (1985, 1992) appear to support this mixed picture. There is some evidence that workers are getting more training, particularly skills improvement training. In 1991, 41 percent of workers reported having received training to improve their skills, compared to 35 percent in 1983. But the percentage of workers reporting qualifying training was only slightly higher, at 57 percent in 1991 compared to 55 percent in 1983. Perhaps the most dramatic change between the two surveys occurred in employer-sponsored training. Employers sponsored significantly more skills improvement training in 1991 (for 16 percent of workers) compared to that in 1983 (11 percent). These findings would be consistent with a movement within firms to jobs that require more highly skilled workers. At the same time, the 1991 survey also reveals that the United States is far from an economic structure in which most jobs require and most workers receive significant amounts of training. Barely half of all workers reported

TABLE 1.3 Changing Organizational Patterns in U.S. Industry

Old model: mass production, 1950s and 1960s	New model: flexible decentralization, 1980s and beyond

Overall Strategy

Low cost through vertical integration, mass production, scale economies, long production runs	Low cost with no sacrifice of quality, coupled with substantial flexibility, through partial vertical disintegration, greater reliance on purchased components and services
Centralized corporate planning; rigid managerial hierarchies	Decentralization of decision making; flatter hierarchies
International sales primarily through exporting and direct investment	Multimode international operations, including minority joint ventures and nonequity strategic alliances

Product Design and Development

Internal and hierarchical; in the extreme, a linear pipeline from central corporate research laboratory to development to manufacturing engineering	Decentralized, with carefully managed division of responsibility among R&D and engineering groups; simultaneous product and process development where possible; greater reliance on suppliers and contract engineering firms
Breakthrough innovation the ideal goal	Incremental innovation and continuous improvement valued

Production

Fixed or hard automation	Flexible automation
Cost control focuses on direct labor	With direct costs low, reductions of indirect cost become critical
Outside purchases based on arm's-length, price-based competition; many suppliers	Outside purchasing based on price, quality, delivery, technology; fewer suppliers
Off-line or end-of-line quality	Real-time, on-line quality control
Fragmentation of individual tasks, each specified in detail; many job classifications	Selective use of work groups; multiskilling, job rotation; few jobs classifications
Shop-floor authority vested in first-line supervisors; sharp separation between labor and management	Delegation, within limits, of shop-floor responsibility and authority to individuals and groups; blurring of boundaries between labor and management encouraged

TABLE 1.3 *Continued*

Old model: mass production, 1950s and 1960s	New model: flexible decentralization, 1980s and beyond
Hiring and Human Relations Practices	
Work force mostly full time, semi-skilled	Smaller core of full-time employees, supplemented with contingent (part-time, temporary, and contract) workers who can be easily brought in or let go, as a major source of flexibility
Minimal qualifications acceptable	Careful screening of prospective employees for basic and social skills and trainability
Layoffs and turnover a primary source of flexibility; workers, in the extreme, viewed as a variable cost	Core work force viewed as an investment; management attention to quality-of-working-life as a means of reducing turnover
Job Ladders	
Internal labor market; advancement through the ranks via seniority and informal, on-the-job training	Limited internal market; entry or advancement may depend on credentials earned outside the workplace
Governing Metaphors	
Supervisors as policemen, organization as army	Supervisors as coaches or trainers, organization as athletic team. (The Japanese metaphor: organization as family)
Training	
Minimal for production workers, except for informal, on-the-job training	Short training sessions as needed for core work force, sometimes motivational, sometimes intended to improve quality control practices or smooth the way for new technology
Specialized training (including apprenticeships) for grey-collar craft and technical workers	Broader skills sought for both blue- and grey-collar workers

SOURCE: U.S. Office of Technology Assessment (1990:115).

receiving *any* kind of qualifying training, and only two-fifths took training to improve their skills.

While this book analyzes training policies, creating a future of skilled jobs for skilled people requires paying attention to employer demand and to the pattern of developing technology as well. Simply increasing the skills of workers will not ensure a more prosperous future for American society. As suggested in the last section, it is not enough to focus on the supply side of the labor market: the nation will need to consider diverse policies that affect the level and composition of labor demand as well. These include human resource development strategies by firms (Kochan and Osterman, 1991); differential investment in physical capital or intangible assets such as research and development; organizational development, such as supplier relationships for firms; macroeconomic growth policies; and efforts to increase national savings and reduce the deficit. That both demand and supply affect outcomes does not, however, reduce the imperative to assess seriously weaknesses in the training of the work force and to try to improve the way the United States trains its workers.

The following chapters show that postsecondary preparation is not all that it could or should be. Inadequate work force skills can impede firms' efforts to adopt advanced technologies and transform themselves structurally so that they can use these technologies most effectively (Levy and Murnane, 1992:1373). Without adequate skills among the work force, the economy will be slow to move along a high-growth, high-wage path, regardless of changes elsewhere in the economic system. Even if the high-wage, high-skill future that most analysts want to see develop in the United States is more a dream than a reality, better training will, at the minimum, raise the wages and enrich the lives of those workers who learn those skills. America needs to ensure, therefore, that its institutions and programs for postsecondary training function as well as possible.

STRUCTURE OF THE REPORT

Although postsecondary training is not primarily a federal responsibility, the multibillion-dollar expenditures of the federal government on postsecondary training can influence the direction and efficiency of skill formation throughout the country. At present, however, there is too little thinking about how federal programs affect the training system, and too little attention is being paid to whether the various parts accomplish what they are supposed to. The remainder of this volume lays out how federal expenditures affect postsecondary training and offers suggestions for improvement.

Chapter 2 describes how postsecondary training is provided in the United States and the kinds of postsecondary training current federal programs were designed to support. It shows how the existing array of federal programs developed one at a time, over several decades, to meet the needs of particular subsets of the population. Chapter 3 examines how well postsecondary training is being carried out, in order to pave the way for a discussion of whether the federal government needs to do more in the future to shape the overall contours of the system or to provide more postsecondary training directly. The evidence shows that, in a number of ways, this system does not operate well. Individuals and society will be better off if ways can be found to make it work better. Chapter 4 describes several key features of training in four other countries. Chapter 5 presents the committee's general conclusions about whether a change in the federal approach to postsecondary training is needed. If change is needed, what kinds of activities are most appropriately undertaken at the federal level and how can the federal government most effectively exercise its influence, given the limits on national policy in a system largely determined by state and local officials and private firms? We discuss these issues in Chapter 5, which sets the stage for the presentation of our more specific views on desirable changes in federal policies and programs in Chapters 6 through 8.

NOTES

1. Federal assistance provided to students through grants and loans is greater than federal expenditures on grant and loan programs because the loan programs to date mostly involve government guarantees and interest subsidies rather than the direct provision of loan capital. Capital comes largely from banks, though some schools and state agencies also put up capital for federally guaranteed loans. In fiscal 1992, $15.6 billion was lent to students in the various loan programs authorized by the Higher Education Act; federal expenditures on loans in that year amounted to $7.3 billion. Changes in the loan programs enacted in 1993 will shift the source of capital in the future. By academic year 1998-1999 60 percent of loan volume will come in the form of direct federal loans rather than federally guaranteed private loans.

2. This observation needs to be qualified, in terms of the BLS surveys, by the fact that the job classifications used are frequently imprecise. "Accountants," for example, can mean anything from bookkeepers to professional certified public accountants. Nevertheless, it remains true that pathways to many jobs in the United States are remarkably diverse. For example, among electrical and electronic technicians, only 63 percent reported having received their qualifying training in schools (about two-thirds in vocational schools or community or technical colleges, but some in high schools and some in 4-year colleges). Twenty percent cited company training, 31 percent on-the-job training, and 16 percent training in the armed forces (Bureau of Labor Statistics, 1992:54). (Percentages do not add to 100 because workers could report more than one source of training.)

3. This is in part the problem of general versus firm-specific skills, first explored by Becker (1964). General skills are valuable not only to the employer providing the training, but to other employers as well. Specific skills are of value only to the employer who gives the training. Firms will be reluctant to provide general skills training if they believe that trained workers can move easily to other employers. Moreover, if job mobility is high, firms may also be reluctant to provide even specific skills training because of the fear that the employee will leave before the employer recoups the training investment.

4. One such effort is Freeman (1994).

2

Overview of Postsecondary Training Institutions and Programs

Federal programs supporting postsecondary training for work cannot be understood apart from the institutions where this training takes place. The federal government does not directly provide training except—and it is a major exception—for training for its own employees, including the military. Instead, federal programs operate through a set of diverse institutions over which Washington has varying (and often quite limited) influence and which frequently have multiple purposes in addition to those established by federal mandate.

This chapter presents an overview of these institutions and examines the array of federal programs that have grown up to support postsecondary training. The following chapter identifies and assesses concerns that have arisen about the ability of these institutions and programs to provide the nation with a highly skilled work force.

INSTITUTIONS OF POSTSECONDARY TRAINING

The landscape of postsecondary training has become increasingly complex. At midcentury, vocational education was found predominantly in high schools. High school vocational programs have recently faded in importance as enrollments declined. They have declined for a variety of reasons, including the continuing low status of vocational education, the emphasis on academic achievement during the 1980s, and changes in state policies, such as increasing the number of academic courses required to receive a high school diploma.

Meanwhile, occupation-oriented education has become a key course of study at community colleges and postsecondary technical institutes, supplemented by training in area vocational schools that enroll both secondary and postsecondary students. In a wide variety of fields, profit-making, privately owned proprietary trade schools offer courses that require from a few months to 3 or 4 years to complete. Short-term job training programs, funded by both the states and the federal government, have spurred the establishment of special community-based training organizations that serve the clients of these government programs almost exclusively. Employers provide a great deal of formal and informal training to their employees and contract with vendors and consultants as well as with schools for additional courses. Employers also cooperate with labor unions to sponsor apprenticeship programs for individuals seeking to enter certain occupations. In addition to these major providers of training, which we will examine more closely below, other organizations, such as professional associations, also help give people needed job skills.

Community and Technical Colleges

The most noticeable change in the landscape of American postsecondary education in the past 30 years has been the phenomenal growth and increasingly vocational orientation of publicly funded 2-year colleges. Community and technical colleges have grown and expanded more quickly than any other level of postsecondary education. Enrollment at such institutions grew from 740,000 in the fall of 1963 to 4.9 million in the fall of 1990.

Of all undergraduate enrollment in 2- and 4-year colleges and universities more than 40 percent can be found in community and technical colleges. In the fall of 1990, part-time students accounted for 65 percent of public, 2-year college enrollments (National Center for Education Statistics, 1992c). Because many students at these institutions are not enrolled for a full academic year, the total number of students who participate at some point in the year is quite a bit larger than that reported in annual fall enrollment statistics. For the academic year 1989-90, the National Center for Education Statistics (1992a:xxiii) estimated a full-year enrollment in public, 2-year institutions of just over 7 million students.

There are approximately 1,000 community or technical colleges in the United States. This represents a meteoric increase: there were 297 in 1949 and only 520 in 1967 (National Center for Education Statistics, 1992c:237). These colleges are now spread fairly evenly across the nation, although the percentage of the population enrolled varies from state to state.

Despite the existence of some large institutions, most community colleges are fairly small. Thirteen percent reported a head-count enrollment of under 1,000 in the fall of 1990; two-thirds had fewer than 5,000 students.

Notable exceptions include Miami Dade Community College, with nearly 44,000 full- and part-time students, and the Houston Community College System, with over 36,000 students (National Center for Education Statistics, 1992c:212-213).

Historically, most public, 2-year colleges were created by the local community. Community colleges often evolved from junior colleges with an academic transfer orientation or from technical colleges. Two-year postsecondary institutions were often administered by local officials along with the public primary and secondary schools. They became increasingly comprehensive in the 1970s and 1980s, offering a broad menu of liberal arts, technical, and vocational education. This is true even of many institutions, such as those in South Carolina, that continue to be called technical colleges. Tuma (1992:44) estimated that by 1990 over two-thirds of the students in public, 2-year colleges who had selected a course of study were in vocational programs.

Community colleges, to a greater degree than other colleges and universities, are creatures of state and local governments. On average, they get two-thirds of their revenues from these sources, while 18 percent come from tuition and only 5 percent from the federal government (National Center for Education Statistics, 1992d:16). Their dependence on local governments has declined over the past 30 years, while state support has grown. In 1958, localities provided just under 45 percent of all community college revenues (Breneman and Nelson, 1981:17), but, by 1990, that had fallen to under 15 percent. Today, in at least 18 states, community colleges no longer receive *any* local funding. State governments now provide more than half of all community college revenues (Honeyman et al., 1991:7-8). State and local funding is usually given through formula-driven allocations based on enrollments (for the majority of the funds) and through special appropriations linked to other state initiatives, such as economic development or worker retraining.

Community colleges are unique in higher education for their open-door status. They are comparatively inexpensive: annual tuition and fees for in-state residents averaged $962 in the academic year 1991-1992 (National Center for Education Statistics, 1992c:308). Since most students enroll part-time, costs are even lower. State and local governments generally do not explicitly restrict or cap enrollment, although most now limit enrollments at their 4-year institutions. Thus, community college enrollments tend to reflect student demand.

Virtually all community college students commute to the college campus, so the college must appeal to the local citizens. To increase enrollment, the college must draw from the local population. The college must either increase the participation rate of traditional students, appeal to adults or other nontraditional groups, or ride a wave of population growth. Over half the students are 25 years of age or older, and, in 1990, 22 percent of community college students were racial minorities and 57 percent were women (National Center for Education Statistics, 1992c).

Community colleges might accurately be described as service conglomerates. They provide many different kinds of services to many different kinds of students. Community colleges offer both credit programs leading to associate degrees (typically requiring 2 years of full-time study) and shorter certificate courses in a variety of fields. In the hierarchy of programs within vocational education, those offered by community colleges are clearly at the top; they are longer than those offered by other institutions, more intensive, with relatively more programs in sophisticated and capital-intensive areas like electronics, computing, and computer assisted design/computer assisted manufacturing (CAD/CAM), and with more extensive requirements for related academic coursework as well as general education or "breadth" requirements. In most communities, these institutions are the only providers of postsecondary credit courses (those that can be counted toward baccalaureate degrees). Other providers tend to offer only noncredit courses.

Technical colleges or institutes, where they exist, have much in common with community colleges, although they may remain more narrowly focused on vocational fields of study and offer relatively few academic courses. They usually offer 2-year degree programs leading to an associate of science or associate of applied science degree as well as shorter certificate programs.

Community colleges also provide a menu of other services, including remediation, English as a second language (ESL), retraining for displaced workers, training for the hard-to-employ, assistance to local economic development initiatives, and recreation and community service programs. Remediation occupies a large chunk of the curriculum at most community colleges (though much of this coursework is noncredit).

Some community colleges also play an important role in providing education and training through federal retraining and second-chance programs like the Job Training Partnership Act (JTPA), Job Opportunities and Basic Skills (JOBS), and adult education. Program administrators often choose community colleges to provide occupational classroom training because these colleges offer a variety of courses at low cost to the federal government (thanks to institutional subsidies from state and local governments). Increasingly, many community colleges work with businesses to provide customized or contract training programs designed to meet the specific needs of individual firms. Customized training courses are usually relatively short (lasting anywhere from several hours to a few weeks) and are often devised by modifying existing courses to fit the specific needs of the sponsoring company. These courses may take place at the contractor's worksite, which enables the college to use the company's own, perhaps more advanced, equipment.

Community colleges, therefore, are the one type of training institution in America that can truly be said to cover the range of training needs that we identified in the first chapter. Their activities attest to the entrepreneurship present in many such institutions. This characteristic potentially puts community colleges in competition with other providers of training in their local areas, at the same time that it creates a wider variety of offerings within the colleges themselves to meet the needs of a wider range of students. Some community colleges, however, are decidedly less entrepreneurial than others, dedicated almost entirely to promoting transfers to 4-year colleges.

The contribution of community colleges to qualifying training is growing, according to training surveys conducted by the Bureau of Labor Statistics (BLS) (1985, 1992). The proportion of workers citing "junior college or technical institute" as a source of qualifying training for their current jobs increased from 5 to 8 percent between 1983 and 1991.

In summary, although their diversity makes it difficult to generalize, community colleges have several salient characteristics that explain much of their behavior and performance:

• The location and character of each community college reflect *local* decision making and, more recently, *state* planning and rationalization of service areas. The federal government has had almost no role in the planning or operation of these institutions.

• Enrollment is *local* and reflects consumer demand, not centralized planning. Although overall enrollment growth in the last 30 years has been meteoric, the typical community college has experienced considerable fluctuation over this time.

• State funding has become the most important revenue source. Traditionally, state funding patterns have given community colleges a very strong incentive to increase enrollment.

• The typical community college is a service conglomerate; it provides many different kinds of services to many different kinds of students and often offers all four of the different types of postsecondary training for the workplace identified in this report.

Proprietary Vocational Schools

Proprietary schools are for-profit educational institutions that offer primarily short-term, intensive, occupational programs in a single subject or a few related subjects: secretarial and clerical training, computer programming, certain trades, truck driving, cosmetology, and so on. These schools have private owners who run them as profit-making businesses; while they must have state licenses, they have historically operated outside of and largely invisible to the traditional collegiate world and public oversight bodies. Even more than the technical institutes described above, they focus on providing students with highly structured, occupation-oriented courses of study that stray very little from the skills specifically needed by the occupation in question. While most proprietary programs last less than a year, there are some schools that offer associate and even baccalaureate degrees.

Precise information on enrollments in the proprietary sector is difficult to come by, and revenue statistics are largely nonexistent. Until 1987, the federal government, which has annually collected basic statistical data on colleges and universities for many years, did not include proprietary schools in its surveys. Sporadic, ad hoc attempts to collect information on this sector suffer from serious problems of comparability and coverage. Nevertheless, a recent study of the sector (Lee and Merisotis, 1990) reveals that the history of profit-making trade schools dates back well into the nineteenth century and that nearly 1,000 schools enrolled over 300,000 students in the years immediately following the First World War.

The U.S. Department of Education estimates that 722,000 students were enrolled in about 4,700 proprietary schools in the fall of 1989 (National Center for Education Statistics, 1992b:7).[1] Since programs of study are often short, and new courses begin frequently throughout the year, a larger number of people (1.4 million) were enrolled over the course of the 1989-1990 academic year (National Center for Education Statistics, 1992a:xxiii). While some schools are very large (for example, DeVry Institutes of Technology and Business Training International each enroll over 10,000 students annually), the median fall enrollment was 64 in 1988 (Apling and Aleman, 1990:8).

Because they receive no direct government subsidy as community colleges do, proprietary schools are comparatively expensive. Since the Second World War, their fortunes have been tied in important ways to the availability of federal subsidies for their students, first through the G.I. Bill (and its successors) and then through student grant and loan programs that were originally established for students in colleges and universities in the mid-1960s (Lee and Merisotis, 1990:10-11). In 1989-1990, almost 80 percent of the students enrolled half-time or more received grants or loans from federal student aid programs, compared to a little under half of the students at private, nonprofit colleges; about one-third at public, 4-year institutions; and about one-fifth at community colleges.[2] (Federal student aid, which will be discussed below, is largely limited to students enrolled at least on a half-time basis.) No reliable statistics are available on the overall revenues from various sources received by these schools, but it is clear that the federal government is of major importance to them.

Proprietary schools enroll somewhat disproportionate numbers of women, minorities, and low-income individuals. They do not appear to be heavily involved in federal second-chance programs like JTPA and JOBS, although some do obtain contracts to serve JTPA and JOBS clients. This tends to occur when lower-priced services are not available through community colleges or other local training organizations. They are also less apt than community colleges to work with businesses on customized training, although again there are exceptions. Because they are highly entrepreneurial (so long as outside funds are available) and unfettered by the rigidities of the academic calendar followed by many community colleges, they can be flexible and responsive in ways that the colleges may not.

Area Vocational Schools and Adult Education Schools

Following the implementation of the Vocational Education Act of 1963 (VEA), states began to use federal funds to establish new, locally operated vocational schools. In fact, President Johnson was explicit on signing the VEA that states could use the funds made available to them for this purpose (Gallinelli, 1979). Although there are no recent figures available, by 1979 there were over 1,300 such institutions nationally (Galladay and Wulfsberg, 1981).

Area vocational schools have changed in nature since their creation. Most of them were established in the 1960s and 1970s as secondary schools, designed to provide richer vocational programs than individual high schools could offer. In the 1970s and 1980s, many began serving adult students as well, usually through relatively short, noncredit programs. As secondary vocational enrollments dwindled in the 1980s, for the reasons mentioned above, and adult enrollments expanded, most area vocational schools became, in fact, predominantly adult institutions.

Such schools are not found everywhere, but similar programs are offered in some communities by vocation-oriented adult schools that are also part of the public school system. They offer subjects such as remedial education; preparation for high school general equivalency diploma exams (GED); English as a second language (ESL); avocational and hobby courses; and vocational courses, such as business, marketing, real estate, secretarial, automotive mechanics, air-conditioning maintenance and repair, and other trades. The presence or absence of such schools reflects state policies: in California, they are optional for localities; in Florida, school districts must operate adult schools in 14 counties, while in 14 others the community colleges, rather than school districts, are expected to provide noncredit adult education.

In fact, variation among states is particularly important to understanding these institutions. At one extreme, states such as Delaware have begun to phase out area vocational schools, preferring to incorporate them into existing secondary schools. At the other extreme, Oklahoma attaches great significance to such schools and has developed a set of institutions (the Francis Tuttle School, for example) whose facilities are state-of-the-art.

Community-Based Organizations

Community-based organizations (CBOs) are responsive to specific, geographically, or ethnically based constituencies. The term came into usage in the 1960s to describe private, nonprofit organizations representing ethnic minorities and low-income groups that were run by representatives of these groups and which oriented their services toward meeting the needs of disadvantaged Americans. Many were created in response to the expansion of federal funding for employment and training programs in the early and mid-1960s. At various times, they received special funding priority, for example, under the now-defunct Youth Employment and Demonstration Projects Act of 1977. At that time, an increasingly diverse set of organizations began to consider themselves CBOs; and the term has evolved to mean any private, nonprofit organization that is representative of a community and provides education, training, employment, and social services to that community.

In the employment and training arena, CBOs are still almost entirely dependent on government programs for funding. They provide a range of services, including job development and counseling, job search and placement assistance, classroom skills training, remedial education, vocational exploration and prevocational training, and ESL. Services designed to help clients get jobs are more prevalent in CBOs than are education and training activities (Bailis, 1984), although CBOs account for approximately 20 percent of the classroom training providers in the JTPA program. CBOs appear more likely than other JTPA classroom training providers to serve minorities and high school dropouts. Information on who provided classroom training is missing for at least one-third of JTPA participants who received such training. It is difficult, therefore, to make accurate comparisons among classroom training providers as to the types of clients served or the outcomes of training. Available program data indicate that individuals who receive classroom training from CBOs tend to have shorter stays in JTPA (averaging 21 weeks) and to enter employment at a higher rate than individuals who attend public vocational schools, high schools, and community colleges under JTPA auspices (U.S. Department of Labor, 1992). Given the large number of participants for whom information on classroom training experiences is missing, however, these findings cannot be given great weight.

CBOs provide an added degree of flexibility and responsiveness to the education and training "system" that would not otherwise exist. They are often thought to be particularly adept at certain functions—including recruitment, counseling, and job placement—that more traditional education providers may not wish or be able to provide. Because of their close community ties and commitment to their clients, CBOs provide assistance to groups with marginal access to labor markets who may be bypassed by more mainstream organizations (Grubb and McDonnell, 1991; Bailis, 1987).

Apprenticeship

Apprenticeship, a centuries-old mechanism for teaching a trade, is a comparatively minor source of training in the United States, especially compared to schools, although it remains important in some occupations. Interest in apprenticeship is growing, however, particularly because of the success that other countries have had in preparing youth for work through apprenticeships.

According to the U.S. General Accounting Office (GAO) (1992a:8), apprenticeship consists of "structured, long-term (typically 3 to 4 years), on-the-job training combined with related theoretical instruction, leading to certification of the attainment of journey worker status in a skilled trade."

Apprentices work closely with a particular employer. The employer pays the apprentice wages and provides the training costs. Frequently, employers receive funds for apprentices from both local and national trust funds that have been established jointly by unions and employer associations (U.S. Office of Technology Assessment [OTA], 1990:238). Because of this funding mechanism, apprenticeships are concentrated in a few, heavily unionized industries. Although registered apprenticeships exist in over 800 occupations involving 43,000 apprenticeship programs, half of these programs had no active apprentices during the first quarter of fiscal year 1991. Approximately two-thirds of all apprenticeships in the United States are provided in just 20 occupations, primarily in construction and metal trades (U.S. General Accounting Office, 1992a:2,17).

There were approximately 283,000 civilian workers in registered apprenticeship programs in 1990. In addition, 44,000 apprentices were being trained in the military, and an estimated 100,000 are trained annually in nonregistered programs (U.S. General Accounting Office, 1992a:2; U.S. Office of Technology Assessment, 1990:137). In the overall context of the U.S. work force, these numbers are quite small. In 1987, registered apprentices comprised only 0.16 percent of the civilian work force (U.S. Office of Technology Assessment, 1990:236). Apprenticeship in the United States, according to the GAO (1992a:4), "plays a minor and declining role in training United States workers." In fact, during the 1980s, overall employment increased by 18 million, but the number of registered civilian apprentices dropped by 11 percent. The average age of apprentices in the United States is 29, which means that apprenticeship is not widely used to train students directly out of high school (Clark, 1992:914).

The number of workers trained through apprenticeship is limited less by an inability to attract interested workers than by difficulty finding firms to sponsor apprentices. In some industries, there are generally four applicants for every available opening (U.S. General Accounting Office, 1992a:20; U.S. Office of Technology Assessment, 1990:238). In part, this reflects a lack of infrastructure to support apprenticeships outside the unionized trades.

Minorities and women have traditionally been underrepresented in apprenticeship programs, though, in recent years, minority participation has increased so that it is now approximately equal to minority representation in the work force as a whole. Minorities now comprise 22.5 percent of all apprentices, a 50 percent increase since 1973. The percentage of female apprentices grew from virtually zero in 1973 to 6.6 percent in 1983. Since then, however, the growth has leveled off; women currently comprise just 7 percent of apprentices. Furthermore, both women and minorities tend to receive apprenticeships in the lowest-paying occupations that offer apprenticeships (U.S. General Accounting Office, 1992a:21-28).

The federal government has supported the apprenticeship system since 1934, when it created the Federal Committee on Apprenticeship. Three years later, Congress enacted the National Apprenticeship Act (often called the Fitzgerald Act), under which the federal government began setting standards for apprenticeship programs and officially registering programs that met those standards. Today, federal responsibility for overseeing the apprenticeship system lies with the U.S. Labor Department's Bureau of Apprenticeship and Training (BAT). The BAT's primary responsibilities include promoting apprenticeships, providing technical assistance to potential sponsors, ensuring compliance with equal employment regulations, and registering programs that meet official federal standards. It does not provide direct financial support either to apprentices or to their employers. From 1978 to 1990, BAT's funding (in constant 1982 dollars) and staff size were cut in half (U.S. Office of Technology Assessment, 1990:241).

Twenty-seven states currently operate their own state apprenticeship councils. In addition to supporting apprenticeship programs, the councils are also authorized to register apprenticeship programs that meet federal standards and to bestow certificates of completion to apprentices. Evidence indicates that state certification of apprentices has decreased the portability of apprentice certificates, since certification standards may vary from state to state (U.S. Office of Technology Assessment, 1990:239).

States play a more important role than the federal government in promoting apprenticeships. According to the GAO (1992a:19), states spent close to three times as much as the BAT on apprenticeships in 1990. While the GAO does point out that, in many states, resources for apprenticeships will probably be cut within the next few years, under existing funding patterns the federal government has only limited leverage if it wishes to increase its control over the apprenticeship system (U.S. Office of Technology Assessment, 1990:239).

In spite of funding constraints, the federal government attempted to increase employer interest in the apprenticeship system through a project known as the Apprenticeship 2000 initiative, begun in 1987. The initiative focused on two areas: improving traditional apprenticeships and expanding apprenticeships to less traditional sectors. As noted above, traditional apprenticeships could be improved by making certificates more portable across state boundaries. The initiative also hoped to expand apprenticeship into new industries, initially by funding demonstration projects through the U.S. Department of Labor's recently created Office of Work-Based Learning (U.S. Office of Technology Assessment, 1990:55).

In addition to these extensions of traditional apprenticeship, federal, state, and local governments are experimenting with youth apprenticeships modeled after systems operating in Germany, Austria, Switzerland, and Denmark. The new programs begin as early as the eleventh grade; encompass a 3-year program combining work-site training, high school, and possibly community college; require a contract between employer and student laying out the obligations of each; and lead to a certified competency in an occupational area. Existing demonstration programs are small. According to Jobs for the Future, a sponsor of several youth apprenticeship demonstrations, there were fewer than 2,000 youth apprentices in 1992 (Clark, 1992:922).

Employer-Sponsored Training

Employer-sponsored training is a sizable enterprise, although, as a decentralized and largely private activity, reliable estimates about it are hard to obtain. An OTA (1990:128-130) summary of various studies estimates the costs of formal, employer-provided training to be $30 billion to $45 billion annually; the costs of formal and informal, on-the-job training range from $105 billion to $210 billion annually. For a variety of reasons, however, OTA and others put little faith in the accuracy of these numbers.[3] Nevertheless, it is clear that absolute expenditures are large. On a per-worker basis or as a percentage of gross national product (GNP) or payroll, however, the size of these expenditures appears less impressive. For example, the estimate of $44 billion for expenditures on formal training amounted in 1988 to $385 per worker, less than 1 percent of GNP and 1.8 percent of the total compensation that workers received.

According to training surveys sponsored by the Bureau of Labor Statistics (1985, 1992), the importance of formal company training programs has grown noticeably for workers seeking to improve their skills in their current jobs. In 1983, 11 percent of workers reported having received skills improvement training through formal company programs at some point in their current job. By 1991, 16 percent of workers (nearly 18 million people) reported such training. (Fourteen and 15 percent of workers in the 2 respective years reported receiving informal, on-the-job training.) Moreover, of the 13 percent of workers in 1991 who reported having received school-based training to improve their skills, 42 percent said that their employers sponsored the training. This represented very little change from 1983. Only 3 percent of the 1991 respondents with school-based skills improvement training reported that their training was sponsored by government programs.

The BLS surveys also indicated that two-thirds of 1991 workers who upgraded their skills through formal company programs received training for fewer than 25 weeks. Company training appears to be lengthening, however. In 1983, 72 percent of workers reported that their training had lasted less than 12 weeks; the comparable percentage in 1991 was 33 percent.

Employer-sponsored training is less important but not negligible as a source of qualifying training. Ten percent of workers in 1983 and 12 percent in 1991 reported that company programs provided them with the training they needed to qualify for their current jobs.

Employers provide some of the formal training themselves and arrange with outside providers for the rest. Carnevale et al. (1990:3) suggest that employers provide 69 percent of the formal training they offer and use outside providers for 31 percent. This appears to be a rather rough estimate, but is not far from more precise figures reported by the OTA (1990:137) for federal expenditures on the training of its civilian work force. OTA reports that the federal government spent $1.03 billion on training its employees in fiscal year 1988; 60 percent was for internal training by agencies, and 40 percent covered the cost of training provided by outsiders.

A variety of providers help employers meet their training needs, including equipment vendors; private training consultants; schools; professional, trade, and labor organizations; community organizations; and private tutors and instructors.

Employer-sponsored training is largely a private activity, with little direct assistance from government. Direct aid that is provided is more likely to come from the states than from the federal government. An OTA survey found that, in 1989, 44 states operated one or more customized training programs (U.S. Office of Technology Assessment, 1990:144). Those states had spent about $375 million on customized training projects in their most recently completed fiscal year. These expenditures did not include one-time training subsidies offered as part of the effort to recruit firms to a state; nor did they include indirect state support for customized training provided by public community and technical colleges at the request of firms.

The federal government has not provided significant direct support for employer-sponsored training. It has been involved on a small scale through such efforts as support for training and technology transfer programs from the U.S. Department of Commerce's National Institute of Standards and Technology and from the U.S. Department of Education, through activities encouraging the spread of apprenticeship (see above), and quite recently through demonstration projects aimed at improving basic literacy in the workplace. Federal support for employer-sponsored training is largely indirect through the tax code. Companies incur direct training costs in various ways: through reimbursements to employees for the costs of external education and training programs, for example, and through expenditures on the purchase of materials, support for formal in-house training, and compensation paid to workers during on-the-job training. For the purposes of calculating tax liability, firms may fully and immediately deduct these training costs from revenue (Quigley and Smolensky, 1989:828-829). They are considered part of the costs of doing business. The federal government has also from time to time provided a tax subsidy to training by allowing workers to exclude employer-paid reimbursements for training costs from their taxable income.

Military Training

Like many large, private firms, the U.S. military trains its own personnel. Unlike many private employers, however, the military does not focus predominantly on management-level workers; it provides extensive training to all new recruits (U.S. Office of Technology Assessment, 1990:259).

In fiscal 1992, the four military services expected to provide 217,000 person-years of training for the military's active and reserve personnel at a cost (including indirect expenses such as wages) of more than $19 billion. The military is currently spending 10 percent less on training than it did in fiscal 1986 (U.S. Department of Defense, 1991). Cuts in the number of enlisted personnel entering training and reductions in the procurement of new weapons for which further training would be required suggest that the amount of training the military provides will continue to decline in the future.

The military has been an important contributor to the *middle-level training* that is the subject of this report. More than 55 percent of the person-years spent in military training is devoted to "specialized skill training": occupational instruction and on-the-job training in such areas as electronics and health care provided primarily to enlisted personnel (almost all of whom have a high school diploma and very few of whom have a baccalaureate degree) (U.S. Department of Defense, 1991). With its large training budget of some $3,500 per person (as compared to a few hundred dollars per employee in the private sector), the U.S. Department of Defense can provide the most sophisticated training technology available. Military services train some personnel directly but also contract with local service providers. Civilian contractors may provide training in areas ranging from basic skills to uses of the latest technology (U.S. Office of Technology Assessment, 1990).

The military is also an important source of innovation in the training field. The military uses job analysis to establish specific performance standards for its trainees. Also, military trainers receive constant feedback and opportunities to rotate back into the field (U.S. Office of Technology Assessment, 1990:259).

There has been some debate about the transferability of specialized military training to the civilian sector. However, Mangum and Ball (1987:438) examined data from the youth cohort of the National Longitudinal Surveys of Labor Market Experience and found "significant amounts of skill transfer between military-provided training and civilian employment." They also found that over 30 percent of males enlisting in the military did so primarily to receive training that would be useful after they left military service.

Summary

From this review of the institutions that provide postsecondary training in the United States, several crucial conclusions emerge. At least to the uninitiated, there appears to be a bewildering array of institutional providers, with overlapping responsibilities that vary significantly from place to place. Some of these providers concentrate on one or two kinds of training (e.g., firms concentrate on qualifying and skills improvement training for their own employees; CBOs on second-chance training for the disadvantaged). But other central providers, such as community colleges, are key actors in all four training arenas identified in Chapter 1.

Except for CBOs, the military, and many (although not all) proprietary schools, most of these institutions do not exist primarily to carry out training programs funded by the federal government. Even the institutions that are heavily dependent on revenues from federal programs, such as CBOs that are affiliates of national organizations like the Urban League or La Raza, pursue institutional objectives in addition to the objectives of the public policies they are implementing. Community colleges are even more independent. They are more likely to be responsive to the state and regional objectives of the state systems of which they are a part and the local boards that govern them than to distant federal policy makers whose programs represent only a small part of their activities. Employers train their employees if and when they perceive a business reason to do so; they are not likely to invest their own capital in people or types or training that do not have a clear economic payoff for the firm.

We return to the implications of this institutional structure in Chapter 3 when, after having reviewed the existing array of federal postsecondary training programs, we will bring together the institutional and programmatic perspectives to diagnose the health of the postsecondary training system.

FEDERAL POSTSECONDARY TRAINING PROGRAMS

Intersecting with the institutions described above is a set of federal programs designed to train individuals for work and facilitate their entry into the workplace.

Federal employment policy is often traced to the early 1960s, especially to the passage of the Manpower Development and Training Act of 1962. Government interest in employment and training issues can be found much earlier in the nation's history, however. Cohen and Stevens (1989) found the first public support for labor exchange activities through state and local sources in 1830. In 1917, spurred by the First World War, the U.S. Department of Labor secured funding for a system of local offices that could meet war manpower needs. In the same year, Congress passed the Smith-Hughes Act, which authorized federal aid to states for vocational education in the nation's secondary schools. The Depression years spawned a host of employment-related activities. The Wagner-Peyser Act of 1933 provided federal matching funds to state employment security agencies and created the U.S. Employment Service. Two years later, Congress created the unemployment insurance system as part of the Social Security Act. The Public Works Administration and the Works Progress Administration created jobs through federally funded projects and provided wages to student workers, first through the Federal Emergency Relief Administration and later through the National Youth Administration. After the Second World War, the Serviceman's Readjustment Act (the so-called G.I. Bill) provided funds for education and training to over 2 million returning veterans (Olson, 1974:27,43). So, the federal government indicated a sporadic interest in employment and training policy, even before the rediscovery of poverty in the 1960s spurred the creation of new employment and training programs for the nation's disadvantaged citizens.

Given this brief history, it is no surprise that a major distinguishing characteristic of federally supported training is that it is carried out through many programs that were created over time, when varying perspectives on employment and education and training policy were in vogue. Like the institutions we have already examined, the programs are not part of a coherent structure or a tidy division of labor. Both the institutions and the programs have grown and diversified over the past several decades.

Starting with a list provided by the U.S. Department of Labor, the committee identified several dozen current federal programs concerned with postsecondary training as we have defined it.[4] These programs are divided among seven executive branch departments and accounted for about $20 billion in federal support (see Table 2.1). Most of the federal funds for training civilians, however, are allocated to programs sponsored by the U.S. Departments of Labor and Education and the welfare-related JOBS Training Program in the U.S. Department of Health and Human Services. (This report does not examine further the military's training programs for its own employees; the focus is on policies affecting the nonfederal work force.) Key federal postsecondary training programs have quite distinct goals, support different types of training (although there is some overlap among them), and share funding and administrative responsibilities with states and training providers in different ways.

Student Financial Assistance

Grants and loans provided to students attending proprietary schools and community colleges represent the single largest source of federal support for postsecondary training. The irony is that student aid is perhaps the least often mentioned source of such support. This misperception is directly related to the history of student aid programs: first authorized in 1965, the student aid programs in Title IV of the Higher Education Act were largely aimed at students pursuing baccalaureate degrees in 4-year colleges and universities.

Federal student assistance was created to help equalize educational opportunities and to foster access to postsecondary education for those with limited financial means. As reauthorized in 1992, the Higher Education Act includes, in Title IV, five sets of programs:

Grants to students in attendance at institutions of higher education, which include Pell grants, Supplemental Educational Opportunity Grants (SEOG), State Student Incentive Grants (SSIG), and several smaller programs.

Federal Family Education Loans (FFEL), which include the Stafford Loan Program (Stafford) for students, the Parents Loans for Undergraduate Students Program (PLUS), and the Supplemental Loan for Students Program (SLS). These are federally guaranteed loans financed with private capital.

Federal work study programs.

Federal direct loans, which provide for a direct loan program beginning in 1994 under which some student loans will be made directly by the federal government rather than through the FFEL guaranteed loan program.

Federal Perkins loans, a direct-lending program under which the fed-

TABLE 2.1   Federal Support of Postsecondary Training Programs, Fiscal 1991

Program		Budget Authority ($ million)	
U.S. Department of Labor			
Apprenticeship training		16	
Veterans employment and training		148	
Disabled Veterans Outreach Program	77		
Local veterans employment representative	71		
Trade adjustment assistance		270	
Job Training Partnership Act		4,039	
JTPA Title II-A	1,780		
JTPA Title II-B	683		
JTPA Title III: EDWAA	527		
JTPA Title IV: Job Corps	867		
JTPA Title IV: Migrant farmworkers	70		
JTPA Title IV: Native American education and training	60		
JTPA Title IV: Pilots and demonstrations	36		
JTPA Title IV: Veterans employment program	9		
JTPA Other	7		
McKinney Homelessness Assistance Act		12	
Job training for the homeless demonstration	10		
Homeless veterans reintegration	2		
Targeted jobs tax credit		80	
Tax expenditures (revenue loss)	60		
Administration	20		
Subtotal U.S. Department of Labor			4,565
U.S. Department of Education			
Adult Education Act		242	
Basic grant program	201		
Workplace literacy partnerships	19		
Literacy training for homeless adults	10		
Other adult education programs	12		
Student financial assistance		5,946	
Pell grants	2,419[a]		
Students and parent guaranteed loans (Stafford, PLUS, SLS)	3,339[a,b]		
Campus-based aid	188[a]		
Cooperative education		14	
Perkins Vocational Education Act		417[c]	
Basic grants to states	320[c]		
Tech-prep	63		
CBO grants	12		
Other Perkins	22[c]		
Vocational rehabilitation		1,633	
Subtotal U.S. Department of Education			8,252

TABLE 2.1 *Continued*

Program	Budget Authority ($ million)	
U.S. Department of Health and Human Services		
JOBS		1,000
Refugee and entrant assistance		121
Education and training assistance	83	
Targeted assistance	38	
Vocational rehabilitation		61
Subtotal U.S. Department of Health and Human Services		1,182
U.S. Department of Agriculture		
Food stamp education and training		153
Subtotal U.S. Department of Agriculture		153
U.S. Department of Interior		
Indian education programs		35
Indian training and related programs		22
Subtotal U.S. Department of Interior		57
U.S. Department of Veterans Affairs		
Montgomery G.I. Bill		289
Vocational rehabilitation		132
Survivors and dependents education assistance		104
Post-Vietnam era vets education benefits		92
Benefits for reservists		79
Subtotal U.S. Department of Veterans Affairs		696[d]
U.S. Department of Defense		
Navy specialized skill training		1,974
Army specialized skill training		1,494
Air Force specialized skill training		694
Marine specialized skill training		564
Subtotal U.S. Department of Defense		4,726
TOTAL FEDERAL SUPPORT		19,631

[a]This figure represents an estimate of program share directed toward students at community colleges and proprietary schools. It overstates somewhat the amount devoted to job training, since a fraction of students at community colleges are in academic programs.

[b]This figure represents the proportion directed toward community college and proprietary school students of total aid awarded through the guaranteed loan programs. Actual federal expenditures are lower than the total aid awarded, since the government does not provide the loan money, but rather pays to subsidize some low-interest loans and repays defaulted loans. Data on the percentage of federal expenditures, rather than the percentage of total aid awarded, for community college and proprietary school students were not available.

[c]This figure represents an estimate of Perkins program money provided to postsecondary (rather than secondary) institutions.

[d]Dollar amounts for veterans programs represent funds going to students in all sectors of postsecondary education, including 4-year schools.

SOURCES: Compiled by staff using materials provided to the committee by the U.S. Department of Labor and the U.S. General Accounting Office, as well as the fiscal 1992 budget of the U.S. government, the U.S. Department of Defense *Military Manpower Training Report* for fiscal 1992, and College Board (1993).

eral government provides money to college and universities to lend to students.

SEOG, Perkins loans, and work study are known as the *campus-based programs* because federal appropriations are distributed to campuses, where administrators select recipients on the basis of federal guidelines. Federal student assistance from the Title IV programs represents about two-thirds of all the aid awarded to students from federal, state, institutional, and other sources (College Board, 1993).

Title IV programs provided $22 billion in federal aid to students at all levels in the academic year 1991-1992.[5] Of this amount, we estimate that community college and proprietary school students received roughly $6 billion. As Table 2.2 indicates, proprietary school students received more than one and one-half times as much overall aid as community college students and over three times as much in student loans. (Since most federal aid is based on the financial need of the student, taking into account both educational costs and family ability to pay, students at proprietary schools qualify for more assistance—other things being equal—than do students at comparatively low-priced, state-subsidized community colleges.) Federal

TABLE 2.2　Federal Student Aid Awarded to Community College and Proprietary School Students, Academic Year 1991-1992

Program	Proprietary School Students		Community College Students		All Postsecondary Students[a]
	Aid Awarded ($ mil)	% of Program Total	Aid Awarded ($ mil)	% of Program Total	Aid Awarded ($ mil)
Pell	1,196	20.7	1,404	24.3	5,777
Campus-based	117	5.5	198	9.3	2,126
Guaranteed loans	2,621	18.7	814	5.8	13,993
Total	3,934	18.0	2,416	11.0	21,896

NOTE: Total aid awarded, reported here, is greater than federal expenditures, since the federal government guarantees loans and may provide interest subsidies, but loan capital comes primarily from private lending institutions as well as some schools and state agencies. In addition, this table includes matching funds provided by schools participating in the campus-based programs. Totals in the table refer to academic year 1991-1992 and are therefore not directly comparable to the fiscal year totals reported in Table 2.1.

[a]This column includes aid for all students at all undergraduate and graduate institutions of postsecondary education.

SOURCE: College Board (1993:Tables 1 and 6).

student aid has, until recently, been limited to individuals enrolled in school on at least a half-time basis; very short programs of study (under roughly 3 months for student loans and 6 months for Pell grants) do not qualify. Aid recipients must be making satisfactory academic progress (consistent with the graduation requirements of the institutions they attend) in order to remain eligible for federal assistance.

Over 80 percent of Title IV federal student aid is awarded through the Pell grants, Stafford loan, and SLS programs. We therefore focus on these programs.

The Higher Education Act was first passed in 1965, authorizing grants, loans, and work study assistance through the campus-based programs and creating the Guaranteed Student Loan (GSL) Program, the forerunner of today's Stafford and SLS programs. Initially, only public and private non-profit institutions of higher education were eligible for these programs. For proprietary schools, Congress created the Vocational Student Loan Insurance Act of 1965, closely paralleling the GSL program in content and administration. The House Education and Labor Committee hearing records indicate that the primary reason for creating separate programs was abuses by proprietary schools under the G.I. Bill during the late 1940s and early 1950s. However, in 1968 Congress merged the vocational loan program into GSL, citing duplication of effort and equity of funds availability as primary factors (Fraas, 1990).

GSL was originally aimed primarily at middle-income families who were clamoring for help with college costs and whose appeals had almost resulted in the passage of a tuition tax credit bill in the U.S. Senate in 1964. It grew slowly in the early years, but then, as Table 2.3 indicates, exploded in the late 1970s and 1980s due to a variety of factors, including removal of income restrictions for interest-subsidized loans in 1978 (they were reimposed in 1981); interest rates in the general economy that made student loans quite attractive; and growing use by proprietary school students (Hansen,

TABLE 2.3   Stafford Loan Growth Since 1966

Year	# Loans (thousands)	$ Loaned (million)
1966	89	73
1970	498	457
1975	486	637
1980	2,078	4,335
1985	3,641	8,401
1990	3,609	9,708

SOURCE: U.S. Department of Education (1990a:13).

1991). By the end of the 1980s, the now-renamed Stafford program had become the major student aid program, making over $10 billion available annually. Additional student loans could be obtained through the SLS program, created in 1981 along with a parent loan program.

Today's Stafford loan program allows students in their first 2 years of postsecondary education to borrow $2,625 in the first year and $3,500 in the second.[6] Loans up to $4,000 annually are authorized for students in programs lasting at least 1 academic year under the SLS program (SLS loans are federally guaranteed, but the interest rates are not subsidized as are need-based Stafford loans). Community college students, despite their numbers, accounted for only about 6 percent of Stafford loan volume and 4 percent of SLS volume in fiscal 1991. Proprietary school students, on the other hand, accounted for 17 percent and 29 percent of volume, respectively, in the two programs (College Board, 1993).

Student loans became controversial in the 1980s as costs to the federal government of paying off defaulted loans rose rapidly. (In a guaranteed loan program, the federal government insures lenders against the risk that a borrower will default on his or her loan. The government may or may not subsidize interest rates as well.) Default costs grew because of rising loan volume as well as an increase in borrowing among groups more likely to default. Default costs drew attention as they became a multibillion-dollar item in the federal budget (an estimated $2.7 billion in fiscal 1992, for example) and because of high default rates, particularly in the proprietary school sector.[7]

Congress created what is now the second largest student aid program, Pell grants (originally called Basic Educational Opportunity Grants), in 1972, intending them to serve as the foundation of a student's financial aid package. From the program's inception, students from all sectors of postsecondary education have been eligible for Pell grants. However, because Pell grant recipients must be enrolled in a program of at least 600 clock hours (6 months), many proprietary school students do not qualify.

Although the original authorizing legislation spoke of Pell grants as an entitlement, awards, in fact, depend on annual appropriations from Congress. (Student loans are, by contrast, true entitlements; Congress must appropriate whatever funds are necessary to cover the costs of all who decide to borrow.) Although Pell funding grew throughout the 1980s, it did not keep up with demand or rising college costs. To keep federal expenditures down, federal policy makers have refused to let maximum grant levels grow much. Maximum grants were $2,100 in 1985-1986 and had grown to only $2,400 by 1992-1993. For 1993-1994, the maximum will actually fall to $2,300. This has the effect of increasingly concentrating the available grants on lower-income students.

Student grants and loans are by far the most significant source of federal assistance to those pursuing training to qualify for employment. Workers who can enroll on at least a half-time basis and can qualify on the basis of income can also use these programs for skills improvement training or retraining. As educational vouchers that provide funds directly to students, this aid affords recipients an almost unrestricted choice of school and program of study. Until recently, the federal government exercised a relatively hands-off approach to certifying the eligibility of institutions to enroll federal aid recipients, relying mostly on state licensing and voluntary accreditation. Later chapters will discuss the subject of institutional and program eligibility.

The Carl D. Perkins Vocational and
Applied Technology Education Act of 1990

Today's Perkins Act is the lineal descendant of the Smith-Hughes Act of 1917 that established a program of federal grants to the states for support of vocational education. Originally focused on secondary schools, the act was amended in 1963 to allow states to use federal funds for occupation-oriented programs at the postsecondary level as well. Despite its small size ($941 million to secondary and postsecondary institutions in fiscal 1991) compared to federal student aid, the Perkins Act is usually considered the centerpiece of the U.S. Department of Education's activity in vocational education and training.

The Perkins Act provides funds to state vocational education agencies, which in turn distribute the money to schools and school districts. The act aims at improving the quality of vocational training and ensuring the full participation of individuals who are members of special populations (people with handicaps, disadvantaged individuals, people with limited English proficiency, foster children, and people in correctional institutions). The preponderance of Perkins Act funds are awarded through Title II basic grants to the states. Basic grants, which states must match, can be used for a variety of purposes, including upgrading of curricula, purchase of equipment, inservice training of instructors, guidance and counseling, and remedial courses. The Title III Tech-Prep program, the other part of Perkins of special interest because of its involvement in postsecondary training, was added to the act during its most recent reauthorization in 1990.[8]

States allocate their basic grant funds between secondary and postsecondary education in vastly different ways. A major assessment of the Perkins Act that was completed in 1989 indicated that, in 1986-1987, the share of total funds directed to postsecondary institutions varied among the states from 8 to 100 percent. Overall, 38 percent of basic grants went to institutions at the postsecondary level (National Assessment of Vocational Education, 1989a:8-10). While federal vocational education funds have historically exerted a strong influence over the development of secondary vocational education programs, postsecondary institutions have been far less affected because the federal dollars represent such a small part of their revenues. For example, the current fund revenues of 2-year public colleges in academic year 1989 were $15.5 billion (National Center for Education Statistics, 1992d:16). At the postsecondary level, federal funds were spent mostly on equipment purchases, not on broader program improvement efforts (National Assessment of Vocational Education, 1989b:35).

The 1990 legislation envisioned expansion of so-called Tech-Prep initiatives that emerged around the country in the 1980s. The law defines a Tech-Prep program as one that combines secondary and postsecondary education and leads to a 2-year associate degree or certificate; provides technical preparation in fields such as engineering technology, health, and business; builds student competence in math, science, and communications; and leads to employment (Irwin and Apling, 1991:14). The title Tech-Prep was itself adopted to remove the stigma of the term *vocational education* and to mirror the respected college prep track in high schools. In a well-developed tech-prep program, students pursue coursework in the final 2 years of high school that provides a basic mastery of necessary skills. They then move on to 2 years of coursework at a community college, during which they achieve advanced mastery in a technical subject area. The federal government committed $64 million to the support of state and local tech-prep initiatives in fiscal 1990.

The 1990 reauthorization of the Perkins Act requires states to develop and implement performance standards and measures. Each state's performance standard system must include measures of learning and competency gains in basic and advanced skills; include at least one measure of outcomes of vocational programs (e.g., job placement or school completion rates); provide incentives to encourage serving members of special populations; and capitalize on existing resources for performance assessment, such as those developed under JTPA (Irwin and Apling, 1991:8-9). The legislation does not call for sanctions against program recipients who do not meet performance standards. Recipients who do not make substantial progress must only develop program improvement plans that will indicate how they will improve performance.

Finally, the 1990 Perkins legislation calls for a major new assessment of vocational education, with a final report due in 1994.

Adult Education Programs

Since the mid-1960s, the federal government, through the Adult Education Act, has assisted states in providing educational opportunities for adults who lack basic skills. The core Basic Grant portion of the act supports

Adult Basic Education (ABE: programs designed for adults functioning at or below the eighth-grade level); Adult Secondary Education (ASE: instruction for adults functioning at the high school level); and ESL. In 1988 the act was amended to supplement Basic Grants with programs designed to improve the literacy skills of people in the workplace and to serve adults with limited proficiency in English. The National Literacy Act of 1991 further amended the Adult Education Act. The highest priority set out in the National Literacy Act is the improvement of programs to ensure the quality of educational services supported by federal funds. This act called for the Secretary of Education to develop indicators of program quality that could be used by state and local programs as models for judging service effectiveness. In addition, the act established a national institute for literacy, state literacy resource centers, work force literacy grants, and optional state literacy councils.

Basic State Grants accounted for over 80 percent of the $220 million in federal funds appropriated for adult education in fiscal 1991. Basic Grants are allocated to states by formula based on the number of adults who have not completed high school in each state. States distribute funds to local education agencies and other public and private nonprofit agencies.

States and localities supplement the funds they receive from the federal government and, in fact, spend significantly more than the federal government. The U.S. Department of Education estimated that, in fiscal 1992, 3.6 million people would be served through a combination of approximately $240 million in Adult Education Act funds and $560 million in state and local funds (Office of Vocational and Adult Education, 1991:2).

In September 1990, the U.S. Department of Education launched a national evaluation of federally supported adult education programs supported by Basic Grants, with a final report due in 1994. In the fall of 1990, a survey of all federally supported providers of adult education instructional service was conducted. This survey presents the best available data on these providers. There were 2,819 in the program year ending June 30, 1990, serving 3.7 million clients during the 1989-1990 program year. Since many individuals participated in the program for less than a year, fewer were enrolled at any one time: about 1.7 million in October 1990, according to the survey. Local programs were diverse in sponsorship and size. They served a median of 168 clients in October 1990, with 12 percent of programs serving over 1,000 clients each and 37 percent serving less than 100 clients each at that time. Sixty-eight percent of the programs were administered by local education agencies and 17 percent by community colleges. Volunteer organizations and community service groups (6 percent), technical institutes (6 percent), and regional educational service agencies or consortia of public school districts (2 percent) accounted for the rest. Sixty-three percent of the students were served by school system programs and 28 percent by programs administered by community colleges (U.S. Department of Education, 1992).

Vocational Rehabilitation

The other major U.S. Department of Education effort with a vocational focus is authorized by the Rehabilitation Act of 1973, as amended. In fiscal 1991, federal vocational-rehabilitation expenditures exceeded $1.5 billion. Rehabilitation is provided to enable individuals with disabilities to prepare for and engage in gainful employment to the greatest extent possible. Individuals of all ages are eligible for services that include evaluation, counseling, physical and mental restoration, training, supportive services, and placement. Supportive services are varied, including, for example, interpreter services for the deaf; reader services for the blind; and tools, licenses, equipment, supplies, and management services for vending stands or other small businesses for individuals with severe disabilities (U.S. Department of Education, 1990b). The Rehabilitation Act authorizes federal allocations to state rehabilitation agencies on a formula basis with a matching requirement.

In fiscal 1991, state rehabilitation agencies funded through the act served over 940,000 individuals and "rehabilitated" over 200,000 individuals. Rehabilitated persons are those who applied for vocational-rehabilitation services, were found eligible to participate, received services, completed their programs, and were found to be eligible for employment upon completion. Sixty percent of the persons rehabilitated were classified as "severely disabled" (e.g., blind, deaf, severe respiratory disorders, etc.) (U.S. Department of Education, 1991).

While vocational-rehabilitation is one of the larger programs in the U.S. Department of Education, its postsecondary training component is comparatively small. The training portion of vocational-rehabilitation may include on-the-job training; occupational training at a vocational-rehabilitation center; adjustment training (e.g., interviewing skills, job search assistance, etc.); as well as classroom training in a community college, area vocational school, proprietary school, or 4-year college or university. There are no reliable national estimates for the utilization of these services. However, conversations with state and national vocational-rehabilitation officials indicate that 10 to 15 percent of vocational-rehabilitation participants receive training through a 2- or 4-year college or proprietary school. When participants do receive training through one of these institutions, they must first use Pell grant funds before vocational-rehabilitation funds will be committed.

The Job Training Partnership Act

The Job Training Partnership Act (JTPA), first enacted in 1982 and administered by the U.S. Department of Labor, is the latest in a series of federal programs dating back to the 1960s that were designed to provide training and employment assistance to disadvantaged individuals and dislocated workers. It is the major federal program specifically aimed at improving the training and employability of those without jobs.

JTPA serves disadvantaged adults and youth through activities authorized under Title II, dislocated workers under a program authorized under Title III (see the following section), and special populations (veterans, Native Americans, and seasonal and migrant farm workers) under Title IV provisions.[9] The Job Corps, a largely residential education and training program for youth, is also authorized under Title IV. States have primary responsibility for programs under Titles II and III; the federal government directly administers Title IV programs.

Funding for JTPA was $4.1 billion in fiscal 1993, about 10 percent higher (in current dollars) than when the program was created. Funding declined somewhat in current dollars throughout the 1980s for the Title II programs, but Title III and the Job Corps under Title IV grew from $233 million and $640 million, respectively, in program year 1984 to $567 million and $966 million in fiscal 1993.

Nonetheless, JTPA funding is significantly lower than federal spending on the Comprehensive Employment and Training Act (CETA), which JTPA replaced. This is true even after excluding CETA expenditures on public service employment (Levitan and Gallo, 1988:19).[10] Title II is the centerpiece of JTPA, accounting for about three-fifths of JTPA spending. It and the Job Corps together account for over 80 percent of JTPA funds.

In program year 1991 (July 1, 1991–June 30, 1992), 533,100 persons were newly enrolled in Title II, and 526,000 were terminated. Title II services for unemployed adults and out-of-school, unemployed youth included classroom training, on-the-job training, job search assistance, work experience, and other services. Table 2-4 indicates the relative incidence of these services. In reaction to criticisms that CETA funds were spent too heavily on nontraining activities, JTPA originally restricted nontraining expenditures on administration, allowances or stipends, and supportive services to 30 percent of program costs. (The 1992 amendments to JTPA raised this level to 50 percent.) Unlike CETA, which assumed that the poor would need income support while they pursued training, JTPA in practice almost eliminated such assistance in many areas (Levitan and Gallo, 1988:62-63).

Several features distinguish JTPA from most other federal training activities. Most important, Title II is similar to a block grant to the states, with important administrative responsibility vested in the states and discretion about whom to serve left to local officials. Worried that too few beneficiaries were seriously disadvantaged, Congress amended JTPA in 1992 to require that, besides being economically disadvantaged, at least 65 percent of the adults and youth served by Title II had to have at least one

TABLE 2.4 Principal Program Activities of JTPA IIA
Terminees, 1991

Type of Training	Percentage of Terminees Receiving Training
On-the-job	15
Classroom/occupational	29
Classroom/basic education	15
Work experience	6
Job-search assistance	15
Other[a]	20

[a]Refers to participants who received services that could not be considered as one of the above activities, *or* participants who received
significant amounts of more than one type of activity.

SOURCES: U.S. Department of Labor (1993:8), supplemented by information provided to the committee by the U.S. Department of Labor.

barrier to employment (such as basic skills deficiencies, receipt of cash
welfare payments, disabilities, homelessness, or criminal records).[11]

Nevertheless, JTPA retains a strong emphasis on state, local, and private sector involvement and responsibility. Title II funds are allocated to
the states on the basis of the number of people in poverty and concentra-
tions of unemployed individuals. States pass on about four-fifths of these
funds to more than 640 service delivery areas across the nation, based on
the same federally determined factors. Each area is overseen by a Private
Industry Council, a majority of whose members, appointed by the chief
elected officials of the service delivery areas, must represent business. Private Industry Councils and local officials together select an administrative
agency to run the program; this can be the council itself, a government
agency, or a nonprofit organization. The administering agency can provide
services directly but typically contracts them out to schools, community-
based organizations, and private vendors.

JTPA is a voluntary program; participants hear about it through word of
mouth or advertising or are referred by state welfare and employment agencies. After completing applications to establish financial eligibility and
assessments to measure academic preparation and job readiness, individuals
are assigned to one of the various program services noted above. Youth
assigned to classroom training usually utilize services provided by area
vocational and high schools; adults tend to get their classroom training from
community colleges and, to a much lesser extent, proprietary schools. Some
youth and adults receive classroom training from community-based organi-

zations. When JTPA participants are referred to community colleges and proprietary schools, they may be placed in regular classes alongside the schools' regular students, or the service delivery area may contract for special classes limited to JTPA enrollees.

Another distinguishing feature of JTPA is the use of performance standards in Title II. In its early years, JTPA was directed from the federal level with some restraint. Congress instructed the U.S. Department of Labor to develop performance standards to measure the results of local service delivery area activity. The development of performance standards actually began in the mid-1970s under CETA and has characterized JTPA since the outset. The standards used in the first years of the program specified desired outcome levels for the proportion of adult participants entering employment; the proportion of adult welfare recipients entering employment; average hourly wages; and costs per placement; all measured at the point when participants left (or terminated from) the program. Standards for youth included the proportion entering employment, the positive termination rate, and the costs per positive termination. (A positive termination is one with a positive outcome, such as the participant returned to school or attained specific competencies upon termination from the program.) These standards have been modified over time to emphasize longer-term rather than immediate postprogram results and to eliminate the cost standards. Cost standards were widely viewed as encouraging service delivery areas to "cream"; that is, to serve the most job-ready and easiest-to-place applicants to minimize costs rather than to select individuals who would be harder and more expensive to serve. Governors can modify federally determined standards by using optional adjustment models that allow for differences in expected performance based on participant characteristics and local labor market conditions. Service delivery areas that fail to meet the performance standards are given technical assistance by the state but may ultimately be removed from the JTPA program. Service delivery areas that succeed are given financial awards based on the extent to which they exceeded standards.

The performance standard system is further advanced in JTPA than in other federal training programs, although the approach is spreading. Follow-up standards since 1989 have replaced termination-based standards for adults and welfare recipients. Youth standards have also shifted to emphasize competency more strongly (see Chapters 3 and 6).

In 1992 Congress passed JTPA amendments that made the first major changes to Title II since the program was enacted in 1982. The legislation emphasized targeting services, enhancing program quality, moving toward a comprehensive human service delivery system, and increasing fiscal integrity. Some of the changes in eligibility requirements have been described above. The amendments also require individualized assessments of education, skills, and service needs of each participant so that service strategies can be tailored and managed individually and provide more intense and comprehensive services to each client. Performance standards were changed to emphasize actual acquisition of skills in addition to job placements. The amendments require better documentation and reporting of costs and stronger procurement and contracting procedures. They promote a greater level of coordination among human resource programs through support for state human resource investment councils (see Chapter 3).

The Job Opportunities and Basic Skills Training Program

The Job Opportunities and Basic Skills (JOBS) Training Program was created in 1988 as part of the Family Support Act, a major reform of the nation's leading welfare program. That reform, while continuing unchanged cash benefits for poor adults and their dependent children under the Aid to Families with Dependent Children (AFDC) program, "sought to shift the balance between permanent income maintenance and temporary support toward the latter" (Gueron and Pauly, 1991:1). JOBS was created to provide adults receiving AFDC with the education, training, and employment that would help them avoid long-term dependence on welfare. To accomplish this, the JOBS program not only required that AFDC recipients undertake education and training in preparation for stable employment, but also provided the necessary supportive services, such as child care, transportation, and medical assistance, to facilitate the goal.

JOBS operates as a capped entitlement, with $1 billion authorized for 1991, rising to $1.3 billion in 1995. In September 1991, approximately 560,000 individuals were participating in JOBS (Greenberg, 1992:3). Over the years, states are supposed to include an increasing proportion of the welfare caseload in their JOBS programs, with the percentage rising from 7 percent in 1991 to 20 percent in 1995.

Unlike JTPA and other education and training programs, JOBS is at the same time a service and a welfare reform program, in that it seeks to condition welfare receipt on participation in employment-directed services. This mandatory element distinguishes the program from other related activities, although, in reality, limited funding has substantially restricted the mandatory nature of the program. JOBS and JTPA overlap in important ways. Welfare administrators frequently refer JOBS participants to the local JTPA program for training, and JTPA also frequently uses JOBS to pay for supportive services such as child care and transportation. JTPA legislation requires that welfare recipients be served on an equitable basis relative to their incidence in the population.

JOBS operates as a significant partnership between states and the federal government. The U.S. Department of Health and Human Services provides broad guidelines to states about the makeup of state JOBS programs. All state JOBS programs must include four basic services: educational activities below the postsecondary level, job skills training, job readiness activities, and job development or job placement activities. State JOBS programs must also include two of the following four components: group and individual job search, on-the-job training, work supplementation, and community work experience. Postsecondary education is one optional activity among many that states may offer. Within these guidelines, states have much flexibility in developing programs. In particular, the law provides that states must meet program requirements "to the extent that resources permit." Thus, there are significant state-to-state differences in the character of JOBS programs (Gueron and Pauly, 1991:56). Overall, however, states have opted for greater emphasis on investment in human capital than on work attachment strategies.

The responsibility for financing JOBS is also shared among federal and state governments. Whereas JTPA is fully funded by the U.S. Department of Labor, states must provide matching funds to be able to draw down their portion of the JOBS-capped entitlement. The federal matching rate is 90 percent up to each state's Work Incentive (WIN) Program allocation for 1987. Above that amount, the federal government matches JOBS expenditures at the Medicaid rate or 60 percent, whichever is higher. Thus, the $1 billion allocated to JOBS for 1991 represents funds available for state matching. Due to state budget constraints, states have not been able to draw down their entire allocation. Of the federal funds available in 1991, states spent only $591 million. State allocations in that year ranged from $1.2 million in North Dakota to $160 million in California. Expenditures as a percent of available funds ranged from 11 percent in Mississippi to 100 percent in several states (Greenberg, 1992:Appendix D).

Of particular interest to the committee is the extent to which JOBS participants are offered postsecondary training opportunities in community colleges, proprietary schools, or area vocational schools. While much of the education and training in JOBS takes place below the postsecondary level (because there are substantial numbers of young high school dropouts on AFDC), a JOBS participant can enroll in postsecondary training in two ways. First, if an individual is deemed eligible for, but is not already attending, a postsecondary institution prior to JOBS participation, the state may assign that individual to a postsecondary activity. Second, if an individual is already attending a postsecondary institution prior to participating in JOBS, the state may approve the activity as self-initiated education and training, thereby making the participant eligible for support services. In either case, attendance at a postsecondary institution is at the discretion of the state.

One important difference between these two modes of entry into a postsecondary institution is the mix of services and activities for which the state either can or must pay. Whether the postsecondary activity is self-initiated or referred, the state must pay for necessary child care and transportation costs. If the state refers the participant to the postsecondary activity, the state may pay the cost of the activity (i.e., tuition and fees). If the state approves the postsecondary activity as self-initiated education and training, JOBS regulations do not allow the state to pay for the cost of the activity. Greenberg (1992:i) found that approximately 25 percent of JOBS participants were attending a postsecondary institution, whether referred or self-initiated.

In many states, basic education is the largest JOBS component activity. In September 1991, 32 percent of all participants were assigned to this category. Basic education includes high school or GED completion for adults, high school completion for teen parents, and ESL (Greenberg, 1992:7-8).

While states have operated under requirements relating to program participation rates since JOBS' inception, the program does not yet use performance standards of the type found in JTPA. The Family Support Act requires the Secretary of Health and Human Services to make recommendations to Congress on performance standards for the JOBS program by October 1, 1993.

Dislocated Worker Programs

The federal government provides assistance to dislocated workers through a number of mechanisms, including those targeted at dislocated workers as well as those provided to all individuals in need. The two major federal programs aimed specifically at dislocated workers are Trade Adjustment Assistance (TAA) and the Economic Dislocation and Worker Adjustment Assistance Act (EDWAA), both of which are administered through the U.S. Department of Labor (National Commission for Employment Policy, 1991a). A variety of smaller discretionary grant programs have been created in recent years under programs such as Defense Conversion Adjustment (1990), Clean Air Employment Transition Assistance (1990), and Defense Diversification (1992). The National Governors' Association (private communication) has estimated that there are at least 18 different federal dislocated worker programs, each with different eligible grantees, administrative structures, eligible participants, allowable services, and performance goals. Not all of these programs provide training, however. We concentrate here on the two main dislocated worker programs that have a training focus, TAA and EDWAA.

TAA was established in 1962 and has been amended several times, most recently by the Omnibus Trade and Competitiveness Act of 1988. TAA provides two types of services. First, TAA funds trade readjustment allowances, which extend unemployment insurance benefits up to 52 additional weeks for workers certified by the U.S. Department of Labor as having become unemployed or underemployed as a result of increased imports. Under the 1988 amendments, workers must participate in an approved job training program in order to receive readjustment cash benefits, unless they receive a waiver that job training is either inappropriate or unavailable. In fiscal 1990, the federal government provided close to $100 million in cash benefits to 19,545 displaced workers. One recent study (Corson et al., 1993) found that over 85 percent of readjustment recipients came from the manufacturing sector.

In addition to cash benefits, TAA also funds job training services for certified dislocated workers. As part of its job training program, TAA offers occupational information and counseling, on-the-job training, vocational-technical training, remedial education, job search assistance, and relocation allowances. In fiscal 1990, 19,867 displaced workers received some form of job services, the bulk of them in the form of direct training, rather than job search or relocation assistance.[12] While the state employment agencies usually offer the job search assistance and relocation allowances directly, they usually contract for the training services from both public and private vendors. Although TAA training is an entitlement program, training costs are subject to an annual $80 million cap.

Currently, TAA is considerably smaller than it was at its height in 1980, when it provided some 500,000 people with trade readjustment allowances totaling over $1.6 billion (Levitan and Gallo, 1988:107). Only a handful of these received any readjustment training. The next year, however, the elimination of payments that increased weekly unemployment insurance benefits and the limitation of trade readjustment allowances to an extension of unemployment insurance benefits—passed as part of the Omnibus Budget Reconciliation Act of 1981—significantly reduced the number and cost of trade readjustment allowances.

EDWAA became operational in 1989 and replaced the original Title III of JTPA through legislation in the Omnibus Trade and Competitiveness Act. EDWAA changed Title III significantly by emphasizing rapid response capabilities to assist workers before a plant closure or major layoff occurs, including labor-management cooperation to prepare for layoffs; a mandated role for the substate areas that deliver EDWAA services—at least 60 percent of the state's funds are to be passed down to substate areas; intensive retraining services to dislocated workers; and improved linkages with the unemployment insurance system, the Employment Service, and TAA. With federal appropriations of $527 million in program year 1991, EDWAA served about 330,000 people.

EDWAA provides for such services as job search assistance, on-the-job training, occupational skills training, entrepreneurial training, and basic skills training. The substate grantee may provide all or some of the services directly or may contract out for them to a variety of public and private organizations.

Community colleges and vocational-technical schools are the most frequent providers of occupational classroom training. Most substate areas supplement public service providers with proprietary schools, which offer shorter, more intensive training with more flexible scheduling. CBOs and unions also provide classroom training, although far less frequently than community colleges, vocational-technical schools, and proprietary schools (Corson et al., 1993).

TAA and EDWAA both address the needs of similar populations, offer similar services, and are administered by the U.S. Department of Labor. Yet, the two programs have developed distinctly different characters. EDWAA strongly resembles JTPA Title II and is characterized by training programs of comparatively short duration. TAA, on the other hand, emphasizes longer-term training and provides cash benefits so that workers have the flexibility to undertake longer-term training.

Summary

The federal government, through these and other programs, is an active partner in postsecondary training. As these program descriptions indicate, though, the federal approach is piecemeal. Goals, services, and financing and administrative arrangements are quite variable. Federal oversight and administration is divided among numerous executive departments; congressional responsibility is equally decentralized among many committees and subcommittees. There is no one place in the federal structure where postsecondary training as a whole is considered. Instead, this array of programs intersects with the assortment of providers described earlier in the chapter to compose a complex matrix of postsecondary training opportunities. We will now turn to the question of how well or badly this matrix of activities meets the training needs of the nation.

NOTES

1. Enrollment estimates from the National Center for Education Statistics, while the best available, probably understate proprietary school enrollments. The Center's enrollment survey is sent to just a sample of less-than-2-year proprietary institutions and the results are "weighted up" statistically to determine enrollments for the universe of such schools. Since proprietary schools open and close at a rapid rate, it has been difficult to keep the sampling frame up to date so that it yields reliable estimates.

2. These data were tabulated by the committee using data from the National Postsecondary Student Aid Study, 1989-1990, sponsored by the U.S. Department of Education.

3. Some of the reasons for this include poor response to surveys from firms, unreliable memories and perceptions of training on the part of individuals queried in employee surveys, and the difficulty of distinguishing between "training time" and "work time" when employees

are trained informally on the job (U.S. Office of Technology Assessment, 1990:128). In addition, many firms do not know what they spend on training, and data that are available are usually not comparable from firm to firm (Kochan and Osterman, 1991:22).

4. The exact number of programs depends on how one defines the term *program*. The JTPA, for example, includes a number of different programs for disadvantaged youth and adults. Likewise, student financial assistance includes several grant and loan programs and a program that provides work-study support for students. We have not attempted to develop the definitive list of activities that can be distinctly identified as separate programs. The activities that we identify in Table 2.1 as supporting postsecondary training are part of a broader set of federal activities that provide training and other employment-related services to adults and youth. In a July 24, 1992, letter to Senator Edward M. Kennedy, Chair of the Senate Labor and Human Resources Committee, the General Accounting Office (GAO) listed 125 programs (not counting the U.S. Defense Department's training of active-duty personnel, which we include in our calculations) with funding of $16.4 billion in fiscal 1991. Most programs were quite small—under $50 million each.

5. See footnote 1, Chapter 1, on why the amount of federal assistance available to students exceeds the costs of that assistance to the federal government.

6. Students enrolled in short programs of study have lower loan limits.

7. For example, 23 percent of all Stafford borrowers attended proprietary schools, but 42 percent of Stafford defaulters came from the proprietary sector (U.S. General Accounting Office, 1988:7). In another study, the GAO found that of 1.1 million students from accredited proprietary schools who were in loan repayment status in 1989, nearly 300,000 individuals owed over $712 million in defaulted loans (U.S. General Accounting Office, 1990a).

8. The act's name was also changed, adding "applied technology" to the historical emphasis on vocational education.

9. Until the 1992 JTPA amendments, Title II-A combined year-round programs for adults and young people, and Title II-B authorized a summer employment and training program for youth during the school vacation period. The reauthorization restricted Title II-A to adults and created a new Title II-C authorizing year-round programs for both in-school and out-of-school youth. Not less than 50 percent of those served under Title II-C are to be out-of-school youth. Title II-B continues as a summer youth program.

10. Public Service Employment, a job creation program, began in the mid-1970s as a response to rising unemployment rates. It became quite controversial, however, and was eliminated when JTPA was created. Amendments to JTPA in 1992 added permanent authority for up to $15 million annually to be used for a small program of public service employment for disaster relief.

11. While Title II primarily serves economically disadvantaged youth and adults, Congress has created a special 10 percent window that allows up to 10 percent of participants within a given service delivery area to be people who are not economically disadvantaged, but who face a serious barrier to employment.

12. Since workers receiving cash benefits are also required to participate in job training unless they receive a waiver, there is clearly a significant amount of overlap between individuals receiving cash benefits and those receiving job training. Corson et al. (1993:xviii) found that 47 percent of readjustment recipients received training through TAA. This means that just over 30,000 people received at least one kind of service (either cash benefits through trade readjustment allowance, or training through TAA, or both) in fiscal 1990. More workers received job services than trade readjustment allowances because such services were provided to dislocated workers who were still receiving regular unemployment insurance benefits and were thus not eligible for trade readjustment allowances.

3

Diagnosing the Health of Postsecondary Training

Postsecondary training in America is a large and multi-faceted activity, as Chapter 2 described. Is it working well or badly? Answering this question about so diverse an enterprise is not easy. There are areas of strength and areas of serious weakness. An accurate diagnosis, however, is crucial to the committee's ultimate goal of assessing the need for new or revised federal policies.

In evaluating the health of postsecondary training, the committee found itself struggling with two sometimes opposing tasks: analyzing each institution and program or evaluating postsecondary training as a system. It is easier, and tempting, to assess the performance of each institution and each program and to recommend how each should be improved. This is the way most research and analysis in the field has been done. But such a piecemeal perspective begs the critical question: Is the sum of all the activities embodied in existing institutions and programs a postsecondary training system that is accessible, effective, efficient, and adequate to America's needs in a rapidly changing and ever more competitive global marketplace?

While not ignoring the evidence about the individual parts, the committee chose to approach its diagnosis by giving primary emphasis to the system perspective. We will therefore evaluate the postsecondary training institutions and programs by organizing our discussion around five questions relating to the characteristics of a well-functioning system: Is training accessible, and do people have the information they need to select among training options? What do we know about the results of different kinds of training and what works for which people? Do the incentives in the system encourage efficiency and effectiveness, or do they leave elements open to abuse or inadequate performance? How and how well is training connected to employers? How well are the diverse pieces of a fragmented system articulated and coordinated with one another?

ACCESS AND INFORMATION

Osterman (1990:258) has observed that "the array of institutions [devoted to postsecondary training in America] is impressive" and that a strength of this diverse system is that it "is very much driven by individual initiative, and a person who wants to change careers or gain new skills can find numerous ways to do so. . . . [E]arly choices are not binding and the system provides chances (for those with the resources) to start over or change direction." Most people live close to a community college, where prices are relatively low and a variety of training options is often available. Numerous other opportunities for training exist in most areas.

Nevertheless, access to different kinds of postsecondary training is quite variable, and information about the options available, which would enhance access for individuals seeking training, is often inadequate.

Access to Qualifying Training

Postsecondary training that qualifies individuals for jobs, when offered on a formal rather than informal basis, is heavily school-based in the United States. Thanks to the wide availability of state-subsidized community colleges and vocational-technical schools with few or no admission requirements and to financial aid to help cover the costs of unsubsidized training programs in private and proprietary schools, there is generally good access to postsecondary qualifying training.

Two recent studies, which approach the issue in very different ways, confirm the general accessibility of postsecondary qualifying training.

McPherson and Schapiro (1991:188) undertook a comprehensive evaluation of the affordability of postsecondary schooling and the effects of student financial aid policy, reviewing earlier research as well as conducting original econometric analyses on the effects of the net price of an education on enrollments. They concluded that "the combination of state institutional subsidies and federal student aid makes *some* form of postsecondary education financially accessible to a wide range of Americans." Because prices are very different in different sectors of postsecondary education, however, access to various kinds of postsecondary experiences are constrained by incomes, with low-price community colleges the most readily accessible choice for lower-income people. This does not limit access to training for these people, since many vocation-oriented programs are offered at community colleges. Access to baccalaureate-level education, which takes longer to complete and occurs in more expensive institutions, is more likely to be uneven. Nevertheless, there are some state-to-state differences even in access to training-oriented institutions: not every state has an extensive community college or technical college system, and the willingness and ability of states to subsidize these institutions varies. In general, however, qualifying training is quite accessible for most people, even the economically disadvantaged.

Tuma's (1992) review of cross-sectional national data on enrollments in postsecondary schools supports this conclusion. He conducted a detailed analysis of participation in vocation-oriented schooling in the academic year 1989-1990, using the National Postsecondary Student Aid Study (NPSAS) data generated by the National Center for Education Statistics (NCES).[1] Like McPherson and Schapiro, he found that vocation-oriented postsecondary schools, even relatively expensive ones like proprietary institutions, were especially accessible to individuals with economic, educational, and other disadvantages.[2]

Several qualifications should be placed on this generally positive picture, however. Resource constraints at the state and federal levels are affecting both institutional subsidies and the availability of financial aid, which increases the net costs of postsecondary training to individuals and places higher economic barriers in the way, particularly for lower-income people. Restrictions on access to schools that provide postsecondary training are especially worrisome in light of the fact that there are few alternative routes to school-based qualifying training in the United States. Moreover, even if access to schools remains good, there is reason to believe that the relative absence of nonschool-based options is a problem.

The Massachusetts Institute of Technology (MIT) Commission on Industrial Productivity (Dertouzos et al., 1989) studied the routes from school to jobs in two sets of countries. The first set, called "pattern A" countries, included the United States, Sweden, and Britain, all of which rely on formal educational institutions for most of the job-oriented preparation of their work forces, including teaching specialized as well as more general skills. In "pattern B" countries, such as Japan and Germany, both general and specialized skills are usually learned on the job. The commission found that "pattern B countries find it easier to produce workers with the flexibility and skills needed to respond to rapid and unpredictable changes in technology and markets" (Dertouzos et al., 1989:84).

Whether worker training is best provided in schools or in firms is an old debate in the United States (Osterman, 1990:269-270). The question has become salient again, particularly because of deep concerns about the shortcomings of American secondary education and widespread interest in the so-called dual system in Germany, which involves the majority of young people in firm-based, 3-year apprenticeship programs. It is generally acknowledged that many school-based training programs in the United States are divorced from the needs of the workplace, with no connection either to the knowledge and skills needed at work or to the ways in which knowledge and skills are used in the workplace.[3]

Learning in work-based rather than school-based settings is thought to have a number of advantages, especially for young people (Hamilton and Hamilton, 1992:18). Learning at work seems real and has an immediate payoff that is easy to identify. Knowledge and skills acquired in the context in which they will be used are learned more effectively and powerfully. Work-based preparation occurs among adults, which makes work and learning seem more serious and also allows young people to develop relationships with older mentors.

However, the question of whether work-based or school-based training is more desirable is controversial. Berryman and Bailey (1992) cite a number of concerns about work-based learning. The current failure of many employers to provide much formal training to their employees, especially younger and less-educated ones, casts doubt on their interest and ability to serve as major providers of qualifying training. The quality of work-based learning can vary from excellent to awful, depending on the training skills and expertise of those doing the training. School-based educators have been slow to understand and adopt research findings about how to create powerful learning environments; it is unclear why employers would be likely to do better.

Scribner and Sachs (1991) show that the key issue for the workplace as a learning place is no different than for school-based learning. Whether in the workplace or the schoolroom setting, what is emphasized and encouraged helps learners develop either a conceptual understanding or a highly routinized, inflexible set of responses. For example, a company that organizes work or a school that organizes learning as a set of segmented tasks will limit what its workers or its students learn. Companies organized for mass production will be more apt to structure learning as segmented tasks. Since most companies still organize work for mass production, America may face a Hobson's choice between two worlds, schools and the workplace, neither of which is well designed for powerful learning.

Whether or not work-based training on a massive scale would be better than the current school-based system, the committee recognizes that the absence of significant work-based alternatives is unfortunate. Chapter 2 showed that traditional apprenticeships in the United States are not usually open to people in their late teens to early twenties and that innovations such as youth apprenticeships are still in the demonstration stage, reaching relatively few people. Cooperative education, where students alternate schooling and work, involved fewer than 3 percent of community college students in the academic year 1989-1990 (U.S. General Accounting Office, 1991:19). The evident success of work-based approaches to qualifying training in Germany and elsewhere (see Chapter 4) as well as the unsatisfactory state of much of school-based training in the United States suggest that a more experimental strategy utilizing both approaches is called for.

Access to Skills Improvement Training

Unlike the other forms of training considered in this report, decisions about the extent of skills improvement training are left almost completely to the private sector; that is, to firms and their employees. Not surprisingly, then, access to skills improvement training for currently employed workers is extremely uneven. Some firms have embraced training as fundamental to their success and promote participation by a large proportion of their work forces. In some unionized companies, joint union-management programs mandate set-aside funding for training that involves substantial funds. More typical, though, appear to be the findings of the MIT Commission on Industrial Productivity (Dertouzos et al., 1989:86), which discovered in interviews with managers in many industrial settings that companies had low regard for training. The commission found "a systematic undervaluation in this country of how much difference it can make when people are well educated and when their skills are continuously developed and challenged."

Chapter 2 indicated that expenditures by firms on employee training are sizable. The evidence indicates, however, that the receipt of training is quite uneven for different categories of workers and for employees of different firms. Women, minorities, young people, employees of smaller firms, lower-level workers, and workers with lower levels of formal education tend to receive disproportionately low amounts of skills improvement training (Kochan and Osterman, 1991:26-27; Lynch, 1992).

Many firms, especially small and new companies, appear reluctant to invest in training for a variety of reasons (Stern and Ritzen, 1991; Lynch, 1994; National Research Council, 1993). Chapter 1 described some general features of the American labor market that help explain this reluctance. In addition, small and new companies confront special problems. They face capital constraints that prevent them from borrowing. Borrowing to invest in training—even training that can be shown to be a good investment—is also likely to be difficult because of the uncertainty associated with training investments and because of its intangibility, which means there can be no collateral for such loans. Small firms also face deterrents because of their small size. Training programs require certain fixed costs (determining what training is necessary, developing an appropriate curriculum or teaching method), regardless of how many individuals are to be trained; as a result, training at small firms will cost more per worker than similar training in large firms.

One partial solution has been for community colleges and other training providers to offer standardized courses—in, for example, literacy, English as a second language, the math necessary for statistical process control, or total quality management—in which small firms can enroll their employees without incurring high fixed costs. Here, though, another problem surfaces: inadequate information. Firms may not be aware of what is available or be in a position to judge its quality or its potential payoff to the company.

In addition, shifting from one "equilibrium" to another can pose problems. To use the terms of *America's Choice: High Skills or Low Wages!* (Commission on the Skills of the American Workforce, 1990), a distressingly large number of firms appear to be in what can be characterized as a *low-skills equilibrium*: they are profitable and endure with a relatively undereducated labor force. In such workplaces, firm-based training is rare and largely confined to upper-level managers and professionals, and production methods have been adapted to the low skill level of the labor force. While there may be another, high-skills equilibrium—characterized by greater skills, a different organization of work stressing greater responsibilities for front-line workers, and more education and training—there may be no good way for firms to move from one equilibrium to the other on their own. Such a change would require too much lost time in reorganizing production and retraining workers; it would be impossible to obtain loans to cover the capital and training costs; there would be serious problems of timing, deciding in what order changes in technology, organization, and skill development should take place; and competitive pressures would make it difficult for managers to chart a long-run strategy.

Access to Retraining

Access to the two major federal dislocated worker retraining programs is currently limited, primarily by the need for dislocated workers to meet specific eligibility criteria and the size of appropriations to finance the training. The ability of individuals to participate in the programs may also be limited by amount of income support available and the timeliness of service offerings.

Of the two federal programs, the Trade Adjustment Assistance (TAA) program has the more restrictive eligibility requirements. Workers are eligible only if a significant number of workers in a company have lost (or are threatened with the loss of) their jobs because imports of like or directly competitive products contributed importantly to a decrease in that company's sales or production. Other dislocated workers in the same community who may have lost jobs because of a local economic decline resulting from layoffs at the affected company are not eligible. Similarly, workers dislocated from separate companies supplying the affected company are not eligible.

The other program, Economic Dislocation and Worker Adjustment Assistance (EDWAA)—Title III of Job Training Partnership Act (JTPA)—can provide services to all unemployed workers who lack the job search and basic and occupational skills necessary for reemployment. However, all workers losing jobs because of a plant closing or substantial layoff are eligible without having to demonstrate a lack of those skills. The emphasis in EDWAA is to provide a rapid response to the needs of the latter workers. As with TAA, workers who lose jobs because of the secondary effects of a plant closing or mass layoff do not have the same access to EDWAA services.

Appropriations can also limit access to these programs. Although TAA job training is an entitlement, it is currently subject to an $80 million appropriation cap. The fiscal 1991 appropriation for EDWAA was $527 million.

Lack of income may also inhibit dislocated workers from using job training assistance. TAA provides income support to eligible dislocated workers for 52 weeks after exhausting unemployment insurance. Although EDWAA also allows some income support, few participants receive any (U.S. General Accounting Office, 1992b). The GAO reports that, in the three states it examined, TAA participants were more likely to enter and remain in longer-term training than EDWAA participants. However, since the final 26 weeks of TAA income support is dependent on enrollment in training, it is not clear whether the income support enables the training or the training enables the income support.

Meaningful access to training may also be dependent on the speed with which assistance is provided. The GAO report indicates that, while over 50 percent of EDWAA participants entered training within the first 15 weeks of unemployment, substantially more than 50 percent (97 percent in one state) of TAA participants did not get training services until they had been unemployed for at least 15 weeks. The GAO concludes that the necessity to certify the cause of dislocation is an important reason for the delay in the TAA program. Although the U.S. Department of Labor is required to complete action on a worker's petition for certification within 60 days, it also takes time to prepare a petition for filing and to inform workers of eligibility after approval. Moreover, the GAO (1992c) found that the 60-day requirement has forced the department to take shortcuts; as a result, 63 percent of the petitions that were investigated in 1990 and 1991 were flawed.

Access to Second-Chance Training

Like retraining programs, access to second-chance training programs is limited because benefits are targeted to specific populations and funding has never been adequate to meet the needs of those who meet the eligibility requirements. This is particularly true of the three largest second-chance programs: Title II training for youth and adults in JTPA, the Job Opportunities and Basic Skills Act (JOBS), and adult education programs.

JTPA funding has never been adequate to serve more than a small fraction of an eligible population that is defined quite broadly. The version of JTPA Title II-A in effect prior to the 1992 reauthorization established five broad criteria under which an individual could be considered "economically disadvantaged" and therefore eligible for JTPA services. Sandell and Rupp (1988:34-36) used these criteria and data from the Job Training Quarterly Survey for program years 1984 and 1985 along with information from the Current Population Survey to estimate JTPA participation rates. They found that an average of 39 million people met formal Title II-A criteria each year. Of this total, 31.7 million were 16 through 64 years old. Within this age group, only 12 percent were unemployed, both without jobs and actively seeking work; thus there were 3.9 million unemployed eligibles actively seeking work. These were the people most likely to be interested in JTPA services. In program year 1985, JTPA II-A served 498,800 unemployed people aged 16 to 64, or just 13 percent of the eligible population most likely to take advantage of the program. In that same year, JTPA II-A served 738,200 of the 31.7 million eligibles aged 16 to 64, a participation rate of just 2.33 percent.

When Congress created the JOBS program in 1988, it enacted specific participation rate goals and timetables. Aid to Families with Dependent Children (AFDC) recipients between the ages of 15 and 59 are required to participate in the JOBS program, unless they have been exempted. (Recipients working at least 30 hours a week, attending high school, or caring for young children are among those exempted.) Congress set a schedule that states had to meet of gradually increasing, minimum participation rates. Under the schedule, states were required to serve 7 percent of the total number of nonexempt AFDC recipients within the state during fiscal 1991.[4] Because of the stringent definition of *participation* used in JOBS, many more people are involved in the program than are actually counted as participants. The required participation rate rises to 11 percent in 1992 and 1993, 15 percent in 1994, and 20 percent in 1995. States not meeting these rates stand to lose a portion of their federal funds for JOBS programs. For fiscal 1991, all but one state met the 7 percent minimum each month (U.S. General Accounting Office, 1992e). Early indications are that many states will not have the money to meet the 20 percent participation requirement.

A serious gap between the size of available programs and the need for services also exists in the field of adult basic skills training. Estimates of the number of adults in need of basic skills education vary, but the number is generally believed to be more than 20 million (Chisman, 1989; Grubb et al., 1991). In findings incorporated into the National Literacy Act of 1991 (PL 102-73), Congress put the number at closer to 30 million. Whatever the exact number, it is clear that existing programs do not meet the potential demand for services. Chapter 2 showed that fewer than 4 million people annually have been served by the programs authorized by the Adult Education Act. In the National Literacy Act, Congress said that public and private literacy programs taken together serve approximately 19 percent of those in need of help. As with other programs, of course, not all of those officially considered to be in need of help may have an interest in receiving services. Nonetheless, one study from 1987 (Mikulecky, 1989:221-222) reported waiting lists for 30 percent of literacy programs nationwide and for 47 percent of programs in urban areas.

Information About Training Options

We began our discussion of access to and information about postsecondary training by acknowledging the benefits of multiple providers and multiple routes into occupations. A drawback of this approach, however, is that the variety of options available can be confusing, and information to help individuals make appropriate choices is often either unavailable or difficult to use.

Various kinds of information would be useful to those contemplating training, such as an overview of the training opportunities available in a geographic area, the success of various training providers in preparing people for jobs, the training and certification requirements of specific occupations, the likely demand by employers for new workers with specific kinds of training, and the wages and career paths that characterize various fields of work. Though we did not as a committee undertake a careful study of the information issue, experience tells us that quite a bit of information exists, thanks in part to requirements of various federal programs, such as the Perkins Act and JTPA; a federal and state data system operated under the auspices of the Bureau of Labor Statistics; and the work of the federally supported National Occupational Information Coordinating Committee, its state counterparts, as well as state and private efforts. Nevertheless, the pieces are not complete in terms of the needs of potential trainees. They are not easily available to many who need them, especially adults. And there are important gaps, such as information on training results (see below) and the needs of the local labor market.

Later in this chapter, we briefly discuss information needs from the viewpoint of employers, who also lack easy access to many things they would like to know about trainees and trainers. Chapter 6 returns to the subject of information at greater length.

RESULTS[5]

A key question about all training institutions and programs is, What difference do they make? Training is ultimately supposed to help people get better jobs at higher pay than they would without it. But does it help and how much? And what kind of training makes a difference, and for whom? It is frustrating that, for much of the American system of postsecondary training, the answer is all too often "we don't know." With the exception of the major second-chance programs, which have been increasingly subject to formal evaluations based on experimental designs, surprisingly little effort has been directed at assessing the results of postsecondary training (Mangum et al., 1990).

Assessing the results of training is not easy. Even comparatively straight-forward information on outcomes (What proportion of trainees finish programs? How many get jobs? How much are they paid? Do the jobs reflect the skills individuals obtained in training?) is hard to find. The necessary record-keeping is often not done by training providers. Where public funds are not involved (as in firm-based skills improvement training), there is no requirement that any data be kept, and often they are not. Most publicly supported institutions and programs have some kind of record-keeping requirements. These naturally vary, given the decentralization of training among the many institutions that must be responsive to widely varying state and local rules as well as to differences in requirements among multiple federal programs.

Going beyond outcomes to determine what impact (or "value added") training has is even more difficult. What we would really like to determine is not just what happens to trainees, but whether the training itself is responsible for whatever difference we can observe between those with training and those without. Evidence about impacts is often lacking, even in instances where something is known about training outcomes. In this case, the ability to determine what difference training makes depends on judgments about whether outcome data reveal useful information about the value added by training. The next section explores this issue in more detail.

The absence of good information about results has several implications. As suggested above, it means that individuals seeking training have to select among available options without knowing much about the track record of different training routes or providers. The lack of reliable evidence regarding impacts also makes it impossible to judge the cost effectiveness of much of postsecondary training. This would be true even if sufficient information on costs were available, which is frequently not the case. Finally, this lack of information about results makes it difficult for policy makers to allocate public resources to programs that are most likely to help their intended audiences.

These comments should not be taken to mean that there is no evidence on the results of postsecondary training. Rather, the evidence is less complete than we would like and is often more indirect than direct. Nevertheless, using the framework described in the next section, we have evaluated what the available evidence can tell us about the benefits of training.

A Framework for Analysis: Value Added Versus Outcomes

Our interest in assessing the success of existing training efforts centers on their impact or value added, i.e., *the change in relevant outcomes due solely to the training experience.* In other words, value added is the increment in the proportion of people getting a job *as a result of training* as opposed to the percentage of program trainees getting a job. That percentage may or may not be the result of training. Value added is the increment in the wages of trainees—the gain in wage *due to the skills they learned in training* relative to the gain comparable individuals would make without the program—not their absolute wage level or their wage compared with some crude alternative. This definition distinguishes between the value that training adds, on the one hand, and simple outcomes as measured only by the behavior of people who were in a training program, on the other.

The best way to determine the value added of training is through a random assignment, controlled experiment (Betsey et al., 1985; Burtless and Orr, 1986; Job Training Longitudinal Survey Research Advisory Panel, 1985; Barnow, 1987). In such an experiment, applicants for training are randomly assigned to a treatment group that is allowed access to training or to a control group that is excluded from training. Random assignment ensures that the treatment and control groups do not differ in any systematic way except in their access to the program. Therefore, any subsequent differences in outcomes between the two groups can be confidently attributed to the training.[6] Increasing evidence on the feasibility and credibility of this approach (Gueron and Pauly, 1991; Hollister et al., 1984; Wiseman, 1991) has prompted the use of random assignment in many government- and foundation-sponsored evaluation efforts, particularly for JTPA and welfare-related training programs (see, e.g, Gueron and Paul, 1991; Bloom et al., 1993; Manpower Demonstration Research Corporation, 1980; Bell et al., 1987; and Puma et al., 1990). Where they exist, we rely on random assignment experiments as the best indicator of program effectiveness.[7]

But it is not always possible to do a random assignment experiment. For instance, it is impossible to forbid some students from going to community colleges. As a result, almost all research on the results of school-based postsecondary training has been limited to nonexperimental studies in which statistical methods are used to attempt to correct for pre-existing differences between training participants and a nonrandom comparison group. Evidence from such studies is limited to differences in outcomes between those who go through training and those who do not. We distinguish between raw differences—the difference in earnings or employment of those with training and those without—and differences adjusted for factors aside from the training that might make trainees different workers than nontrainees. These factors include school achievement, test scores, family background, location, age, sex, ethnicity, previous training, and work experience. When data that follow the same person over time exist, analysts can look at changes in outcomes for those with training and those without training—differences in the differences between the groups before and after training.

Without a controlled experiment, there is always uncertainty about the causes of differences in outcomes, because trainees may differ in various ways from nontrainees. They may be more able or motivated and would do better in the job market even without training. Still, most evidence on education and training comes from nonexperimental data. The weight that we place on nonexperimental data depends on the nature of that evidence. There are several circumstances that are more likely to yield positive correlations between outcome differences and the value added of programs:

1. *When the world produces a "natural experiment" that brings some people almost randomly into a program and leaves others out.* These cases come close to a random assignment, controlled experiment in that the people who have had training are unlikely to differ in major ways from those who have not. For instance, when one state increases the age at which students can legally leave school and another does not, the students have relatively little choice. Differences in earnings of students of the same age between the states would likely reflect the true effects of schooling (Angrist and Krueger, 1991).

2. *When a difference in outcome changes greatly over time.* Consider what happens when the earnings of existing technicians rise sharply relative to that of other workers. This might be due to greater market demand for technicians' work. While technicians may earn more than others, in part because they have more ability or are more motivated, the increase in earnings reflects the greater value society places on their work and thus indicates a rise in the value of technician training. The ability or motivation differences between the technicians and others have not changed.

3. *When comparisons are between people who are similar demographically and in measures of previous academic skills and ability, or when these differences are controlled in the analysis.* We put more weight on analyses of training that compare persons with and without training who have the same age, sex, years of schooling, test scores, who work in the same area, etc. than we do on comparisons that compare persons with and without training who may differ along any of these (or other) dimensions.

4. *When there are objective measures of skills related to the training.* Since training is supposed to increase skills, we feel more confident attributing differences in outcomes between trained and untrained persons to the training when we have additional information indicating that trainees can do something they could not have done without the training. For example, if a person takes a course in driving a big truck and passes a licensure exam, we would be more confident that any difference in earnings between that person and a classmate who did not take the training was due to the skills learned at the truck-driving school than if there was no objective evidence to substantiate that claim.

There is one circumstance in which we are particularly uneasy about using outcome indicators as a measure of success: when program managers can affect outcomes by creaming, or selecting individuals who are the easiest to train.

These considerations helped the committee interpret the evidence on training results and are important to the analysis in Chapter 6, which discusses how to improve the results of training.

The Evidence

"At its root, training is an act of faith" (Mangum et al., 1990:82). The evidence we have does not call this faith into question, although it is often insufficient for a ringing endorsement of training's benefits. Read judiciously, however, the evidence tells us where steady if not dramatic improvement is taking place, and it sometimes points up areas of training where public programs do not seem to be accomplishing their intended purposes.

Community Colleges and Proprietary Schools

Where qualifying training is concerned, the big questions center on what happens to people who enroll in community colleges and proprietary schools. To answer these questions, researchers have had to rely primarily on cross-sectional surveys of income or longitudinal sets of data that have followed three high school graduating classes for a number of years.[8] The cross-sectional data provide evidence for the population as a whole, but existing high school longitudinal studies inadequately reflect the results of training for the large number of older students who enroll in community colleges and proprietary schools.

The available data indicate that large fractions of students who enroll in community colleges and proprietary schools fail to acquire any credentials—either associate degrees or certificates—and that many of these students complete very few courses (see Grubb, 1989, 1993b; Carroll and Peng, 1989; and Dougherty, 1987).

However, the interpretation of these findings is in dispute. Many students do enroll in such institutions for avocational purposes. Some are "experimenters" (Manski, 1989) trying out postsecondary education to see whether it suits their interests and goals. For some, leaving college may be a rational decision. However, many advocates for community college argue that virtually all those who leave do so because they have achieved their goals; for example, by learning enough to advance at work or find an entry-level job. Those who appear to be dropouts are therefore really "completers." While this may be true for some students, there is no evidence about the fraction of those leaving community colleges who have attained their goals, and the completer argument explains away what may be a serious problem.[9]

Another crucial issue has received even less attention: whether students in community colleges, technical institutes, and proprietary schools enter jobs for which they have been trained. Particularly for students in vocational programs, who are presumably being trained for specific occupations, this question is critical, because their education may have little or no economic value if they fail to find related employment. Some preliminary results suggest that about one-third of students with certificates and vocational associate degrees find related employment within 6 months after leaving the training institution. The fraction is substantially lower, between 11 and 17 percent, for those leaving community colleges without a credential, and somewhat lower for students leaving technical institutes and private vocational schools without credentials (Grubb, 1989).

Other results based on the same methodology suggest that the fraction having related employment at age 32 is higher—about 76 percent for males and 67 percent for females—for those earning certificates than it is for those earning associate degrees, among whom approximately 22 percent of men and 45 percent of women were in related employment. (There is a difficult timing problem here, however: "relatedness" was measured as the relation of employment at age 32 to the field in which an individual received his or her highest credential an unspecified earlier time.) Furthermore, among those who have entered community colleges and proprietary schools but have failed to complete the program, coursework tends not to be related to future employment (Grubb, 1992). Since the returns to related education are substantially higher than the returns to unrelated education (Grubb, 1992), there is reason to be concerned about the implications of these findings. However, the ways of matching education to occupations have not been carefully examined, and there has been no effort to determine the sensitivity of any conclusions to the various ways of matching education to jobs. Furthermore, the dynamic issues related to such matches have not

TABLE 3.1 Differences in Mean Earnings for 1991 Between Individuals with Associate Degrees and Those with High School Diplomas (in dollars)

Age	Male				Female			
	All	White	Black	Hispanic	All	White	Black	Hispanic
25-34	4,912	4,576	5,644	4,520	5,346	5,518	3,589	5,355
35-44	9,007	8,792	9,590	8,656	6,485	6,279	5,403	n.a.
45-54	7,974	8,595	n.a.	n.a.	4,696	4,362	8,198	n.a.
55-64	1,028	1,013	n.a.	n.a.	7,540	7,824	n.a.	n.a.

SOURCE: Bureau of the Census (1992b:Table 29).

been studied. Therefore, these findings on the relatedness of training must be considered extremely preliminary.

Researchers have attempted to estimate whether training at community colleges and proprietary schools raises the earnings of those who attend. Available data sources frequently fail to distinguish between academic and vocational associate degrees from 2-year colleges, and data on other credentials besides degrees (certificates, for example) are not consistently reported. The results below must therefore be read carefully to determine the limits of the findings.

Recent data from the Current Population Survey (CPS) indicate that individuals with associate degrees (either academic or vocational) earn more than individuals with only high school diplomas or the equivalent. Table 3.1 shows that the differences in mean 1991 earnings held for all age groups and were substantial. For men, the earnings advantage from an associate degree increased and then decreased with age, suggesting that the degree opens additional opportunities for advancement through mid-career. For women, the earnings advantage was actually highest among the 55-64 age group.[10]

Older data from the Survey of Income and Program Participation (SIPP), which distinguish between holders of vocational certificates from proprietary schools and high school graduates, also indicate that holders of the postsecondary credential earn more. Table 3.2 shows age-related earnings differences ranging from $636 for younger individuals to $6,360 for older ones.

These differences may reflect preexisting differences between holders of associate degrees and vocational certificates from proprietary schools, on the one hand, and high school graduates, on the other, rather than the effect of the postsecondary credential itself. Several researchers (Grubb, various dates; Hollenbeck, 1992; Horn, reported in National Assessment of Vocational Education, 1989b; Kane and Rouse, 1993; Lyke et al., 1991) have

TABLE 3.2   Differences in Mean Earnings
for 1987 Between Individuals with Proprietary
School Vocational Certificates and Those with
High School Diplomas

Age	Earnings Difference (per year)
25-34	$ 636
35-44	$1,728
45-54	$3,900
55-64	$6,360

NOTE: Figures are based on a 4-month average from the spring of 1987.

SOURCE: Bureau of the Census (1990:Table 2).

used detailed data from longitudinal studies sponsored by the U.S. Department of Education to control statistically for preexisting differences and to investigate more thoroughly the earnings differences among individuals who pursued various postsecondary schooling options.

In brief, these studies indicate that, in 1985, vocational associate degree holders who attended a 2-year college had an earnings advantage over high school graduates of $1,800 to $4,000 at age 24 to 32. Where academic and vocational associate degrees were combined, little difference between associate degree holders and high school graduates was found, suggesting that vocational associate degrees may pay off more (at least in the first years after graduation, when the surveys were conducted) than academic associate degrees. Earnings differences based on the receipt of a vocational certificate, rather than an associate degree, were more mixed. These certificates appeared valuable for women, but not for men. When work experience since high school was controlled, earnings differences between holders of postsecondary credentials and high school graduates decreased.

The estimated 1985 earnings advantage for proprietary school graduates over high school graduates, statistically controlling for family background and prior school achievement, range, in various studies (Grubb, 1993b; Hollenbeck, 1992; Kane and Rouse, 1993; Lyke et al., 1991), from $1,000 to $2,000 at age 24 to 32. Lyke et al. found that men who completed training at proprietary schools had the same employment rate as those who graduated from high school, a rate lower than those who completed a community college program. Men completing training at proprietary schools had higher earnings than high school graduates and the same as community college students, but that advantage was due to other characteristics and not to the fact of attending those schools. Among women, the employment rate was higher for those completing proprietary schools than for high school graduates and about the same as for women at community colleges, but, again, the advantage was due to other factors. Women from proprietary schools had higher earnings than high school graduates, even controlling for other factors.

Returns vary substantially according to field of study (Grubb, 1992). People employed in the health and technical fields have substantially higher earnings than those in agriculture, marketing and retail, business (for women), education (for men), or public service occupations (for women), for whom such credentials provide no significant benefits compared to a high school diploma. Furthermore, as one might expect, there appear to be essentially no returns to those in jobs unrelated to their field of study.

Given the high rate of noncompletion at community colleges, it is important to know whether it pays to take courses without completing a degree or a certificate, or whether longer-term, more intensive training is required if positive results are to be achieved.

The results here are less clear. Grubb (1992), using data from the National Longitudinal Study of 1972, found that coursework that does not culminate in a degree or certificate increases wage rates but not annual earnings. Kane and Rouse (1993) looked at the same data with somewhat different specifications and found that such coursework increases wage rates, annual earnings, and occupational status. Several methodological decisions made by Kane and Rouse deflate the value of credentials compared to coursework, but the difference between the two analyses remains puzzling.

Given the large numbers of individuals in community colleges, technical institutes, and proprietary schools who do not acquire credentials and who leave with very small amounts of coursework completed, the lack of convincing evidence supporting the benefits of small amounts of postsecondary education is troubling. It suggests that the conventional lore among advocates—that students who leave these institutions without earning credentials have met their own goals—needs to be tempered.

Skills Improvement Training

By skills improvement training, we mean training for existing employees that enhances their skills so they can assume positions requiring more sophisticated abilities, a wider range of capacities, or greater responsibility.

A review of the literature on economic returns to training by Mangum et al. (1990:67-69) noted the sparse evidence on returns due to employer-sponsored training. Lynch (1993) reiterates how little direct evidence there is on how private-sector training affects wages or how training strategies affect firm productivity and competitiveness. Individual employers have historically made little effort to measure increases in trainee income or employer profits resulting from training efforts. Firm-based studies tend to be subjective, unstandardized, and dependent on before-and-after comparisons without the use of control groups that would allow the effects of training to be disaggregated from other influences.

Most of what is known about the results of skills improvement training, therefore, comes from analyses of national databases, such as the Current Population Survey, the Panel Study of Income Dynamics, the Employment Opportunities Pilot Projects Survey, the National Longitudinal Study of the high school class of 1972, and various cohorts of the National Longitudinal Surveys of Labor Market Experience. Studies using these sources focus on economic returns to individuals and indicate that company-based training has an impact on earnings "in the range of 10 to 30 percent [that] persist[s] over about 13 to 14 years, depending on the data base employed, the controls used, and the dependent variable analyzed" (Mangum et al., 1990:60). Economists usually conclude from such findings that skills improvement training clearly benefits the individuals receiving it, and, on the assumption that wages and earnings reflect productivity, that such training increases productivity on the job as well.

For the most part, these studies have had to infer the impact of training on wages from the shape of wage profiles, because most of the available data sets were inadequate to permit a direct examination of training effects. Thus, many questions about employer-sponsored training have been largely unanswerable. These include questions such as what types of training programs are provided and where, how firm-specific or portable company-provided training is, and how company, on-the-job training results differ from those of off-the-job and apprenticeship training.

Some of these problems are avoided in Lynch's (1992) work using the youth cohort of the National Longitudinal Survey, because this particular data set reconstructs the entire formal training history of the individuals in the survey and permits distinctions among different sources of private-sector training. She analyzed young people (age 14-21 in 1978) who were not college graduates, had completed school by 1980, and had wages when they were interviewed both in 1980 and 1983. She found that company training (on the job) increased the average recipient's wage rate by 9 to 11 percent and that apprenticeship increased wage rates by 13 to 17 percent. She also found that company training appears to have firm-specific rather than general effects, since on-the-job training acquired before the current job had no impact on current wages. That finding supports the view that employers primarily provide training useful to themselves rather than giving individuals capacities that are transferable to other firms.

Recent studies by Bartel (1992), Bishop (1994), and Weiss (1994) contribute to the sparse literature on how training affects the productivity of firms. Weiss used data monitoring the output of new hires over a 6- to 8-

month period in four electronics assembly plants that have no formal training programs. While informal training (or learning by doing) generated large productivity growth in the first month of employment, 6 months later there is little evidence of any positive productivity changes associated with this form of training. Bartel and Bishop, by contrast, studied formal training in firms; both found sizable effects of such training on firm productivity (on the order of 9 to 17 percent, depending on whether the formal training was provided by the current or a previous employer). Bishop's study also indicated that formal training improved workers' ability to be innovative.

It is difficult to tell from the available studies how much of the benefits from company training result from selection bias. Firms may select the most able, motivated, or disciplined individuals to receive training, and individuals may select such training themselves, where it is an option. Lynch, for example, does find some evidence of selection bias for those in her sample of people who have had some on-the-job training.

Other potential evidence is available on the effectiveness of skills improvement training: virtually every state supports a program to fund short-term, firm-based training, and much of the training that goes on in such programs involves existing workers in skills enhancement. Unfortunately, there is little evidence about the effectiveness of such efforts (Creticos and Sheets, 1990), though the positive results of Holzer et al. (in press) for Michigan's MJOB/Upgrade program are an exception. (Batt and Osterman [1993] also describe some exemplary programs, and Bassi [in press] reports the favorable opinions of managers in firms with workplace education programs.)

Retraining

Rather late in our deliberations, we came to the realization that retraining for displaced and dislocated workers needed to be included in the typology of postsecondary training described in Chapter 1. We did not have time, therefore, to undertake a thorough investigation of existing programs and their outcomes and impacts. Our impression, however, is that there is scant evidence about the results of worker retraining programs, and that the quality of this evidence is often weak.

The JTPA Title III EDWAA program has never been evaluated. The U.S. Department of Labor is in the third year of a 3-year implementation study to determine the extent to which the goals of the 1988 legislation authorizing the program have been achieved, but the department does not have any plans to conduct a formal evaluation of the program design using a quasi-experimental method. The outcome data for the most recently completed program year, 1991, indicate a nationwide placement rate of 68 percent at an average wage of $8.49 an hour; 90 days after termination, 70 percent of the program's participants were employed at an average wage of $8.75 an hour.[11]

In April 1993, Mathematica Policy Research, Inc. (Corson et al., 1993) completed a formal evaluation of the Trade Adjustment Assistance (TAA) program, the other major dislocated worker program administered by the U.S. Department of Labor. The study did not yield placement and average wage data comparable to the data collected for the EDWAA program, making performance comparisons between the two programs difficult.

The evaluation tracked trade readjustment allowance recipients (some of whom received training as well as allowances under TAA) for 12 quarters following their initial unemployment insurance claim. A control group of people who had exhausted their unemployment benefits and were dislocated from similar industries, but who did not receive readjustment allowance benefits, was used for comparison. The study documented substantial earnings losses (approximately $46,000 during the 3-year period) associated with trade-related dislocation. Even by the 12th quarter, the earnings losses averaged nearly $3,000 for readjustment allowance recipients. The total value of TAA, readjustment allowance, and unemployment benefits per client was less than one-quarter of their average earnings losses.

The study concluded that the program design had successfully targeted those workers with barriers to reemployment. It also showed that most readjustment participants switched occupations or industries upon reemployment, and those that switched had greater earnings losses than those who did not. Readjustment allowance recipients lost more in wages over the 3-year period than the control group, but most of that difference can be explained by higher prelayoff wages for that group. The jobs found on reemployment by the two groups paid similar wages.

The Mathematica evaluation also examined the postlayoff experiences of people who received TAA training benefits compared to readjustment recipients who did not participate in training. TAA trainees had employment rates and an average earnings level below that of other readjustment recipients for most of the 12th quarter period. By the 12th quarter, the trainees showed better results than the nontrainees, but the gap was due largely to differences in observable characteristics between them. As a result, the study concluded that, if training has a substantial positive effect on employment and earnings, it occurs no earlier than 3 years after the initial unemployment insurance claim.

Mangum et al. (1990:65-67) reviewed the literature on returns to dislocated worker training programs and found the most important evidence in studies of various demonstration projects that preceded the passage of EDWAA. Much of that evidence is weakened by problems, such as the failure to match comparison groups by personal characteristics or to use controlled experiments in projects attempting to duplicate early results. One rigorous evaluation in Texas in the mid-1980s assessed a sequence of job-search assistance followed by classroom training in occupational skills or on-the-job training for participants who did not find employment. The results were modest but not statistically significant, and the gains appeared to come from job-search assistance that led to earlier employment. Mangum et al. cited several other studies that also appear to suggest that job-search assistance and early intervention are most likely to result in positive impacts and cost effectiveness in programs for dislocated workers.

Osterman (1988:161) reached similar conclusions based on his reading of the evidence on programs going back as far as some 1960s retraining efforts aimed at displacement:

> The general lesson from these efforts is that success is strongly age-related, with older workers faring poorly, that placement is at least as important as retraining, that a major issue is teaching workers who have labored for years in sheltered markets how to function in an external market . . . and that hastily designed last-minute programs usually fail.

Second-Chance Training

Major evaluation research has been conducted on welfare-related, second-chance programs and on employment and training programs (JTPA and its predecessors) for low-income or unemployed adults and out-of-school youth. Not much is known about the effects of adult education and literacy programs on their recipients (Grubb et al., 1991; see below).

As indicated earlier, second-chance welfare and job-training programs have been subjected to research using strong, quasi-experimental designs and, more recently, random-assignment experiments to measure their impacts. In addition, researchers have been able to go beyond the effect on earnings to study the kinds of cost-effectiveness questions that elude analysts of other forms of postsecondary training. At the same time, much of what occurs in second-chance welfare and employment programs has not been job training per se, but activities such as job search, work experience, and (especially in the JOBS program) basic remedial education. This limits what research can reveal about the effects of expanding the training components of these programs.

It also makes findings on the results of JTPA and JOBS not comparable to our earlier findings on results of vocational training in community colleges and proprietary schools. There are other reasons as well as to why findings on JTPA and JOBS cannot be compared to those on training at these postsecondary schools: most importantly, the personal characteristics of those receiving training are likely to be quite different, with JTPA and

JOBS participants having more educational and economic disadvantages than community college and proprietary school students.

In the early 1980s, Congress changed the decade-old, Work Incentive (WIN) welfare-to-work program to give states new flexibility to design their own approaches to moving welfare recipients into employment. States responded by creating a variety of innovative model programs; and random-assignment evaluations were conducted on a number of them. The results, summarized in Gueron and Pauly (1991), proved influential in the federal legislation that resulted in the creation of the JOBS program in 1988 (Wiseman et al., 1991).

The evaluations found that the welfare-to-work programs of the 1980s, almost all of which focused on single women on welfare, produced rela-tively consistent and positive results. Increases in average annual earnings ranged from $268 to $658 in the last year of follow-up for welfare recipi-ents in what Gueron and Pauly labeled "broad coverage" programs. In "selective-voluntary" programs, the gains ranged from $591 to $1,121 above the average earnings of the control group. A part of the estimated differ-ence between the two types of programs probably resulted from the fact that the effects of broad coverage programs were averaged over all eligible individuals, many of whom never actually received services under the wel-fare-to-work program. Individuals in the selective-voluntary programs, by contrast, were highly likely to have been active participants in welfare-to-work activities.

Earnings impacts were found in both low-cost and higher-cost programs and tended to be sustained for at least the 3 years after program enrollment, when the studies ended. There is limited evidence that programs with higher costs and more intensive components (usually education and skills training) led to higher earnings gains. Earnings gains, however, did not always mean savings in welfare expenditures. When both increased taxes on earnings gains and welfare savings were considered, though, many wel-fare-to-work programs were cost effective; the investment in services was offset by subsequent taxes and reductions in welfare and related expendi-tures. The most cost-effective programs were the low-cost, less intensive ones. While more intensive programs showed some tendency to result in larger earnings gains, the added costs led to a lower impact per dollar spent (Friedlander and Gueron, 1992). Because of the difficulty of designing experiments to assess the differential impact of different services, relatively little is known about just what aspects of various programs contributed most to the positive results achieved.

A different, more intensive approach to training for welfare recipients was tested in the (AFDC) Homemaker-Home Health Aide Demonstrations. This set of seven state demonstrations, conducted between 1983 and 1986, provided the volunteer participants 6 weeks of classroom training and practicum experience as homemaker or home health aides, followed by up to a year of subsidized employment in a regular home health agency. A random-assignment evaluation found annualized earnings gains of $1,200 to $2,600 in the second post-program year in five of the seven states (Bell et al., 1987). Net social benefits exceeded the cost of the program in at least four of the states. Further analysis of these data showed that the significant earnings gains persisted for at least 5 years after program entry (unpublished research, Larry L. Orr and Stephen H. Bell, Abt Associates, Inc., Bethesda, Md.). The study suggests that close linkages between occupational training and specific employers may be an important key to sustained training results.

For the purposes of the committee's deliberations, a crucial aspect of existing welfare-to-work evaluations is the limited information they provide about the kind of education and training now being encouraged by the JOBS program. The emphasis on improving the human capital of welfare recipients that characterizes JOBS was not found in most of the innovative welfare programs of the 1980s. One exception is California's GAIN (Greater Avenues for Independence) program, which began in 1986 under WIN and is now the state JOBS program. It had an unusually heavy emphasis on education for pre-JOBS programs and has been the target of a large-scale, random-assignment evaluation that began in 1988. Interim results (Friedlander et al., 1993) indicate second-year earnings gains for single parents (usually women) of $520, or 24 percent above the control group, and for heads of two-parent families (usually men) of $370, or 12 percent above the control group. Since the program is a broad-coverage one, these earnings impacts understate the effect on those who obtained jobs, because the results are averaged over all people in the study, including participants, nonparticipants, and people who did or did not work. There were also corresponding welfare savings. Within subgroups of people on welfare, some evidence suggests that GAIN sometimes had a positive impact (increasing earnings and reducing welfare payments) on people who needed basic education, and thus were likely to have participated in adult basic education, GED preparation, or English as a second language programs.

With the exception of GAIN, however, existing evaluations say relatively little about whether expanded education and training services will lead to larger program impacts (e.g., higher earnings, greater welfare savings) and greater gains that justify the added costs. Here, again, the operative motivating force is faith, rather than knowledge. Experimentation and evaluation in the 1980s suggest that this faith may well be justified. The extensive research planned over the next decade to assess the results of different JOBS approaches will provide more definite answers.

Programs to improve the job prospects of unemployed and disadvantaged adults and youth have also been extensively evaluated. The 1973

Comprehensive Employment and Training Act (CETA) authorized several kinds of programs for adults and youth, including classroom instruction and training in a private-sector job. Barnow (1987) summarized the results of quasi-experimental studies using the Continuous Longitudinal Manpower Survey (CLMS). These studies found annual earnings effects of CETA participation as of the late 1970s that ranged from negative to gains of $1,500 (compared to a matched sample developed using data from the Census Bureau's Current Population Survey). Generally, women benefitted more than men. The results were about equally divided as to whether classroom training or on-the-job training produced bigger effects, but most of the findings indicated that on-the-job training paid off more for minorities than for whites.

There was great variation in estimated impacts among the different studies of CETA based on CLMS data, due in large part to different procedures for selecting matched comparison groups and modeling the process by which individuals were selected into CETA programs. These problems and contradictory findings contributed to the dissatisfaction with quasi-experimental evaluations and led to the decision to evaluate CETA's successor, the 1982 JTPA, through the use of random-assignment research.

Preliminary results from the National JTPA Study, begun in 1986 (Bloom et al., 1993), indicate that overall the program has had modest positive impacts on the earnings of adults, but zero or even negative effects on the earnings of youths. The evaluation divided program participants into three groups on the basis of service recommendations at program intake: those recommended for classroom training in occupational skills; those recommended for on-the-job training; and those recommended for other, less intensive services (e.g., job-search assistance, work experience, basic education).

Both adult women and adult men enrollees recommended for on-the-job training showed significant earnings gains of $1,200 to $1,300 over the first 18 months after entering the program. For both men and women, the gains persisted at a relatively uniform level throughout the 18-month follow-up period. Adult women recommended for classroom training in occupational skills experienced annualized earnings gains of $900 to $1,200 in the last several quarters of the period. There were no statistically significant impacts on earnings for men assigned to classroom training or for either women or men assigned to less intensive services.

The effects of JTPA on the earnings of youths (21 or younger) were much less positive. There were no statistically significant impacts on the earnings of female youths in any of the three service groups, and the only significant impacts for male youths were negative effects on the earnings of those recommended for on-the-job training or less intensive services. JTPA participants within these groups lost approximately $2,000 in earnings relative to the control group over the 18-month follow-up period. This earnings loss was relatively uniform over the follow-up period; it was not concentrated in the period when participants were in the program. Further analysis revealed that the earnings loss for male youths was primarily attributable to the subgroup of male youths who had been arrested prior to entering the program.

The final report of the National JTPA Study, due at the end of 1993, will follow the sample for an additional 12 months to see whether the trends evident in the first 18 months persist. It will also examine program impacts on welfare benefits and will include a benefit-cost analysis of each of the three service subgroups.

The findings for out-of-school youths in the National JTPA Study are not inconsistent with those from the other two existing experimental studies of employment and training programs for out-of-school youths. The first, the youth component of the National Supported Work Demonstration, evaluated an intensive work experience program for severely disadvantaged youths (Manpower Demonstration Research Corporation, 1980); the second, JOB-START, evaluated intensive education, employment, and training services provided through JTPA (Cave and Doolittle, 1991). The Supported Work Study found negligible program impacts on the earnings of participants, most of whom were males. Preliminary results from JOBSTART showed negligible short-term impacts for female youths and large short-term negative impacts for male youths over the 2-year follow-up period, as in the National JTPA Study. However, Cave et al. (1993) report that, in the 4th year after entering the program, young men in JOBSTART earned approximately $500 more than people in the control group. While this was not statistically significant, the much larger impact for the particularly disadvantaged group of young men with prior arrest records (over $1,500 in year 4) was significant. Impacts for women were somewhat smaller. Results for the combined youth sample approached statistical significance.

The only program to show positive impacts on the earnings of disadvantaged, out-of-school youths is the Job Corps. Originally authorized by the Economic Opportunity Act of 1964, it was incorporated into CETA in 1973 and then into JTPA in 1982. Betsey et al. (1985) summarized results from an evaluation of the program by Mathematica, Inc. Although participants were not randomly assigned to the program and comparison group, the comparison group was matched on various characteristics and was taken from geographic areas where participation in the Job Corps was low. Gains in earnings for Job Corps participants were more than $600 (in 1977 dollars) in the second year after they finished or left the program and remained just under $400 2 years after that. While these results are encouraging, the quasi-experimental nature of this single evaluation and the fact that the data are now 15 years old has tempered the willingness of many observers to assert that the Job Corps makes a difference for youth. The U.S. Department of Labor has recently announced plans to conduct a new evaluation of the Job Corps based on random assignment.

In summary, research findings about second-chance welfare and employment or training programs offer a wealth of information, some encouraging and some not, about the United States' ability to design effective services for the disadvantaged. Most programs work for adult women; they have modest impacts and are cost effective. This is true of both low-cost and higher-cost programs, although low-cost programs do not have much effect on the most disadvantaged. Moreover, the results have been relatively consistent across sites and studies.

There is less evidence about impacts on adult men. Studies of welfare-to-work programs have found some positive effects (Friedlander et al., 1993; Gueron and Pauly, 1991). Early results from the JTPA evaluation are modestly positive. One reason that programs may be less effective for men than for women is that men tend to do better on their own; that is, they are more likely to find jobs without the help of program services than women are.

Finally, relatively few programs for out-of-school youth have been studied using random-assignment designs, and even fewer have been found effective. The Job Corps is generally viewed as an exception, although the evidence for that is weaker; the recent results from JOBSTART are also somewhat encouraging. The final results from the JTPA study will be particularly critical, since early short-term findings suggest that the program may actually harm, rather than help, some subgroups of young male participants, especially those with arrest records.

More evidence is becoming available on the impacts of second-chance welfare and employment and training programs. Forthcoming studies include large-scale studies of JOBS programs in a number of sites, studies of second-chance education and training programs for teenage mothers on welfare, further results from the JTPA evaluation, and studies of programs for noncustodial parents of children on welfare.

An important area where little is known about outcomes and impacts is remediation: basic education and literacy programs for post-high-school individuals with severe educational handicaps. Grubb et al. (1991) surveyed providers in 23 regions within 9 states in an effort to determine what kinds of programs were offered, by whom, and with what results. There are isolated examples of apparently effective remediation programs: for example, some community college "developmental education" efforts where completers survive and perform in regular college courses almost as well as students not needing remediation. Overall, however, the findings are more discouraging, particularly about remediation in adult education, JTPA, and welfare-to-work programs. Grubb et al. (1991:v) concluded:

> [T]here is almost no information about [the] activities and effectiveness [of the existing system of remediation]. Some providers cannot even tell how many individuals are enrolled in remedial programs; almost none can provide any systematic information about completion rates (though they are clearly low); evaluations of subsequent effects are almost nonexistent; and most evaluations are methodologically flawed. The result is that there is almost no evidence to suggest which of the many programs now offered are effective and still less information that would enable teachers and researchers to improve current practice.

They further conclude, using indirect arguments in the absence of direct evidence, that the dominant teaching methods used in remedial programs (which they label "skills and drills") violate what they believe to be the conventions of good practice in adult education programs. While alternative pedagogical approaches exist that promise to remedy some of the persistent problems in remediation (motivation, programs that are perceived to be boring or irrelevant to subsequent education or job training), they have not been codified or standardized, nor has their effectiveness been established.

As noted in Chapter 2, the U.S. Department of Education began a national evaluation of federally supported adult education programs in September 1990. Final results are due in 1994. Among other things, the evaluation is expected to provide information on learning gains, service costs, and employment outcomes.

INCENTIVES, ACCOUNTABILITY, AND QUALITY

Incentives and accountability mechanisms in postsecondary training have often been criticized as focusing on inputs rather than outcomes or value added; therefore, it is said, they do little to encourage strong performance and quality training. The absence of effective mechanisms to ensure quality has left at least one major federal program, student financial aid, open to significant problems of fraud and abuse. At the same time, our discussion about what is known and unknown about the results of training suggests some of the reasons why quality assurance mechanisms are not more fully developed.

Much of school-based postsecondary training is funded through formulas that lead to a preoccupation with enrollments rather than with outcomes or value added. This is true of state subsidy formulas for public schools and colleges as well as federal student aid funds, which, for the most part, are awarded to individual students to take to whatever school they attend.

School eligibility to participate in federal programs has been heavily dependent on state oversight and private accreditation. While these mechanisms do not necessarily foster high performance, they have generally ensured minimum standards. The exception has been proprietary trade schools, where the combination of unusual dependence on federal funds and lax oversight by state regulators and accreditors led, in the 1980s, to rampant charges of fraud and abuse of federal student aid funds (see, for example, U.S. Senate, 1991, and Banerjee et al., 1989). A study by the State Higher Education Executive Officers (1991:xi) found that all states exercised oversight of proprietary schools through licensing or approval mechanisms but confirmed the "growing belief that many states do not have adequate laws and regulations to protect students and the taxpayers who have invested their money in those students." The study recommended strengthening state licensing provisions and proposed that state licensing be given a more central role in the determination of institutional eligibility for federal student aid. A version of this idea was adopted in the Higher Education Amendments of 1992 (see Chapter 7).

A desire to focus attention on what programs accomplish instead of just on inputs has led to a growing interest in performance-management systems for publicly supported activities. Barnow (1992:278-279) defines performance management as

> a system whereby programs are systematically judged against specified objectives. A formal performance management system is generally characterized by the following elements:
>
> • Performance measure(s). An obvious requirement of a performance-management system is the use of one or more measures of how well the entities being judged are performing. . . .
> • Method of setting the standards. For each measure, specific standards of acceptable performance must be established . . . . To be most useful, the standards should be set rationally and developed in a manner understood by the programs that will be judged.
> • Rewards and sanctions. Performance management systems usually include some method of rewarding programs that meet or exceed the standards and sanctioning programs that fail to meet the standards. The rewards and sanctions may be monetary in nature, may involve loss of the right to operate programs, or may simply involve receiving praise or criticism.

In the training arena, performance management is most developed in JTPA (Barnow, 1992). Efforts to develop performance measures and standards began under JTPA's predecessor, CETA; and the original JTPA legislation included provisions establishing a performance-management system. The basic goals to be achieved were specified in the statute: increased employment and earnings of participants and a reduction in their welfare dependency. The U.S. Department of Labor, in consultation with state and local program officials, developed a series of separate measures and standards for adults and youth participating in the program by which the activities of each local service delivery area could be judged. Governors decided which of the measures and standards to adopt. The department also developed adjustment models that governors could use to modify expected performance to take account of differences in participant characteristics and local labor-market conditions affecting individual delivery areas.

While the existence of performance measures and standards added to the credibility of JTPA (no small feat, given problems with the reputation of CETA), implementing them has also illustrated the difficulty of designing standards that in fact lead to desirable behavior. Cost and outcome standards in JTPA, for example, appeared to lead to "creaming" (selecting recipients who were the most job-ready and the least expensive to train); cost standards were eventually dropped.[12] Over time, standards were also modified to replace measures of the status of participants at termination by postprogram measures, because the former appeared to encourage short-term approaches such as job-search activities rather than longer-term education and training. New measures were added, and the adjustment models were refined by adding variables to make them increasingly sensitive to differences in participant characteristics.

Despite the complexities suggested by the JTPA experience, the performance-management approach to ensuring quality is spreading to other training programs. The Family Support Act of 1988, which created the JOBS program, requires the Secretary of Health and Human Services to report to Congress on performance standards in JOBS by October 1, 1993. The 1990 reauthorization of the Perkins Act requires each state board receiving assistance to develop and put into effect a statewide system of core performance measures and standards. Educational institutions participating in student assistance programs are required to report certain outcome data for the first time under the Student Right-to-Know Act of 1990. What might be called rudimentary performance standards (e.g., provisions denying eligibility to participate in student loan programs to institutions with default rates above a specified level) have been adopted in recent years as part of federal efforts to crack down on default problems in student-assistance programs. In addition to these congressionally mandated steps, measurements and standards are being incorporated into other federal programs by administrative action.

Although the popularity of the performance-management approach to quality assurance is growing, we found no evidence from the evaluation research on JTPA and the welfare-to-work experiments of the 1980s that programs with performance standards produced greater impacts than programs without them. In fact, performance management is not oriented toward impact or value-added. As discussed earlier, outcomes and impacts are not necessarily correlated with one another. Barnow (1992:279) explains the reason for performance management's emphasis on outcomes:

> Performance management should also be distinguished from evaluation. Programs can be evaluated in terms of their impacts on an occasional or one-shot basis, but performance management is an ongoing feature that continuously provides feedback to the program managers and the agencies and organizations responsible for monitoring the programs. Thus, while evaluations often include one or more years of post-program follow-up, performance management systems must rely on shorter post-program periods to provide reasonably quick feedback.
>
> While evaluations answer the question "What is the impact of the program?" performance management systems generally seek answers to simpler outcome and process questions that are associated with the goals of the program; the issue is more one of accountability than impact. Finally, evaluations of human service programs are generally costly and require the use of comparison or control groups to identify what would have occurred in the absence of the program. Performance management systems are generally less intrusive, but they then must sacrifice including impact measures.

The use of performance-management systems is growing, even though very little is known about how institutions respond to different approaches and the varying incentives and disincentives they create. The objectives cited above by Barnow are praiseworthy. Yet the fact that program outcomes and program impacts are not always highly correlated creates a profoundly important dilemma: Does the spreading influence of performance management systems actually lead to more effective programs? This issue is crucial; Chapter 6 analyzes the complexities involved in deciding how best to develop mechanisms for ensuring the quality of postsecondary training.

CONNECTIONS WITH EMPLOYERS

A well-functioning training system needs to be closely connected to employers. In general, employer connections with training, except for the training that they themselves sponsor, tend to be weak in the United States. There are different kinds of possible connections, though, and it is useful to distinguish among them in evaluating existing arrangements.

A key role for employers is as *customers* for the "products" of the training system. The evidence is mixed as to how much employers consider postsecondary training when they make hiring decisions. The generally positive economic returns to qualifying training, at least for those who get degrees or certificates, suggest that employers do place value on what schools teach. On the other hand, research by Grubb et al. (1992) indicates that, in what they call "sub-baccalaureate" labor markets, employers often rely more on experience than schooling in making hiring decisions. This tendency is encouraged by the relative absence of information at the local labor-market level about who is being trained in what kinds of programs. (As Grubb et al. note, sub-baccalaureate labor markets are almost entirely local.) Further complicating the picture is the general lack of information about the content of training programs and the hiring requirements that employers must follow. Nationally recognized credentials or occupational-skills standards would provide information about program content, but these exist in only a few fields. Licensing requirements similarly serve to connect employers and providers, but they exist only in health and a few other occupations in the sub-baccalaureate labor market.

This mixed picture about the value employers place on training in their hiring processes has been identified as one reason why many students are not highly motivated to do well in school. Bishop (1990) has discussed the effects of the failure of American employers to utilize transcripts and other indicators of school success when making hiring decisions. While his attention has been focused on the high school, there is no evidence that employers place more emphasis on performance in postsecondary schools. As we shall see in Chapter 4, this contrasts strongly with the message German and Japanese firms convey to young people about the importance of taking their schoolwork seriously.

Participants in second-chance training have been stigmatized in the eyes of employers by their enrollment in programs labeled as serving the disadvantaged. Osterman (1988, 1990) has emphasized the stigmatization problem in job training. Eisner (1989) cites evidence that workers labeled disadvantaged have been less likely to be hired by employers in other public employment programs, such as the Targeted Job Tax Credit. Similarly, use of the U.S. Employment Service by employers as a central labor exchange fell dramatically after the mid-1960s, when the service's emphasis was altered to focus on the hard to employ (Bendick, 1989).

Employers can be connected to training in various ways besides hiring. They can provide work-based training and instructors for school-based training; make state-of-the-art equipment available to students; contribute to training curricula and pedagogy by helping educators understand industry and occupational skill demands; serve on advisory and governing boards (including boards of directors at large proprietary schools with corporate structures); and exert quality control over training by helping to define industry skill standards and rewarding skill certificates in their hiring processes. Employers do all of these things, but there is very limited data about how often or how well. For example, although there is no national system of defining and certifying boards for occupational and industry skills, some, but not many, industries have established standards and certificates. Similarly, there are widely varying reports about how extensively employers influence the curricula of community colleges. Grubb et al. (1992:41-42) say that employer advisory committees were not very active in this regard in the four labor markets they studied. But the U.S. Office of Technology Assessment (1990:148) observed that community colleges in North Carolina match their curricula to the changing needs of employers through a process called DACUM (developing a curriculum). The process involves employees working with a college coordinator to identify lists of competencies needed in a specific occupation. Members of the committee observed the same process in use in community colleges in South Carolina.

We should note that employer contributions to school-based training curricula need to be viewed cautiously. Ironically, with some notable exceptions, employers are often poor sources of information about the skill demands of their industry or occupations. Economic studies of restructuring companies find substantial variation within the same company in response to questions about what generic skills the company needs. The variation is related to the respondent's position within the company (Thomas R. Bailey, Columbia University, personal communication). Studies of on-the-job training find that employers often do not recognize the cognitive complexity of their own jobs, especially when these jobs are perceived as "low skill." Employers often do not understand the skill implications of restructuring in their own workplaces. For example, they may introduce just-in-time inventory arrangements, but they do not appreciate how such changes increase the skill requirements of such jobs as stockroom clerk (Scribner and Sachs, 1990).

Despite these cautions, we agree with the general view that employer involvement in the planning and design of occupation-oriented programs is important and below optimal levels in the United States. This involvement is needed to ensure that the skills developed will be those needed in the workplace and that the available training programs match the likely needs of the local labor market. We also note strikingly positive findings in the welfare-recipient training area in two studies of sites that were particularly attentive to working closely with private-sector employers: Riverside County in the GAIN evaluation (Friedlander et al., 1993) and the Center for Employment Training in the JOBSTART and Minority Female Single Parent studies (Cave et al., 1993; Burghardt et al., 1992).

OVERLAP, DUPLICATION, COORDINATION, AND ARTICULATION[13]

The fragmented, decentralized nature of training institutions and programs has led to somewhat of a preoccupation, especially among federal policy makers, with overlap, duplication, and the need for better coordination among publicly supported programs. The observation is frequently made by both scholarly and policy-oriented observers that the United States does not have a true training system, but a loose collection of relatively autonomous parts operating within a variety of local delivery structures. We found that fragmentation is not as bad as it appears on the surface. At the same time, we found a number of reasons to believe that improved training requires a much more systematic approach than currently exists.

Grubb and McDonnell (1991) have discovered that, despite fragmentation and program proliferation, existing institutions and programs in fact often behave in a variety of system-like ways. But there are many imperfections in these informal systems that develop in ad hoc ways in local communities.

Contrary to conventional wisdom, at the local level there is considerable coordination among programs. In most communities, administrators of every program are familiar with one another, and extensive referral and contracting among programs takes place. In the most typical pattern—what Grubb and McDonnell call the standard model—secondary and postsecondary vocational programs are linked by articulation agreements and so-called two plus two plans linking the last 2 years of secondary and the first 2 years of postsecondary; JTPA and welfare-to-work programs subcontract with community colleges to provide some (though not all) of their classroom-based training and remediation, with adult schools usually providing the lion's share of remediation; and community colleges provide customized training with their own resources as well as funds from state economic development efforts and payments from sponsoring firms.

There are, to be sure, variations among communities. In another pattern, educational institutions are linked through articulation agreements while JTPA and welfare-related programs collaborate, but the educational "subsystem" and the JTPA and JOBS programs do not interact much. Still another pattern emerges in a few communities, whereby a local community college dominates all education and training services. And, of course, there are some communities where programs operate virtually alone, and coordination is almost absent, but these appear to be quite rare.

Such coordination among programs, which can be described as collaborative service delivery, is typically the result of local initiatives rather than that of federal requirements or state policies for collaborative planning. The motives for local collaboration vary. These include cost-shifting, where programs with limited funding (especially JTPA and welfare programs) refer clients and thereby shift costs to community colleges and adult schools with enrollment-based, open-ended funding or student aid funds; the general dislike of competition and a pervasive feeling that cooperation will increase total resources; the search by most programs for distinct niches where they need not compete with others; and local brokers—including coordination councils, chambers of commerce, other business groups, and sometimes Private Industry Councils—that serve to link different programs.

Where coordination fails to take place, the barriers include differences in the choice of services offered, particularly where JTPA and welfare programs have concentrated on job-search assistance and on-the-job training rather than the more intensive programs typical in community college; dissatisfaction with particular providers, especially in communities where the community college is viewed as too academic and rigid in offerings and scheduling; JTPA performance standards, which have discouraged some educational institutions from competing for contracts;[14] and local politics, which dictate the allocation of JTPA resources in some communities and create a cleavage between educational institutions, on the one hand, and JTPA and welfare-related programs, on the other. These barriers are not the kind that can be overcome by federal or state coordination mandates. They are more fundamental, embedded in the basic purposes and structure of different programs.

In another sense, communities have systems of education and training: a wide range of services are available. Virtually every community, at least in urban and suburban areas, has a continuum of remediation programs leading to the GED (within adult education) or college-level courses (within community colleges); a variety of job-specific training ranging from short-term, entry-level programs in area vocational schools and community-based organizations to 2-year associate degree programs in technical and other well-paid fields; and ancillary services, like job-search assistance and placement services. In theory, individuals can enter various points in this system, make their way through a variety of programs (including remedial programs as necessary), and emerge with various kinds of occupational credentials or with the academic requirements to transfer to 4-year colleges and the rest of the educational system.

Finally, a system of specialization often operates at the local level that avoids the duplication of services and the resulting waste and inefficiency so worrisome to federal policy makers. Grubb and McDonnell (1991) found, in fact, that there are remarkably few cases of outright duplication in vocational education and job training. One reason is that programs vary in their services, with vocational programs concentrating on longer-term certificate and associate programs, while JTPA and welfare programs emphasize short-term training, on-the-job training, and job-search assistance. Institutions and programs also specialize in the individuals they serve: community colleges and technical institutes serve those students not attending 4-year colleges, as well as those in search of retraining, and experimenters trying to decide about their futures (Manski, 1989); JTPA serves a group with less formal education and labor-market experience; JOBS provides certain services for welfare clients; and adult education serves those in need of basic skills remediation and English as a second language. In addition, an overall shortage of resources means that there is generally greater demand than existing programs can supply. Where apparent overlap and duplication exist, especially in federal programs, it tends to occur because programs put different weight on seemingly similar goals. Given these differences in emphasis, duplication in resulting activities or conflicts between like-sounding offerings are not surprising and indeed may be legitimate.

On the other hand, there is reason to be concerned about problems of coordination and the lack of a systematic approach. One issue is the proliferation of federal programs that state and local training providers face. Table 2.1 details several dozen postsecondary training programs; these are only a fraction of the 125 employment and training programs identified by the U.S. General Accounting Office (1992d). While only a few of these programs are substantial, the existence of so many multiplies the administrative and coordinating tasks facing state and local program officials. GAO found that of 125 employment and training programs, 4 had annual funding of over $1 billion each, but 72 had funding of less than $50 million.

Even in the larger programs, a patchwork of incompatible federal requirements inhibits state and local efforts to plan and deliver services in a coordinated fashion. A survey of state and local human resource administrators and policy makers by the National Governors' Association (1991) identified a variety of barriers to coordination created by federal laws and regulations. Major impediments included the lack of common or compatible definitions; procedures for determining eligibility; and fiscal, administrative, and planning requirements.

Despite the large amount of coordination and referral that in fact occurs at the local level, there is also reason to be concerned about the near absence of mechanisms following individuals through the postsecondary education and training system, helping them make transitions among programs, providing them assistance if they falter, providing them information about the alternatives available, or helping them gain portable credentials that demonstrate competencies valued by employers. As a result, referral among programs—e.g., from JTPA to adult education, or from JOBS to the local community college—is likely to result in individuals becoming lost. This happens commonly even in welfare-to-work programs, where case workers are responsible for tracking individuals (Riccio et al., 1989). In a few communities, the dominance of the community college (or, less often, a particular adult school) has consolidated all services in one institution, facilitating tracking and referral among services; and some states, notably Wisconsin, have experimented with one-stop education and training centers. Such efforts have, until recently, been rare, however. In most communities, what could be a well-articulated system with a continuum of remedial and job-specific education has proved to be a patchwork of disconnected pieces for those who want training.

Years of mandating various coordination requirements among training and employment programs and creating ad hoc working arrangements among federal departments have not adequately alleviated these problems. Marion Pines, who headed a JTPA advisory committee to the U.S. Department of Labor that stressed the need for more coordinated human investment approaches and a more rational human resource delivery system in the United States, recently observed (Pines, 1992:30):

> Many states and local areas are working assiduously to make their diverse systems "user-friendly" by developing one-stop intake, assessment, and case-managed resource brokering to individuals and families. But they are doing it with much pain, and a degree of risk for audit exceptions. The variety of [federal] legislative initiatives that have been enacted have created the kinds of barriers to service integration that many prudent and conscientious people fear to buck.

We find the continuing federal barriers to systemic planning and coordination particularly disturbing, because we, like Pines, are hopeful about new state efforts to restructure their approaches to training.

A spate of recent developments suggests that a number of states are moving aggressively to weave the fragments of their own and federal training programs into integrated work force development systems. Governors and business leaders closely involved with such endeavors recognize the importance of decentralizing decision making to the substate level so that solutions can be tailored to the needs of employers and individuals within local labor markets. Nevertheless, they have also recognized the need to restructure state approaches to training, to ensure more comprehensive and coordinated planning, and to "shift the state role from a regulatory one to one of policy guidance and capacity building" (National Governors' Association, 1992:10-11).

They have done so in various ways. Even before the 1992 JTPA amendments granted governors the discretion to establish human resource investment councils, which consolidated numerous advisory councils required by various federal human resource programs, at least 10 states had established "super councils" of one sort or another (National Governors' Association, n.d.). Thanks to the JTPA amendments, this approach seems certain to spread. Some states have rationalized responsibilities for training programs within and among state agencies. New Jersey, for example, has consolidated 64 programs previously operated by 6 departments into 15 program areas in 3 departments. At least one state, Indiana, created a new, consolidated, executive branch department. The Indiana Department of Workforce Development brings under one roof the Commission on Vocational and Technical

Education, the Indiana Department of Employment and Training Services, and the Office of Workforce Literacy. Many states are also strengthening their information and accountability systems and developing new ways of assessing the outcomes of training programs (see National Alliance of Business, 1992, and National Governors' Association, 1992).

These initiatives typically involve strong leadership from governors and enlist the business community as important partners. They go beyond the requirements for coordinating and advisory councils that are often found in federal training programs. They appear to be vigorous, creative, and promising approaches to the problems that we have identified in this study.

We find these new state developments extremely encouraging because it is clear that states occupy the key position in giving public coherence and direction to postsecondary training. Most of the public funding for training institutions is theirs or flows through them. They are in a far better position than the federal government to oversee the development of arrangements that will result in systematically available training opportunities that are attuned to the specific and varying needs of local labor markets. The federal government, as an important player in the postsecondary training arena, must find ways to support these efforts and not inhibit their development.

SUMMARY

This chapter is long and complicated, but its major conclusions can be briefly stated. The United States does not have a true postsecondary training system. We have a variety of providers and programs that supply very good training to some citizens, but less effective or no training to many others. Qualifying training is readily accessible to many people, though the range of options is undoubtedly confusing to some. Qualifying training relies on schools almost exclusively, and many individuals who enroll do not complete any formal credential, though it is not clear how much the failure to stay enrolled long enough to earn a postsecondary training credential hurts individuals in the labor market. Opportunities to use workplaces as learning sites are inadequately developed. For different reasons, skills improvement training, retraining, and second-chance training are all less widely available. Evidence about the results of training is less thorough than we would like, but on balance the results are positive, if sometimes modest. Some kinds of training, particularly for disadvantaged youth, do not appear to be working. The quality of training is mixed, and the institutional structures for ensuring quality are underdeveloped. Linkages to employers need improvement. At the crucial level of local labor markets, programs and providers work together in more harmony than the fragmented national picture would suggest, but the pieces do not add up to anything that can be described as a system. The federal government, with its proliferation of programs and lack of unifying approach, bears part of the blame for this situation.

NOTES

1. While it would be preferable to examine the access question using longitudinal studies that include nonenrolled as well as enrolled individuals, existing longitudinal studies are dated and involve much smaller samples than NPSAS. NPSAS results, while limited by their cross-sectional nature, are recent and revealing.

2. He concluded that "the financial aid system works relatively well at removing the direct economic barriers to postsecondary enrollment" and observed that the vocation-oriented schools were more accessible "not only because of less restrictive admissions practices and lower direct costs [than 4-year schools], but also because they offer short-term programs and flexible scheduling (for example, part-time enrollment) that reduce the opportunity costs that students must incur" (Tuma, 1992:iii-iv).

3. Lynch (1993) has summarized several papers from her forthcoming volume on training and the private sector that use data from the United States, Britain, the Netherlands, and Norway to show that firm-based training results in greater economic payoffs to individuals than does school-based training (see Blanchflower and Lynch, 1994; Elias et al., 1994; and Groot et al., 1994). The committee was not able to examine these studies, but we note that the U.S. data on school-based training apparently are based on secondary-level vocational education and exclude training received in postsecondary schools such as community colleges and proprietary institutions.

4. According to guidelines set by the U.S. Department of Health and Human Services, countable participants as a group must be scheduled for an average of 20 hours a week of JOBS services and must attend most of those hours. States may serve exempted welfare recipients who desire services and may include them in order to meet the minimum participation rate.

5. Parts of this section are taken from a background paper prepared for the committee by David Stern.

6. The major shortcoming of nonrandomly controlled research designs stems from what evaluation experts call the problem of selection or selectivity bias. There may be unmeasured differences (in motivation levels, for example, or in job-relevant capabilities not measured by standardized admission or ability tests) among individuals choosing different training paths or between training participants and nonparticipants. Unmeasured differences may affect subsequent success on the job, thus confounding efforts to determine how much impact training itself has on job success. The evaluation problem created by the selection process is well-documented for welfare-to-work and mainstream employment and training programs (Gueron and Pauly, 1991; Ashenfelter, 1987; Burtless and Orr, 1986; Betsey et al., 1985; Lalonde and Maynard, 1987; Job Training Longitudinal Survey Research Advisory Panel, 1985). Selection bias also occurs among those pursuing various postsecondary schooling options (Grubb, 1990; Hollenbeck, 1992; Kane and Rouse, 1993), though these authors find that selection effects do not affect the estimates of the returns to schooling. From a research standpoint, however, it is clear that the study of selection effects in education has not advanced very far, and that further investigation into selection biases in nonexperimental studies on returns to school-based training is needed.

7. For all their advantages, however, random assignment experiments share some of the shortcomings of nonexperimental research. For example, because the experiment does not have laboratory control conditions, results from one study may not be valid for other circumstances (a training program may work better when the job market is tight but not when it is very soft); few studies follow people long enough to determine if there are permanent changes

in circumstances; and many follow trainees and controls for just 1 or 2 years, requiring extrapolation of end-period results into the future. Manski and Garfinkel (1992) and Heckman (1992) question the emphasis that has been given to random assignment field experiments, and we will see that they may not be practical in some circumstances and may not address all of the relevant policy questions. Still, where it exists, we believe that evidence from the experimental approach is the best available.

8. Cross-sectional income data are found in the Current Population Surveys and the Survey of Income and Program Participation, both conducted by the Bureau of the Census. The U.S. Department of Education conducted two longitudinal research projects, the National Longitudinal Study of the high school class of 1972 and High School and Beyond, studying the high school classes of 1980 and 1982.

9. For example, Adelman (1992) presents evidence from the National Longitudinal Study of 1972 on the infrequency of degree completion. He then concludes that students "seemed to make of the community college what they wanted to make of it," but without any evidence from the data that those who leave have in fact achieved their purposes.

10. The research findings cited in this and subsequent paragraphs relate to average earnings effects. Katz and Murphy (1992) have pointed out that earnings inequality *within* groups defined by education, age/experience, and gender is substantial and has been steadily rising, reaching a level in 1987 that was 30 percent higher than the level in 1970. This suggests that the returns to education vary significantly among students.

11. Data from the U.S. Department of Labor, unpublished 5-year analysis of JTPA Title III program performance, March 23, 1993.

12. Barnow (1992:297) indicates that performance standards likely led to creaming in JTPA but acknowledges that it is difficult to separate out the influence of performance standards from other factors that could also have encouraged the selection of easy-to-place participants. These include the increased role of the private sector in overseeing local implementation and limitations on supporting services and stipends.

13. Parts of this section are taken from a background paper prepared for the committee by Richard F. Elmore.

14. However, the discouraging effects of performance standards are clearly much weaker than often claimed, since the most common form of cooperation between vocational education and JTPA involves JTPA subcontracts with community colleges and technical institutes.

4

U.S. Training in
International Perspective[1]

In the preceding chapter we examined postsecondary training in the United States and found it wanting in many ways. Our concern about these shortcomings is heightened by a number of studies suggesting that many American workers receive less effective training than their overseas counterparts (see, for example, Dertouzos et al., 1989; U.S. Office of Technology Assessment, 1990; Lynch, 1991, 1993; Commission on the Skills of the American Workforce, 1990; Kochan and Osterman, 1991; Kolberg and Smith, 1992; Marshall and Tucker, 1992; National Academy of Engineering, 1993). The committee could not in the time available for its work evaluate the effectiveness of American in comparison with foreign training.[2] We do believe, however, that in an increasingly competitive international economy, the United States should not ignore possible lessons from the education and training practices of its principal trading partners.

Those who extol the virtues of training abroad frequently cite three key features of foreign training systems: close connections to employers, national systems of skills standards and skills certification, and pathways along which young people move in comparatively straightforward fashion from school to work. To get an idea of the different ways training systems might design these features, we looked at the approaches used in Australia, Britain, Germany, and Japan.[3]

It is critical to note, however, that national differences in the design of education and training institutions and in political, economic, and social environments preclude any simplistic notions of comparability and transferability of foreign training practices. The most obvious difficulty is that postsecondary training as we define it in this report does not have a direct analog in other countries (Organisation for Economic Co-operation and Development, 1989:Ch. 2). Even when educational or training institutions appear to be similar, differences in levels of prior preparation confound comparison. In Japan, for example, some observers note (e.g., Marshall and Tucker, 1992:52) that the average high school graduate reaches a level of achievement in the native language, science, and mathematics equal to or higher than that of the average American baccalaureate degree holder. If there are wide differences in achievement levels of secondary school graduates, it becomes harder to compare the performance of different postsecondary training systems by comparing student outcomes (Stevenson, 1992). In addition, school-trained Americans will be likely to have different sets of skills than their company-trained German and Japanese counterparts (Marshall and Tucker, 1992). Good data for comparing postsecondary training and skill levels across nations are lacking, in part because of the difficulty of collecting equivalent and reliable information on such topics as school achievement, formal classroom training within firms, and informal, on-the-job training (Kochan and Osterman, 1991:17; Bradburn and Gilford, 1990:6-9).

Difficulties in comparison also result from national differences in political, economic, and social structures and traditions. Government policies supporting high minimum wage levels, as in Germany, give employers a larger stake in training highly skilled workers who can justify high wages than the stake of employers in countries where they can pay less. Lifetime employment guarantees, a tradition in large Japanese firms, similarly encourage employers to provide training without fear of losing their investment if workers leave. Osterman (1988:Ch. 6) describes many other differences in institutions and behavior patterns that can "redirect and mutate" training models as they are transported from one country to another.

Given that a careful and comprehensive evaluation of comparative training systems and their results was beyond the committee's charge, we set modest goals for our international analyses. We looked at overseas training systems in the hope of learning something about how other countries approach the three key features noted above. We aimed at broadening our perspective rather than finding definitive answers to the problems we have identified in American training.

CONNECTIONS TO EMPLOYERS

Foreign training systems feature strong links to employers. In the countries we examined there are efforts to involve employers in training and to require businesses to invest in training, both for entering and for current workers.

Qualifying training in those countries is characterized by far greater employer involvement than is true in the United States. Germany and Japan have well-established, though quite different, approaches, with the former relying on work-based training and the latter emphasizing close ties between schools and firms. Australia and Britain have over the past 15 years sought to engage employers in preparing people for the workplace, though they chose quite different methods and experienced varying degrees of success. As in the United States, training for individuals already at work is largely the responsibility of firms, but we find evidence in Australia, Britain, Germany, and Japan of public policies that encourage or require employers to invest in training.

Qualifying Training

Germany

The clearest and most widely cited example of employer involvement in preparing young people for the workplace is found in Germany, with its "dual system" in which young people train as apprentices on the job under the tutelage of experienced masters while also pursing classroom instruction for 1 or 2 days per week.

The German apprenticeship system builds on a centuries-old tradition. The national government took steps in 1969 to strengthen the system, in reaction to a declining interest in vocational training among young people and to union concerns that apprentices were being exploited. The reforms were successful in revitalizing this work-based approach to training. By the late 1980s 60 percent of the German work force had completed an apprenticeship (U.S. Office of Technology Assessment, 1990:87). About one-quarter of all firms sponsors apprentices (U.S. General Accounting Office, 1990b:17). A 1975 law requires all businesses to pay a tax of up to 0.25 percent of company payroll if in any year the total number of apprenticeship openings is not 12.5 percent above the number of students applying for apprenticeship positions. The tax has never been levied (Kolberg and Smith, 1992:59).

At age 15 or 16, upon completion of mandatory full-time schooling, most youths enter one of about 380 apprenticeships in crafts and trades, industries, and business. Would-be apprentices have strong reasons to perform well in school because the best students are awarded the highest quality and highest status training slots (Soskice, 1994). After serving as apprentices for 3 years and passing a written and practical national exam, apprentices become journeymen. After 3 more years of taking courses and working on the job, a journeyman may take an exam to become a master. Only masters are allowed to open businesses.

Employers pay the costs of training at the work site, including the time of the masters doing the training; they also pay wages to the trainees, although wages are only about one-third of the adult unskilled wage rate (Lynch, 1993:17). Further, smaller firms receive some assistance from both the federal and the state governments for training costs. The apprenticeship training curricula, examinations, and certification procedures are developed nationally through industry-union-government collaboration. (See below for discussion of approaches to standardization and quality.)

German apprenticeships have such a high reputation for quality that they are able to attract even very academically prepared young people. Each year, a significant fraction of youth completing the matriculation certificate (*Abitur*), which would allow them to enroll in universities, choose instead to become apprentices (although many will later pursue a university education).

Despite the considerable success of apprenticeships as qualifying training, concern over the increased importance of theoretical knowledge is shifting the typical age of entry into apprenticeship upward, to 18 or 19. In Germany, it is increasingly common for students to attend a year in a vocational or special preparatory school before becoming apprentices (Casey, 1991).

Japan

Japanese firms also are strongly involved in qualifying training, through quite different means than in Germany. In Japan, employers are very influential primarily by their hiring practices, coupled with a large commitment to on-the-job training for new employees.

Japanese young people are required to attend school for 9 years; 94 percent continue on for another 3 years of secondary school (U.S. General Accounting Office, 1990b:17). Twenty-six percent of youths aged 15-18 attend vocationally oriented high schools; the rest pursue academic courses (Kochan and Osterman, 1991:29). Employers do not expect secondary schools to emphasize technical skills, and for this reason the Japanese educational system is often thought to be very little involved in occupational training. In fact, though, the entire schooling process has a "vocational cast" (Kochan and Osterman, 1991:28) because schools are closely linked to employers through unique labor recruitment practices (Rosenbaum and Kariya, 1989).

High school students not planning to continue their educations find jobs through their schools. Employers typically form links with a few high schools; they offer jobs to those schools, and teachers nominate and rank students for those jobs. Employers interview nominees and make final selections. How a student performs in school is very important in determining whether he or she will be nominated for a desirable job. This approach to linking schools and firms is also found (though to varying degrees) in

Japanese sub-baccalaureate institutions: private 2-year colleges that are similar to American community colleges and that are largely vocational in nature; technical colleges that combine upper secondary and postsecondary education; and special training schools and miscellaneous schools, which provide a variety of vocational courses.

German apprenticeships and Japanese recruitment practices are well-established ways of linking firms to the process of preparing young people for work. By contrast, Australia and Britain have undertaken major revisions in their training systems in recent years; both have sought to increase the involvement of employers in the training process.

Australia

Australia's reforms began in the 1970s in response to growing unemployment and underemployment among the nearly two-thirds of young people who left high school after grade 10, at age 15 or 16, rather than staying on to complete the narrowly academic 11th and 12th grades. Various changes associated with the inclusion of more general and work-related courses in grades 11 and 12 caused high school completion rates to nearly double in a decade, growing from 34 to 64 percent between 1981 and 1990 (Australian Education Council, 1990).

More recent reforms involve revisions to the Technical and Further Education (TAFE) system that dominates post-high school training for young Australians. The system provides full- and part-time courses for high school graduates and those who leave high school before graduation in TAFE Colleges, which focus heavily on initial vocational courses leading to qualifications in a wide range of trade, paraprofessional, and professional occupations. TAFE is also largely responsible for providing most of the coursework required of apprentices and trainees.

While ongoing reforms to TAFE include efforts to link firms more closely to the training system, Australian employers have a long history of involvement in training through a well-established apprenticeship system and through a newer, smaller Australian traineeship system established in the mid-1980s. About a quarter of Australian young people are apprentices or trainees; for many years apprenticeships were the dominant form of further training for Australian males who did not complete high school. Firms pay apprentices an age-determined proportion of the relevant tradesperson's full-time earnings, but are compensated by the government for the value of apprentices' time spent in TAFE classes. The payment for trainees is similar, though less generous.

Part of the training reform agenda involves strengthening TAFE institutions' ties to local industries. Individual institutions are working with local employers to develop training courses and articulation agreements that link firm-based on-the-job training with accredited TAFE courses. Federal matching grants encourage TAFE institutions to obtain industry contributions for the purchase of equipment. Industry is also involved in negotiations concerning curriculum revisions, the upgrading of credentials, and the development of national, competency-based standards for initial and subsequent vocational training (see below).

The federal government's ability to promote increasing industry involvement in training should be enhanced by recent changes in the governance structure of TAFE, which was historically funded and controlled by state and territorial governments. In 1992, after failing in a bid to take control of TAFE, the commonwealth (federal) government announced a more truly federal model under which a Council of Ministers and a new body—the Australian National Training Authority (ANTA)—will take control of the TAFE system. ANTA will be fully responsible for setting national goals, objectives, and priorities for vocational education and training and, beginning in 1994, will receive all commonwealth funding for TAFE as well as at least some of the state funding. On the basis of principles determined by the Ministerial Council, ANTA will then remit funding to the state training agencies.

Britain

Over the last decade, Britain, too, has actively sought greater employer participation in training its young people, the majority of whom still leave school at age 16. Whereas Australia is trying to engage firms more actively in determining policies for its schools, Britain is attempting to shift more training to the workplace. It created a coordinating mechanism, Training and Enterprise Councils (TECs), that invited firms to participate more in setting policy. These efforts have enjoyed only limited success.

Reform efforts at the postcompulsory level are built on changes made in compulsory schooling (which lasts until age 16). The British government has encouraged business interest in compulsory schooling by recommending that employers constitute at least 50 percent of the local boards of governors that set policies for individual schools. It has also encouraged the introduction of employment-related education into school teaching through "Technical Vocational Education Initiatives" and through the national curriculum developed in the 1980s. Finally, city technology colleges (which, contrary to their name, are seen as secondary rather than postsecondary institutions) have been created under the sponsorship of businesses, with some government funding.

At the postcompulsory level, school-based training takes place primarily in secondary programs for 16- to 18-year-olds and in local colleges of further education. In the secondary programs, which traditionally were highly academic, new courses and new kinds of certification exams with a more vocational bent have been introduced. In addition, it is now required that students have 2 weeks of work experience before leaving school. The national government has also proposed that the further education colleges should become autonomous institutions outside of local authority control with governing bodies that reflect local business interests.

Young people in Britain who do not attend university have historically moved directly into the labor market from compulsory schooling, with no formal training: joining a firm at age 16 or 17 was traditionally the route to many well-paid careers (Vickers, 1991:39). Once employed, individuals have had little incentive to invest in training, and the training that firms have provided tends to be very job-specific, in part because wage differentials associated with skills are lower in Britain than in other European countries. The resulting low levels of training have been of concern to public officials, employers, and employees.

For the moment, government policy is focused on 16- to 18-year-olds and on the unemployed. As in Australia, rising youth unemployment and underemployment in the early 1980s led to training reforms. In Britain, however, training was often controlled by employers rather than by recognized schools and colleges; the changes were marked by disappointing levels of employer involvement and by quality problems (U.S. General Accounting Office, 1990b; Vickers, 1991).

The current Youth Training (YT) program was established in 1990 as an outgrowth of the Youth Training Scheme introduced in 1983. YT provides training and employment opportunities for unemployed young people by encouraging employers to hire and train them for 2 years. The Youth Training Scheme, which initially provided only 1 year's employment, was criticized as being too short, having no clear definition of the training component, and no standardization of the qualification obtained, thus rendering qualifications incomparable and often meaningless. Furthermore, it appeared that firms were taking advantage of the significantly cheaper labor under the program (trainee wages were noticeably lower than those for regular employees or those for apprentices employed before the apprenticeship system collapsed in the economic distress of the early 1980s) to replace jobs that would otherwise have existed. Under YT, local business-controlled Training and Enterprise Councils (TECs) are primarily responsible for regulating the program, thus permitting flexibility in local arrangements; employers are expected to bear more of the costs; and government control and funding is linked less to inputs than to training outputs, which will be measured by new National Vocational Qualifications (see below).

Since 1988 Britain has moved toward putting much of the responsibility for developing training policy into the hands of newly formed TECs. These are private companies, based on American Private Industry Councils, with staff from the government training agency and a board of directors of which two-thirds come from business. TECs are responsible for administering public training programs (such as YT and others) but they are also supposed to promote wider efforts, such as providing help with training to small firms, increasing the involvement of employers with education, and coordinating training policies and finding methods of funding training that will overcome the reluctance of employers to train workers who may then be hired away. Their success will depend on the time and energy devoted by the board of directors, their willingness to help develop a cohesive national strategy rather than pursuing only local goals, and their ability to raise the private funding that will be needed to support efforts (beyond just program administration) to improve the scope and quality of training.

Skills Improvement Training

As in the United States, information on training programs for the current work force, especially skills improvement training for workers that is largely supplied by firms, is not as readily available as information on the preparation of young people for work. The difficulties of comparing direct and indirect training costs and of measuring informal versus formal training make it hard to substantiate the widespread belief that employers in many other countries are more committed to improving the skills of their workers than those in the United States. However, we did find some reasons that this might be so, as well as evidence of government efforts to encourage if not require firms to engage in training.

The distinct cultural, historical, and institutional factors that underlie employers' commitment to qualifying training in Germany and Japan can also help explain why employers might be more willing to undertake skills improvement training. In Germany, the so-called tripartite structure of employers, unions, and government that helps determine national training strategy also helps employers avoid the loss of trained workers to other firms. Local employer associations (called chambers, with similarities to U.S. chambers of commerce), to which every firm must belong, use moral suasion and social pressure to minimize the "poaching" of trained workers (Lynch, 1993:20). Moreover, every German firm with five or more employees is required to have a "works council" to participate in major personnel decisions, which gives workers a voice in deciding the firm's training policies (Kochan and Osterman, 1991:35; Rogers and Streeck, 1993).

In Japan, trained workers do not readily switch firms because the wage gains to quitters are low. Historically, there have also been high social costs paid by firms who lure away other firms' trained employees (Lynch, 1993:6). The tradition of lifetime employment in large firms further increases the benefit to firms from training, although job mobility may now begin to increase as Japanese companies struggle with new and unfamiliar economic difficulties. Finally, Japanese firms, especially large ones, have been enormously successful at integrating training into their production processes—through such practices as on-the-job rotation of workers, team-building and quality circles, and the use of front-line supervisors as trainers—so that training reaches workers as part of what they routinely do.[4]

The German and Japanese governments also explicitly encourage training of the current work force. Germany levies a 4 percent payroll tax—half charged to the employer, half to the employee—to raise funds for the Federal Employment Institute. Although the bulk of these funds goes to unemployed workers, about 15 percent is provided directly to workers for postapprenticeship training, training in new technologies, or retraining. Some German states require firms to give employees 1 or 2 weeks per year of paid training leave to attend outside seminars (U.S. Office of Technology Assessment, 1990:94). In Japan, where the government has played a much smaller role in training policy, there are public subsidies for in-house training, especially for smaller firms (Lynch, 1993:22), as well as subsidies for firms that train older workers (those aged 45 and over) (U.S. Office of Technology Assessment, 1990:95).

As part of its broader training reforms, Australia has also taken steps to promote more systematic and substantial industry investments in on-the-job training. The commonwealth introduced the Training Guarantee Scheme in 1990, requiring all firms whose gross wage outlays exceed A$200,000 per year to make training investments: initially, 1.0 percent of gross wages and rising within several years to 1.5 percent. Firms are also expected to assess their own training obligations and liabilities; to police this, the Australian Tax Office conducts compliance audits. Training programs provided by firms must aim to teach employment-related skills and enhance firm productivity. Employers must identify the skills to be taught, the means by which they will be taught, and the method of assessing productivity increases. One side benefit of the Training Guarantee Scheme is that much better information will become available on what is now a poorly documented, but apparently extensive, system of employer-sponsored training in Australia.

British firms are widely criticized for their low levels of investment in upgrading the skills of the existing work force. Part of the charge to the TECs is to find ways to overcome the traditional reluctance of British employers to train their employees.

NATIONAL STANDARDS AND SKILLS CERTIFICATION

Australia, Britain, Germany, and Japan have national systems that set standards for work-related skills, or certify for those skills, or both, espe-

cially for qualifying training. Some countries are under pressure to standardize so-called further training (what we call skills improvement training in this report) for the current work force as well.

The transition from training to work in Germany and Japan is accompanied by national certifications and national examinations. In both Australia and Britain, governments have recognized that in order to strengthen their training systems they need to establish vocational standards and then to assist in the development of competency-based training programs.

Nationally recognized skills certification is thought to be an important part of successful apprenticeship programs because it provides people with an incentive to participate and to accept lower wages while in training. Employers are more willing to provide general as well as firm-specific training if they are paying apprentices less than regular workers (Lynch, 1993:31).

In Germany, apprenticeship curricula, examinations, and certifications are set at the national level by committees that represent government, employers, and workers. Firms that would employ apprentices have to be approved by local chambers of commerce; internal instructors must be trained and certified through the chambers. To achieve journeyman status, an apprentice must pass national examinations that include written, oral, and practical tests; the tests are administered by committees composed of employers, workers, and vocational instructors (U.S. General Accounting Office, 1990b:38-39). National examinations also determine who can progress from journeyman to master. Training standards are high, and the assessment standards that have evolved over the years are viewed as reliable (Lynch, 1993:17).

Japan, with its greater reliance on on-the-job training and with its tradition of low labor mobility, has less need of national standards and certifications. Instead, many firms have developed internal certification procedures. In an effort to raise the status of blue-collar workers by giving public recognition to the skill levels they had achieved, the Ministry of Labor in 1959 created a national testing system that now covers 130 occupations. In firms, however, ongoing informal evaluations by supervisors continue to carry more weight than formal qualifications (U.S. Office of Technology Assessment, 1990:91).

Australia's recent training reforms included a massive overhaul of the country's credentialing system. The need for such an overhaul stemmed in part from Australia's unique system of industrial relations, which involves a centralized wage-fixing system that establishes "awards" for almost all occupations in both the industrial and the service sectors of the economy. Awards are occupationally specific rulings arrived at through formal tripartite negotiations (government, employer, worker) that stipulate wages and working conditions. Within the industrial awards system, workers' wage entitlements and job definitions depend on their possessing the appropriate certificates, diplomas, or degrees. (Rapid changes in production methods in Australian industry can be impeded by the rigidity of the occupational classifications embedded in the wage awards, so in 1987 the commonwealth committed itself to a major program of industrial reform that focused specifically on award restructuring.) In the metal industry, for example, the overhaul resulted in a change from 360 specific job classifications to 14 levels of competency. Following the change in credentialing came reform of the training system and of the traditional certification system, which had been regulated by a variety of federal and state-based authorities.

Reforms of training standards and certifications are still in process and will take years. Under the leadership of a National Training Board established in 1990, Australia is attempting to develop a competency-based training approach under which a broad range of providers (firm-based and private institutions as well as schools) can have their training programs certified. The National Training Board has decided to establish an Australian Standards Framework of eight competency levels, which will serve as reference points for the development and recognition of competency standards. The implementation of this idea is a major undertaking that will involve analyzing particular jobs to characterize the skills involved, conduct performance-based assessments of worker and trainee skills, and develop new ways of recording achievements that are more flexible and cumulative than the conventional vocational certificates and diplomas.

There appears to be strong support among employers and unions for a competency-based training system and for the registration of a broader range of training providers. Nevertheless, a number of problems have arisen as firms and the TAFE colleges pursue this approach. For example, it is proving difficult to define competencies in nontechnical tasks, and some employers doubt whether standards can be both national and applicable to particular enterprises. There is a concern that the existing formal education and training system will insulate itself from the new approaches and that industry-responsive approaches will only emerge at the margins. Australia's credential reforms have a long way to go, and a sure and steady transition toward a national system of competency standards is not taken for granted (National Board of Employment, Education and Training, 1991).

Britain established its National Council for Vocational Qualifications in 1986 to rationalize and reform the vocational certification system and bring some cohesion to a plethora of training options. The council has developed a national framework of National Vocational Qualifications (NVQs) involving five levels of competence in occupations and professions: the goal is to place all the existing vocational certifications into this framework. The need for such a framework and the challenge in creating it are indicated by the fact that more than 2 million vocational certifications are awarded each year by more than 300 bodies. Within the last several years, the council has also introduced a hybrid form of certification called General National Vocational Qualifications (GNVQs), designed to bridge the NVQs and the traditional A-level exams that are required for university entrance. GNVQs, unlike NVQs, do not imply that individuals are prepared to perform in a specific occupation. Rather, they indicate achievement of a foundation of general skills, knowledge, and understanding that underpin a range of occupations. GNVQs are designed for those pursuing full-time education with limited access to the workplace. They are calibrated to both A-level and NVQ scores and are designed to be an alternative to the academically oriented A-level exams as a pathway to higher education (National Council for Vocational Qualifications, 1993).

As in Australia, the effort to develop a national credentialing system in Britain has drawn criticism. Though the National Council for Vocational Qualifications appears to offer more coordination than existed in its absence, it does not reduce the number of organizations entitled to certify vocational skills, but rather expands it, adding employers and private training agencies to the existing mix of further education colleges and other examining bodies. The NVQs have been attacked for being very low-level and for allowing firms to accredit their own trainees without outside assessment for quality control. This has undermined public confidence in them (Vickers, 1991:45-6).

PATHWAYS FROM SCHOOL TO WORK

Other nations often offer their young people better delineated, more certain pathways from school to work than are available in the United States. As a result, young people (especially men) seeking permanent entry into the labor force accomplish this goal at an earlier age and with fewer interruptions than do Americans.

Americans travel a distinctly different path from education to work than people in major European countries and Japan. In American compulsory education, the academic track dominates, and many young people who do not attend or complete college emerge from school without any clear preparation for work. The postcompulsory period for American youth is characterized by high initial participation rates in postsecondary training, but also high dropout rates, frequent switches between periods of schooling and work, deferred entry to full-time, career-oriented employment, frequent job switches, and relatively low levels of firm-provided training once youths are on the job (Haggstrom et al., 1991). Research has shown that job mobility, especially in the early years of work, is a key way in which young

American men increase their wages and move toward long-term stable employment (Topel and Ward, 1992). Nevertheless, high labor market "inactivity rates" (the percentage of the population that is not employed, serving in the military, or enrolled in school) and the apparent underemployment of many workers with jobs in the years immediately following high school exacerbate the problems and dangers facing some adolescents. A recent National Research Council report (1993:127) on at-risk youths[5] notes that "many high school graduates flounder in the labor market, either jobless or obtaining jobs with low wages and little opportunity for advancement" and observes that these difficulties are most pronounced for adolescents who are already at risk because of their status as minorities or the children of low-income families.

Both the German dual system and the Japanese school-based system with strong links to employers offer teenagers a more direct and certain route into employment. Preliminary analyses of longitudinal data on the school-to-work transition commissioned by the committee suggest that these systems and others like them (such as apprenticeships in Australia) reduce the amount of "milling around" by young people. These analyses indicate, for example, that those who have been apprentices in Germany and Australia switch labor market status comparatively infrequently. That is, they less often change their status from employed to unemployed, employed to student, student to employed, unemployed to student, in-the-labor-force to out-of-the-labor force, etc. Apprenticeship has also proven to be an effective means for youths to gain steady employment after their training period even (as in Australia) when the youth labor market as a whole has experienced significant dislocation and unemployment.[6]

Comparative labor market stability for young adults as it has historically been accomplished in Germany and Japan comes at a price, however. By American standards, young people and their parents frequently make very early decisions about career choices. In Japan, examinations taken at the end of the equivalent of the U.S. 9th grade determine whether a student will enroll in an academic or vocational high school, which in turn is strongly determinative of whether that youth will enter the work force right after high school or pursue additional education. German children take exams at the end of primary school (about age 10) that track them into one of three types of secondary schools. Which kind of secondary school a German attends generally determines what career path he or she will follow.[7] Exam systems that track children into apprenticeship or other vocational pathways can limit their ability to pursue higher education or to switch fields of study. Many European countries, including Germany, have addressed this problem in recent years by opening up their exam systems and allowing each student more options.

The advantages from more structured pathways sometimes accrue disproportionately to young men. Participation in apprenticeship in many countries is dominated by males. In Australia, Britain (before the Youth Training Scheme replaced the apprenticeship system), and Germany, fewer women than men go through apprenticeships. Young women who do become apprentices often find themselves preparing for lower paying occupations and experiencing more subsequent underemployment than men who became apprentices. In fact, gender differences in pathways to work are frequently found in foreign training systems, not just because of tracking but also because of social mores. In Japan, for example, 90 percent of students in private 2-year colleges are female, while 87 percent of the students in technical colleges are male. The differences reflect the lower priority Japanese parents have traditionally placed on the education of their daughters and their preference for keeping them at home: junior colleges offer shorter term programs and are local in nature. Moreover, Japanese companies have historically expected women to work only until they married and have not given them responsible, demanding jobs. They see junior college graduates as more convenient than graduates of longer programs because they will put in more years of work before leaving for marriage, and they will cost less in wages.

CONCLUSION

As stated at the beginning of this chapter, the committee did not undertake a thorough or systematic evaluation of international training practices. We did, however, discover a good deal of information about how other countries that face many of the same issues now being raised in the United States have developed a diverse array of interesting policies and practices. More than that, we take away from our review an impression that other countries are increasingly thinking about training policy in a deliberate, systematic way. The movement in this direction is clearest in Australia and Britain, which historically have been characterized by fragmented, uncoordinated approaches. It is also noteworthy that strategic planning to improve training is not limited to individual countries, but can also be found in multinational entities like the evolving European Community (Glitter, 1992). It is this trend toward active and coordinated national and multinational training strategies, more than the particulars of the practices in individual countries, that impresses us most from our examination of training in an international perspective.

NOTES

1. Unless otherwise cited, information in this chapter is from papers prepared for the committee to describe the institutions, policies, and pathways from school to work in Australia

(Vickers, 1992; Gregory, 1992), Britain (Connolly, 1992a,b), Germany (Rauberger, 1992a,b), and Japan (Rosenbaum and Kariya, 1992a,b; see also Lane, 1992a,b).

2. Lynch (1993:4) notes that an emerging consensus about the relatively poor skills of American workers "is based on limited direct empirical evidence of how skills and skill preparation vary from country to country." This is particularly true of private-sector training, which is a significant part of qualifying training in some countries and is the major source of skills improvement training in most countries. The growing interest in how training is provided overseas and in the effectiveness of foreign training policies is spurring research efforts on these important issues. Some potentially important analyses (e.g., Lynch, 1994) were not available for the committee to consider; moreover, we believe a careful comparative evaluation would be a study unto itself.

3. Our discussion of training policies in Britain refers to England and Wales; Scotland has a somewhat different system, which we did not examine.

4. High levels of training may not be as characteristic of the large numbers of small Japanese firms that perform service work and subcontract with large firms. Large Japanese corporations do provide training assistance to their first-tier suppliers, and smaller firms sometimes benefit from this assistance as well (U.S. Office of Technology Assessment, 1990:90).

5. At-risk youths are defined as "adolescents who engage in high-risk behaviors—behaviors that compromise their health, endanger their lives, and limit their chances to achieve successful adult lives" (National Research Council, 1993:1).

6. In Australia, it will be interesting to see if this advantage carries over to other parts of the training arena as the commonwealth merges its four traditional pathways into work (apprenticeships, traineeships, TAFE courses, and entry-level training provided by firms) into a single system that will involve four vocational certificates, one for each level of training achieved. This so-called Australian Vocational Certificate training system will equate with Australian Standards Framework level 1 to 4.

7. *Hauptschule* involves 5-6 years of secondary schooling and leads primarily to blue-collar apprenticeships. *Realschule* offers 6 years of schooling aimed at training for higher-level but nonacademic occupations; graduates usually enter white-collar apprenticeships or gain admission to technical schools. Graduates of *gymnasium* are eligible, after they complete 9 years of secondary school, for university admission if they pass a qualifying examination.

5

The Federal Role in Postsecondary Training

A desirable system of postsecondary training for the workplace would be coherent, readily accessible, and closely connected to the actual world of work; it would have clearly visible and positive effects on those trained, and be uniformly high in quality. Individuals seeking to enter specific occupations or advance in them would know what kind of training employers value and where to find it. Employers would know what skills and competencies have been developed as a result of training programs. Individuals would have the information they need to gauge their interest in and suitability for various jobs, as well as the likely demand for workers in various fields. Employers would have information about the existing and future supply of trained workers, and they would be able to signal their needs to training providers.

We do not find these attributes to be broadly present in American postsecondary training, despite the existence of many isolated exemplars such as community colleges and proprietary schools offering high-quality vocational programs, employers strongly committed to the continuous improvement of their workers at all levels, or community groups effectively helping welfare recipients move into the work force.

The problems found in American postsecondary training are not new. Almost 30 years ago, a study sponsored by the American Council on Education (Venn, 1964:85) reported that "[o]pportunities for postsecondary occupational education are best described as a sometime thing" and decried the same kind of disjointedness that exists today.

Thirty years ago, however, the consequences of an inadequate training system were less threatening. With the other major industrialized nations still recovering from the Second World War, the United States had no serious economic challengers. Today, there are many challengers, and the industrial, labor-market, and human resource strategies that worked so well for most of this century may not keep the United States at the economic forefront. Thirty years ago, many of the federal training programs studied in this report did not exist: postsecondary institutions had only recently been made eligible for vocational education money; employment training programs were just beginning; welfare-based training was not on the agenda. Now, thanks to new federal and state initiatives, many more training programs exist, but opportunities for postsecondary training remain a sometime thing.

The committee concludes that the time has come for the nation to focus on linking up the various pieces of and partners in postsecondary training. They must be linked in ways that will provide coherent and high-quality training opportunities for individuals at various stages in their working lives. Coherence must ultimately be rooted at the local labor-market level; because they are responsible for many of the training institutions and much of the public funding for training, states are central to developing a training infrastructure that will meet local needs. A national system should, in fact, be composed of a variety of systems that differ somewhat among states and localities but that present potential trainees and employers with integrated training opportunities and information. (The term *postsecondary training system* as used in this report encompasses the notion of a variety of state and local systems.) The federal government has an important, albeit limited, contribution to make in helping such a system come about.

It is important, therefore, to stress at the outset that the federal government needs to change the way it has approached support for postsecondary training in the past. It also needs to improve its existing array of categorical programs aimed at specific needs (see Chapter 7). More important, however, the federal government must move beyond support for individual programs and take the lead in promoting policies that encourage quality and coherence in the training system as a whole. In recommending a change in the federal role, we emphasize that developing a more coherent, high-quality system is a dauntingly complex task, one not readily amenable to quick or blunt policy strokes.

Subsequent chapters discuss in some detail how the federal government could foster high-quality training and be an agent of change. To lay the groundwork for that discussion, this chapter describes how we view the scope of federal responsibility for postsecondary training and why the federal government should adopt a catalytic role in spurring systemic reform.

SCOPE OF FEDERAL RESPONSIBILITY

In Chapter 1 we identified four distinct training needs: *qualifying training*, to prepare people for labor market entry or reentry; *skills improvement training*, to help people improve their performance in their current jobs or occupations; *retraining*, for people whose job skills have become obsolete; and *second-chance training*, for those whose earlier encounters with the education and training systems have been unsuccessful. Responsibilities in each of these areas must be shared among governments at different levels as well as with private actors; moreover, the extent of federal responsibility currently varies substantially among these different types of training, and we believe this differentiation should continue. Finally, the four types of training are distinct enough that no single approach or program is likely to serve all needs well; the existence of multiple programs is inevitable.

In Chapter 3 we described the many and complex functions a training system must serve. The federal government has only limited responsibility for these functions, but it can use its influence to help ensure that the system performs well in:

1. *Providing access to training* for those who can benefit from it. The federal government is key to providing financial access to some kinds of postsecondary training (especially second-chance training), though its role in funding access to other training is not as central.

2. *Providing information about training alternatives and results.* The federal government has a very important role to play in encouraging the development and dissemination of better consumer and career information, but this information must often be produced at both state and local levels.

3. *Providing high-quality, accountable training programs.* The federal government has an important role in encouraging the development of mechanisms for promoting and rewarding quality performance. However, we again emphasize that state and local governments or private groups will usually have the most direct responsibility for improving quality and sustaining high-quality performance.

4. *Involving employers effectively in the education and training system.* The central purposes of the system we are examining include improving people's chances of getting and keeping good jobs and performing well in them. Achieving these purposes plainly requires that training matches employers' needs and expectations. Here again, the federal government should help foster improvements in employer-training connections, while recognizing that many of the connections should be accomplished in decentralized ways.

5. *Improving coordination and articulation among training efforts.* We see two kinds of problems of overlap and poor coordination among training programs, which we call *vertical and horizontal articulation.* By

vertical articulation we mean the availability of well-defined paths by which a person may move through the training system, from less to more sophisticated levels. By horizontal articulation, we mean first, coordination among programs so that individuals have easy access to a comprehensive and clear set of services rather than a fragmented and poorly understood array of choices. Second, we refer to the need for commonly understood workers' credentials that will allow workers to move among employers and across geographic boundaries. Such movement is especially important in minimizing the human costs of changes in economic demand. The federal government can encourage those involved at various levels to coordinate their efforts in productive ways. It can also spur the development of credentials that qualify workers for career paths and that are understood beyond the boundaries of the local labor market where they were earned. Finally, the federal government can guard against the tendency for individual federal programs to impose incompatible requirements that produce unintended barriers to movement through the system.

There is much we do not know about the ideal shape of a system that performs these various functions effectively in a decentralized nation and economy. But there are steps the federal government can and should now take. Throughout American history the federal government has supported preparation for work. Today, another federal push is needed to help American training policies adapt again to changing economic challenges.

POINTS OF LEVERAGE

America's federal traditions and history of shared domestic policy-making responsibility are important considerations in finding the most effective leverage points for federal policies on postsecondary training.

The relationship between the federal and state or local governments has undergone important changes in the last decade or so (Nathan, 1990; Rivlin, 1992; Shannon and Kee, 1989), with implications for the design of an effective training system. After a half-century in which the federal government became increasingly active in domestic policy and increasingly influential in the affairs of state and local governments, the tide turned in the late 1970s and especially with the election of Ronald Reagan to the presidency in 1980. Growing fiscal constraints coupled with Reagan's desire to reduce the size of government led to a sharp decline in the number of and funding for federal grant-in-aid programs to the states and localities. As Table 5.1 indicates, categorical grant programs to state, local, and public and private nonprofit organizations numbered 534 in 1981 and only 392 in 1984. (However, this decline was only temporary.)

There was an ironic and, at least for some, unexpected result. In what

TABLE 5.1   Federal Categorical Grant Programs (selected fiscal years)

Recipient	1975	1981	1984	1991
States only	162	194	153	205
State and local	62	69	42	49
Local only	20	23	14	22
State, local, and public and private nonprofits	198	248	183	267
Total	442	534	392	543

SOURCE: Advisory Commission on Intergovernmental Relations (1992:12).

Nathan (1990:233) has dubbed the "paradox of devolution," state governments were activated and strengthened by the federal retreat.[1] In the 1980s, states were not only willing but also able to redress the balance of power that had been shifting toward the federal government since the 1930s. And, for fiscal reasons if nothing else, the federal government may have a hard time regaining the initiative back for the foreseeable future.

Because of the need to reduce the federal budget deficit, the federal government is unlikely to have large amounts of money to use as leverage on state policies in a period when states are increasingly capable of acting on their own. This also suggests the importance of the federal government using its funds where its leverage can be most effective. This conclusion is also consistent with the recognition that training is largely in state and private hands, as Chapter 2 has shown. Even in programs where federal funding is relatively important (for example, JTPA and JOBS), part of the "paradox of devolution" is that states were assigned important responsibilities in the 1980s for planning and administration. Moreover, there are powerful norms of self-governance and self-regulation (exercised, for example, through accreditation) that condition acceptable federal intervention (Lad, 1992).

To be effective, then, federal training policies must take into account the limits on federal influence, as well as the problems of prescribing uniform requirements for 50 states whose major training institutions (such as schools) vary in critically important ways.

A final consideration is that states are not only better positioned to develop the infrastructure of the first real training *system* that has ever existed in this country, but that *there is growing evidence of their willingness to do so.* We saw in Chapter 3 that, within the past 5 years, a number of states have taken serious steps to address the preparation and quality of their work forces. The federal government ought to nurture this enormously promising development and evaluate whether the promise is indeed fulfilled.

We emphasize that in the United States vocation-oriented training has been, if not an orphan, at least a stepchild. American society has not respected it or given it the status accorded preparation of a more traditional academic nature. Federal postsecondary training programs have usually evolved as off-shoots of programs whose main objectives were elsewhere: vocational education money was targeted at high schools for nearly 50 years before postsecondary schools became eligible; student aid was created with 4-year colleges in mind; the welfare system became interested in training only after many earlier attempts to wean people from the welfare rolls through other methods failed to have the desired results.

The reasons for training's subordinate status are complex and deeply imbedded in our history and culture and conceptions of what it means to be a democratic nation whose citizens' futures are not determined by circumstances of birth or social class but where opportunities and social mobility are open to all. They are further complicated by an economic history that more often found workers and employers pitted against each other rather than collaborating to create both the general skills that give individuals flexibility and the specific skills that employers want.

The stepchild status of training for work may be changing. Chapter 3 described the growing number of promising state initiatives designed to bring business, education and training institutions, and state officials together to restructure education and training systems in order to improve the planning and delivery of integrated work force development services.

The federal government needs to be careful not to unwittingly derail the progress being made in the states; it has the potential to reduce the creativity being demonstrated by state, local, and business leaders. Chapter 3 referred to some of the barriers to state systemic reforms erected by incompatible federal rules and requirements.

Since we believe that the nation still has much to learn about how best to organize training, we argue below and in Chapter 8 for federal policies that encourage the natural experimentation taking place at the state level. Centralization at the state rather than the federal level appears to offer the benefits of system-building, while minimizing the dangers to creativity that could come from overly prescriptive unitary policies dictated at the federal level.

The federal government, with its national perspective, is uniquely able to articulate the goals of the country for better postsecondary training, to act as a catalyst to spur the improvement of training, and to encourage the development of systematic approaches to training. There are at least three reasons why the federal government should take on these tasks, while continuing to support existing programs whose goals of equalizing opportunities and providing second chances are well-established special federal responsibilities.

First, the federal government can bring visibility to the needs of the large middle of the work force between the high-school-educated and the college-trained that has been seriously neglected in this country, just as a decade ago the federal government helped focus attention on high school with its report, *A Nation at Risk* (National Commission on Excellence in Education, 1983). This middle group potentially includes a large majority of all workers.

Second, while states are often wonderful laboratories for developing new ideas and programs (e.g., Osborne, 1990), the federal government has several advantages in fostering the spread of innovation. Innovation in the states tends to occur unevenly; the federal government is ideally situated to provide information and technical assistance on program improvements and to provide incentives that will encourage postsecondary providers to seek out and adopt the best practices. The federal government is in a better position than states to undertake research and evaluation, because of economies of scale and the benefits such research provides to all participants. Finally, even though sub-baccalaureate labor markets are local, some things (such as training credentials, see Chapter 6) should be national in scope to foster worker mobility and spur employer use through a common understanding of what the credentials mean.

Third, the federal government has historically been a leader in shifting the focus of the nation's institutions (especially schools and colleges) as economic changes demanded new ways of preparing people for adult responsibilities. Long before America's citizens and legislators were ready to allow the federal government to give general aid to education, probably the most strongly held reserved power given to the states by the Constitution, they were prepared to support federal aid to occupation-oriented training.[2]

But while the federal government has historically spurred the development of training opportunities, especially for the young, it also bears some responsibility for the fragmentation of the nation's training effort. The federal tendency to proliferate categorical grant-in-aid programs in many areas of social policy has been widely discussed and much bemoaned.[3]

Having helped create the problem, the federal government should help find a solution.

Finally, we believe that the federal government should lead because of the emerging consensus that brain power is the key to economic power and that to compete in the global economy the nation has to have a strategy for investing in people. We looked at the arguments behind this emerging consensus in Chapter 1; here we acknowledge that, in some ways, they are difficult to prove. But, if the principles recommended below are followed, and the caveats heeded, there is little harm in acting as though the consensus finding is true and much risk to the future economic well-being of the nation and its citizens from failing to act until evidence to support the consensus view becomes incontrovertible.

PRINCIPLES TO GUIDE FEDERAL ACTION

We present here seven principles to guide the development of federal policies and programs.

1. *The federal government should refocus its attention, emphasizing the importance of building a postsecondary training system rather than continuing the piecemeal approach that has characterized past efforts.*

The biggest needs in postsecondary training are for systemic thinking about training policy and for structures that can tie together the different parts of training and let individuals move easily among them.

There are no "one-size-fits-all" or "magic bullet" solutions in a country where the responsibility for training is highly decentralized and where the four types of training needed by workers are so different from one another that multiple approaches and programs are inevitable. Federal policies in the past have, as they should, paid attention to the differences.

All forms of training are related, however, as parts of the process of initially preparing and continuously improving the nation's work force. Good public policy now requires the federal government to give attention to linking the parts together in ways that are coherent to both the workers and the employers who need to use them.

2. *While not reducing its commitment to fostering equity, the federal government should give special attention to the problem of ensuring quality, in response to the pervasive sense that the quality of American training is at best mixed and often poor.*

We have seen that too little is known about what is actually accomplished by training and what happens to those who are trained. Too little information about the outcomes and results of training is available to potential trainees and those who would hire them. The problem of ensuring quality is admittedly complex in a decentralized system, but the federal government can encourage improvement in the quality of postsecondary training in ways compatible with our traditions and institutions (see Chapter 6).

Another way of improving the overall performance of the postsecondary training system is for the federal government to respond to the information that is available about what works and what doesn't and to make changes when there is evidence public programs do not seem to be helping those whose lives they are supposed to improve. Youth training programs are a good example. We are not arguing that the nation should abandon its concern for high-risk youth because current youth training does not appear to help participants. But decisions makers should acknowledge forthrightly that current approaches are not working and should aggressively explore new avenues that might help.

3. *The federal government should pursue changes in postsecondary training through policies that emphasize continuous improvement rather than radical reform.*

Much is unknown about what constitutes good practice in training for work and about the effects and outcomes of work-oriented training institutions and programs. At the same time, this is a vital period of innovation and analysis. At such a time, it is more appropriate for the federal government to encourage experimentation, evaluation, and policy evolution than to attempt a radical overhaul of its or the nation's approach to training activities. The approach we propose requires the federal government to think in new ways about how it manages public programs (see Chapter 8). Part of the federal role in continuously improving postsecondary training should be to evaluate the pace at which good practices are adopted and to determine what kinds of technical assistance and incentives might encourage faster diffusion.

One specific area where the federal government can make an important contribution is in encouraging experimentation with and evaluation of promising training practices and structures used in other countries. One example of an approach more prevalent abroad is the use of workplaces rather than schools as training sites for those seeking qualifying training. Other countries also have connecting structures and standard-setting mechanisms that tie the training system together and that may lend themselves to adaptation in the United States.

4. *The federal government should recognize the key roles that states must play in the development of an effective training system.*

State governments are responsible "for structuring and managing a wide range of domestic programs in a way that makes it logical for them to have the lead role in policy implementation . . . . The services that need to be expanded and connected . . . are not the kinds of governmental activities that can be micromanaged from Washington" (Nathan, 1993:125). Moreover, states have demonstrated staying power and the ability to innovate effectively over the past decade in a number of related policy areas, including welfare reform, school reform, and economic development. Fuhrman (1993) cites a variety of actions that states have taken to promote systemic school reform, actions indicating that coherent policy making is being achieved even without fundamental change in the political system which has produced incoherence so often in the past.

5. *The federal government should seek to enhance the involvement and stake of employers in training policies and systems.*

Linkages between employers and the world of training need to be stronger, because the success of training ultimately depends on its usefulness in the workplace. Involving employers in systemic reform efforts is crucial to securing their attachment to the training system. Employers' interests are, though, not the only interests that must be served by training; their needs must be balanced with the needs of those who require not only firm-specific training but broader and more transferable skills as well.

6. *The federal government should resist the temptation to spread its resources so thinly that little or no impact is possible.*

With federal resources constrained by the budget deficit, it is more important than ever to focus available funds where they can do the most good. In addition, focusing resources on successful programs or programs likely to be successful can help (a) create true partners in support of the programs; (b) improve the reputation of training programs and thus reduce the stigmatization of participants, especially those in the second-chance programs; and (c) reduce the complexity created by the existence of dozens of (often very small) federal programs.

7. *"Do no harm": federal policy makers should recognize that it is possible for federal programs to hurt people and should be cautious about extending "help" in such circumstances.*

One way that federal programs can actually harm people can be seen in student loan programs. If individuals whose training offers little hope of giving them the capacity to pay back loans are allowed to borrow, they have a high chance of becoming defaulters. They risk often unpleasant pursuit by loan collectors, finding their credit records damaged, and losing future eligibility for student assistance for which they might otherwise have qualified. We believe that those who would design good public policy should avoid creating situations where individuals are likely to find themselves harmed by participating in a public program.

NOTES

1. Their capacity to pick up the initiative in a variety of policy arenas was in part the result of the modernization of their structure and institutions that occurred during the 1960s and 1970s. The weaknesses in state government that had contributed to the growing role of the federal government in domestic affairs from the Great Depression on were addressed. Guber-

natorial terms of office were lengthened and bans on succession were lifted. Governors were given more power to appoint state officials; historically, many of them had been elected. Staffs were increased in size and became more professionalized. As a result of the *Baker v. Carr* and *Reynolds v. Sims* decisions by the Supreme Court in 1962 and 1964, respectively, state legislatures were reapportioned on a "one person, one vote" basis, reducing the influence of rural areas and increasing representation from cities and suburbs. States and localities strengthened their revenue systems by reducing their dependence on property taxes, using sales and income taxes more extensively, and raising tax rates.

  2. In 1862, the Morrill Act gave states public land or its equivalent to support the establishment of colleges whose teaching would focus on agriculture and the mechanic arts, rather than on the dominant classical curriculum of the day. From this grew a great system of so-called land-grant colleges and universities. In 1917, heeding changes brought about by an industrializing economy as well as fear of falling behind Germany, with whom the United States would soon be at war, the Smith-Hughes Act was passed, promising federal funds to high schools for vocational education in agriculture, trades and industry, and home economics.

  3. As Table 5.1 indicates, this tendency was checked briefly during the early years of the Reagan presidency, but the pause was only temporary. By 1991 there were more categorical federal grant-in-aid programs (543) than ever.

6

Fostering High-Quality Training

The findings in the preceding five chapters have led the committee to conclude that the primary aim of federal postsecondary training policy must be the development of state and local systems of training that provide high-quality and coherent training options to people throughout their working lives.

The committee came to realize that we, like many others, were grappling with a more general challenge of improving the performance of the agencies that administer public programs.[1] This is directly analogous to the situation described in Chapter 1, where private firms are faced with the challenge of restructuring themselves because the old ways of doing business are no longer adequate. We found ourselves, like other critics of "business as usual" in the public sector, searching for management approaches that are compatible with the need to "grope along" (Behn, 1988): we were looking for approaches based on clear objectives, with the knowledge that achieving the objectives will involve continuous adaptation and improvement, not the mechanistic implementation of some predetermined grand strategy.

What might improved public management mean for federal postsecondary training policy? The committee investigation into how to improve the quality of postsecondary training yielded one answer. We gave a great deal of attention to whether performance management and standard-setting, which are increasingly being adopted in federal training programs, are likely to be effective tools to improve the quality of postsecondary training. We concluded that performance-management and standard-setting approaches that produce information useful for continuous improvement and that increase the capacity of training organizations to provide coherent and high-quality training are the most promising tools for ensuring quality in the postsecondary training world.

Moving postsecondary training policy in the direction of high quality and coherence is not an easy task. It demands careful thinking about federalism and about how to coordinate three levels of government, training providers, and employers; it requires marshaling resources from multiple financing sources. To improve quality and coherence, policy makers must focus on adding value that benefits those who are trained and that justifies the costs to those who pay; and changes must include mechanisms that are flexible enough to adjust as the needs of workers and employers change.

Chapter 3 showed that performance management is currently in vogue as a way of using the federal government's financial and political leverage to encourage institutions to move toward high-quality, effective programs. The chapter also demonstrated that this approach does not always have desirable consequences: performance management normally focuses on outcomes, but the performance that should be measured relates to the value added by a program. Outcomes and value added may not be highly correlated. This chapter also shows that the institutional structure of education and training complicates the standard-setting approach in ways that have important implications for how the federal government can help improve the quality of postsecondary training.

THE DEBATE OVER STANDARDS[2]

Using the language of performance management, Chapter 3 defined performance measures as indicators of how well an entity is performing. Performance standards were defined as the specification of acceptable levels of performance. Hill et al. (1993:12) point out that measures and standards can be defined for a host of entities: students, courses, programs, institutions, school districts, regions, and states. The Job Training Partnership Act (JTPA) performance system, for example, sets highly quantifiable measures and standards for service delivery areas. A different kind of standard, this one for curriculum, is growing out of the current policy debate over what should be taught in elementary and secondary schools. Standards in this view are statements embodying a coherent vision of what an individual should know and be able to do at a given stage in his or her educational development.[3] Such standards can also be used to establish the level of accomplishment that must be achieved to receive an award, such as a high school diploma or a certificate of mastery.

The growing popularity of performance management systems coincides with increasing debate over how standards of performance might help to achieve national education and work-readiness goals. Advocates assert that standards of various kinds can produce a variety of benefits.

Standards can provide clearer guidance and direction for education and training institutions. A common critique of American education and training institutions is that they lack a common set of goals or expectations for what students should learn and why. Advocates argue that if standards are based on clearly defined goals, and if these goals are based on realistic appraisals of what students or trainees will need to know in order to perform effectively in society and the economy, then education and training institutions will link what they teach and how they teach to the goals.

Standards can focus education and training institutions primarily on outcomes, rather than inputs. Education and training policies have, until recently, emphasized regulating spending to ensure that money reaches its intended target. This approach meant that institutions had to focus on compliance with regulations rather than on performance. A major theme in the current standards debate is that policy should instead primarily promote and reward higher level performance, allowing institutions maximum flexibility in how they use money, technology, and teaching to meet performance standards.

Standards can encourage greater coherence and coordination among education and training services targeted on similar populations. The variety and complexity of postsecondary institutions encourages each one to think of itself and its clients as unique, rather than as a part of a larger system of institutions organized around a common set of goals. Advocates of national standards, especially standards of student performance, argue that expressing national goals and translating them into standards will emphasize the common purposes of training institutions and produce greater coherence among them.

Standards can improve accountability. Fiscal pressure at the federal and state level, coupled with concern about international economic competition, has caused policy makers to demand greater accountability from education and training institutions. Advocates of standards argue that it will be extremely difficult to make a case for public expenditures on education and training in the absence of solid evidence on performance. They add that evidence on performance has little meaning in the absence of agreed-upon standards against which the performance of individuals and institutions can be assessed.

Standards can improve evaluation and diagnosis. Most policy makers and opinion leaders are convinced that U.S. education and training institutions have serious problems meeting the emerging demands of society and the economy. Yet few agree on what to do about it. Advocates of standards argue that it is impossible to evaluate the effectiveness of particular education and training programs or institutions, much less to assess the overall effectiveness of these institutions, without significant agreement on what they are supposed to do. Standards can provide a set of benchmarks for evaluating the effectiveness of programs and institutions and for diagnosing where the key weaknesses are.

Standards can provide a basis for certifying institutions and establishing credentials for individuals. It is frequently alleged that a major weakness of American education and training is that institutions and individuals often do not know whether they are performing acceptably, because they seldom receive clear feedback on their performance. Employers seldom ask to see school transcripts or the comments of teachers from training programs when they hire new employees (Bishop, 1990). Schools and other training organizations often know little about the immediate effect they have on their students or the long-run effects of their education and training programs. Advocates of standards argue that institutions that succeed in preparing individuals for society and work should be recognized and rewarded for their success, and those that do not succeed should be encouraged to change or close down. Likewise, students or trainees who succeed in learning should be recognized as having achieved important levels of knowledge and skill; those who do not should not be recognized. In this view, agreed-upon standards of knowledge and performance are a basic condition for being able to certify institutions and give credentials to individuals honestly and fairly.

These six purposes—guidance, focus on performance, coherence and coordination, accountability, diagnosis and evaluation, and certification and credentialing—figure prominently in the current debate over national education and training standards. Advocates often disagree on the relative importance of these purposes, however, and even on whether certain purposes should be embraced. Some argue, for example, that standards should be used primarily for guidance and diagnosis, but not for awarding credentials to individuals, because the costs of error in assessing individuals are too great. Some critics of national education and training standards argue that they will lead inevitably to the institutionalization of existing inequalities, because the standards will be manipulated to protect the privileged and exclude the underprivileged. Other critics argue that, while standards are generally a good idea, national standards are suspect, because the responsibility for most governance decisions related to education and training is located at the state and local level.

No one claims that standards alone will improve education and training institutions. Standards are only as good as the measurement and assessment techniques that accompany them. In the absence of incentives and sanctions that reinforce them, standards may be only symbolic. Standards that attempt to influence complex processes, such as teaching and learning, require the organizations and individuals that implement them to have expert knowledge and skills. Finally, standards imply that a standard-setting body commands sufficient authority to influence the institutions that are expected to implement the standards. In sum, standards must be viewed as part of a complex web of factors that must be made to work in parallel in order to influence the delivery of education and training.

Definitions

Performance measures and standards fall into two broad categories: *design*, related to inputs and processes; and *outcome*, related to results.

A design measure for inputs might, for example, be the percentage of a particular client group (low-income, the unemployed) enrolled in a program. The parallel standard, established by law or regulation, would identify the minimum percentage of the client group that the program must enroll in order to perform satisfactorily.

Design standards relating to processes can be used as instruments to improve the quality of services, in contrast to input standards, which are used to target services. Using process-oriented design standards requires the introduction of *benchmarking*. A process-oriented design standard can be based on empirically verified practices that seem to be effective in achieving desired outcomes. This conception of design standards is more similar to the Underwriters' Laboratory's industry standards for safety in electrical appliances, the Society of Automotive Engineers' standards for automobile parts and fluids, or the advanced standards set by certain firms for the processing time of computer hardware. The basic premise is that one can establish a tighter link between quality and performance by making information available about practices that seem to be effective in achieving certain kinds of performance. Leading-edge standards, which will be discussed below, are an application of this idea.

Outcome measures and standards, by contrast, focus on results accomplished. If an outcome measure is how many people are employed 3 months after completion of a training program, for example, the standard for satisfactory performance might be set at 60 percent or better (McDonnell and Elmore, 1987; Bardach and Kagan, 1982).

Recent conventional wisdom has been that outcome standards are preferable to design standards. There are a number of complex problems, however in designing policies that focus on standards with an outcome emphasis.

The Mix of Design and Outcome Standards

The first problem is determining the best mix of design and outcome standards. While conventional wisdom prefers outcome standards to design standards, performance-management systems typically include both. The performance-management system for JTPA illustrates this point. The federal government sets standards for, among other things, the proportion of trainees expected to be employed at the end of a follow-up period and the average wage at follow-up, both of which relate to outcomes. There are also, however, requirements for such design standards as the proportion of welfare recipients to be served and the proportion of funds to be spent on youth.

So when speaking of policies aimed at improving public services, it is important to note that no policy is likely to consist entirely of outcome standards to the exclusion of design standards. It is more accurate to say that such policies shift the balance between design standards and outcome standards, giving more weight to the latter.

Identifying Appropriate Measures

The second design problem in constructing results-oriented policies is determining what measures to use as the basis for judging performance and providing incentives. A fairly robust principle is, "You get what you measure and reward."

We have already discussed one example, the "creaming" problem in JTPA that resulted, at least in part, from cost standards. Welfare policy offers another example, this one stemming from the distinction between outcomes and impacts of programs. An outcome-based assessment of a welfare-to-work program, for example, might reveal that participants with some work experience and income prior to entering the program have an average employment rate of 61 percent after their participation, while those with no prior work experience or income have a 30 percent employment rate. Other things being equal, a service provider rewarded on the basis of outcomes would prefer clients with some minimum amount of work experience.

An impact-based assessment, on the other hand, might give a completely different picture. A comparison of participants who had prior income and work experience with others from similar backgrounds might well reveal that the comparison group had an employment rate of 59 percent without the program, leaving a net impact of 2 percent. At the same time, a comparison of those without prior income and work experience to their peers might reveal an employment rate of 22 percen for nonparticipants, meaning the program had a net impact of 8 percent. Judged in terms of raw outcomes, then, the program would be more effective with participants who have prior income and work experience. Judged in terms of impacts, however, the program would be more effective with participants who have had no prior income or work experience (Friedlander, 1988).

The message of these examples is two-fold: first, outcome standards, while they are relatively easy to administer, may not give a very accurate picture of the actual performance of programs. When outcomes and impacts are not highly correlated, mandating outcomes may focus program administrators in precisely the wrong direction. Second, linking incentives to performance involves complex judgments about what constitutes adding value as opposed to simply learning how to do well within the parameters of the performance system.

Setting Design and Outcome Criteria

The third problem involved in developing standards policies is determining where to set design and outcome criteria. In the literature on the political economy of regulation (McKean, 1980; Stigler, 1971; Zeckhauser and Viscusi, 1979), the problem of standard-setting is portrayed in the following way: administrative agencies have limited resources for monitoring and enforcing standards and, in the case of outcome standards, limited resources for rewards and sanctions. The agencies that are the objects of these standards, rewards, and sanctions—the implementing agencies—have interests of their own. Implementing agencies calculate the costs and benefits of compliance with the administrative standards for them and their clients as well as the likelihood that noncompliance or nonperformance will be detected.

From the perspective of the administrative agency charged with enforcing standards, the central problem is to set standards high enough, taking account of oversight and enforcement costs, to induce implementing agencies to produce desired results. At the same time, the administrative agency must not set standards so high that large numbers of implementing agencies cannot comply.

There are at least three broad standard-setting strategies that administrative agencies can follow. The first might be called the *minimum standards* approach. The agency sets standards to reflect the minimum acceptable level of performance given the political preferences of policy makers and the oversight and enforcement capacities of the agency. The second might be called the *leading-edge standards* approach. This involves deliberately setting standards at a level that only a few implementing agencies can achieve, and investing resources in pulling the rest of the implementing agencies along. Variants of this approach in the private sector are sometimes called *benchmarking*, because they involve setting design and outcome standards for a firm at the leading edge of industry practice rather than at the average level. A third approach might be called *problem-driven*. This approach involves identifying an existing condition that needs fixing and setting standards consistent with a solution to that condition.

The minimum standards approach is the usual solution to most problems, because it is well-adapted to political and administrative constraints. An example of the minimum standards approach is the JTPA performance standards. The performance targets that the federal government and the states set for local service delivery areas and service providers in such areas as placement rates and postprogram wages are, of necessity, based on expectations that it is reasonable to expect the average provider to meet. Hence, these performance targets provide a reasonable standard against which to judge the performance of all providers, with the expectation that a large proportion of providers will exceed the expectations.

In the area of education and training, one can see the clearest evidence of the emergence of a combination of leading-edge and problem-driven standards in a report by the Secretary's (of Labor) Commission on Achieving Necessary Skills (SCANS) (1991). The SCANS standards are leading-edge because they are based on what workplace skills should look like in the future, not on what employers currently demand. They are problem-driven because they are directed at solving the problem of workplace readiness, as defined by evidence on emerging skill needs, rather than being based on a judgment about what regulatory agencies can currently do.

How would one develop standards compatible with the SCANS report? It might seem obvious that education and training programs should be judged on the basis of their success in placing students. But the market for students with the kind of competencies the SCANS report envisions might be limited, as the report admits, because of the time lag in restructuring firms to accommodate people with high-performance skills.[4] Over the long run, economists might tell us, this is a trivial problem; in the short run, however, it presents an important problem of evaluation and standards-setting. Should one continue to push education and training institutions to use leading-edge design standards and benchmarking based on the SCANS model, even though the capacity of firms to absorb the better-trained workers is limited?

Determining where to set criteria in the design of standards systems, then, is a major strategic problem not amenable to simple solutions. A few things seem clear, however. In the absence of strong countervailing political pressures, standards systems tend to gravitate toward the minimum standards approach. Moving standards systems toward the leading-edge or problem-driven approaches requires some clever institutional design. One solution can be found in California, which is implementing leading-edge curriculum frameworks in elementary and secondary education. The state has tried to avoid the minimum standards problem by using experts and leading-edge practitioners to set design standards and by not insisting on short-term compliance, but rather focusing on long-term changes in performance.

Creating an Institutional Structure

The final problem is determining the institutional structure within which standards will be set and implemented. Most analytic discussions of standards-setting ignore the issue of institutional structure, yet, as discussed below, institutional structures have an enormous influence on the way standards work. For example, ignoring for a moment the problem of whether the change resulted in a better program, it is generally acknowledged that JTPA performance standards have shifted the service delivery system's focus on inputs to a preoccupation with mandated outcomes. The institutional conditions of JTPA, however, are almost unique, and the same conditions would not necessarily apply more broadly in the education and training sector. Specifically, JTPA is what might be called a high-leverage program: it is wholly funded with federal money; the system that administers it at the state and local level is devoted primarily to carrying out this responsibility; and the service providers in the system either draw their support mainly from JTPA, or administer JTPA programs separately from other activities in ways that maximize external accountability. One would expect that standards would be quite effective in directing and focusing resources under these institutional conditions.

Imagine what would happen to the development and implementation of standards if these institutional conditions were relaxed. While moving from a single source of funding to multiple sources, for example, different standards are likely to apply to the same or similar functions within a given organization. Moving from a single administrative structure to multiple structures, each with its own governance system, raises other issues: where does the authority come from to set standards and who adjudicates differences among standards? When providers of training no longer draw their support primarily from one source or provide certain services that are funded completely from one source and instead become relatively autonomous actors drawing support from multiple sources, how much leverage can any single funding agency exercise over the performance of any single provider?

Standards imply authority. Where authority is clearly defined and focused, standards seem to be an efficient mechanism of influence and control. Where authority is diffuse, the role of standards in influence and control seems more problematic. Much of postsecondary training clearly falls into diffuse authority category. It is possible to define a role for standards where authority is diffuse. But, as discussed below, doing so requires a broader view of standards than exists in the current approach to performance management in federal programs.

CONCLUSIONS

The impulse behind performance management and the spread of performance standards in federal programs is praiseworthy, but the complexities involved suggest that caution is warranted.

Even in programs like JTPA, where federal authority is clear, the problem of distinguishing impacts from outcomes means that standards-setting is not a simple process. We believe it is important to recognize the dangers involved in tying performance standards to outcomes; to be careful about the use of incentives and sanctions where they may lead administrators to emphasize inappropriate objectives; and to work continuously to develop better ways of measuring impacts and reflecting them in the standards-setting process.

Outcome standards are not always preferable to design standards, especially when design standards are process-oriented and focus on best practice.

Therefore, the federal government, along with improving outcome-oriented standards, should ensure that research and evaluation efforts in federal programs give attention to determining what works. The federal government should also attempt to encourage the adoption of best practices through its standards-setting efforts.

In the many parts of postsecondary training where federal authority is diffuse, the federal government must recognize that much of the delivery system lies outside its direct influence. The standards-setting approach the federal government chooses should reflect the strengths and limits of federal authority as well as the inherent technical complexities of standards design. This suggests that the use of performance management to improve quality needs to go beyond the traditional focus on establishing measures and standards. Performance management should include building capacity into the training system to meet performance standards.

The federal interest in ensuring quality must extend beyond federal programs if the entire postsecondary training system is to improve; this suggests standard-setting should emphasize changing institutions rather than regulating federally funded activities.

Current federal performance management systems assume that any federal effort to set standards should focus on the recipients of federal funds and that money is the federal government's main source of leverage. We prefer an approach that assumes that the federal government's interest in the quality of training goes further. The federal government has two main sources of leverage: its funding and its capacity to set a national agenda and mobilize key institutional interests behind it.

The federal government might pursue at least three strategies in support of a quality assurance system that reaches beyond the providers and recipients of federally funded training: fostering the development of voluntary, national, occupation-based skills standards for job entry and advancement; improving information systems; and helping the providers of postsecondary training increase their capacity for improved performance.

Skills Standards

National skills standards already exist in a few sub-baccalaureate occupations, and the federal government is currently encouraging the development of others through some 20 demonstration projects sponsored jointly by the U.S. Departments of Education and Labor. Skills standards potentially offer a number of solutions to problems we have previously identified in this report:

• Even in the developmental stage, skills standards can turn the attention of providers toward performance, as demonstrated by curriculum standards in elementary and secondary education.
• The effort to develop skills standards often gets key players talking and working together in new ways. In particular, skill standards can become a vehicle for closer communication and joint planning between employers and educators.
• Skills standards can lead to the development of portable credentials for workers that can enhance mobility and improve the job-matching process.
• Skills standards can improve the content of training and provide a measure of accountability for training providers.
• Skills standards can make civil rights enforcement easier by making it more difficult to discriminate against qualified workers.
• If they involve a framework that measures skills at various levels of an occupation, skills standards can create ladders that define career pathways and help document and monitor the progress of people as they move through various kinds of postsecondary training.

The existing federal demonstration-project approach, in our view, fails to provide enough of a framework for the development of a national skills standards system. A number of common questions of definition, structure, and governance should be addressed in more than an ad hoc way. For example, commonly used terms, such as *skills*, *competencies*, *tasks and duties*, *certification*, *occupation*, and *occupational cluster*, need to be defined. Currently they mean different things to different standard-setting groups.

Berryman and Rosenbaum (1992) point out that a system for creating national standards for work preparation must include national skill-defining and skill-certifying entities that they call boards. These boards face common design issues:

- What functions should national boards have? Options include core functions like defining and updating generic or industry and occupational skills, establishing needed levels of performance, certifying individuals, etc. Other possible functions include fostering the adoption of skills standards by employers and educators, accrediting training programs, and designing training curricula.
- When should individuals be allowed to apply for certification? This relates to the kind of foundation skills people will be required to have before being allowed to pursue narrower skills certification. Can they begin after 10th grade? Only after high school graduation? During postsecondary education?
- What framework should boards use to organize skill standards? How broadly or narrowly will occupations or occupational clusters be defined? Should skill standards be restricted to entry level requirements or to the sub-baccalaureate level, or extended to include skilled and professional workers as well? In part, the issue is how useful skills standards will be for experienced workers as well as for new labor force entrants.
- What are the implications of the restructuring economy for conceptualizing skills? Will skills standards reflect the requirements of high-performance workplaces, even when these do not reflect current industry practices?
- How should national boards accommodate existing standards, licensing, certifying, and accrediting processes?
- Should certifying processes be based in any way on completing recognized formal training? Or should individuals be allowed to try for certificates simply on the basis of demonstrated knowledge and skill?
- How should national skills standards boards be governed? Should they be public agencies, some blend of public and not-for-profit organizations, or not-for profits, perhaps linked to professional associations?
- What should be the structure and membership of national boards? How can the boards be organized to ensure that employers have a sense of ownership?
- How should national boards be financed? Is federal subsidy desirable or essential?

The federal government needs a mechanism to address these issues and within which individual skills standards boards can operate. We will propose such a mechanism in the final chapter.

Better Information Systems

A second strategy through which the federal government can help ensure quality is to build better information systems to enhance the influence of consumers (trainees and employers, alike) who are in the market for training services.

We described in Chapter 3 the problems facing would-be trainees and employers in learning enough about the training system to use it well. A great deal of information exists about labor markets and training activities, but it is not always the right information, nor readily accessible. Improving information has several dimensions: improving the federal and state statistical system that provides labor-market data and broadening it to include more useful information about local labor markets; coordinating federal requirements, so that integrated management information systems can be developed at the state level; and improving the availability and accessibility of information to users at the local level.

Information can also become an indirect means for ensuring accountability and oversight by providing details of institutional performance that can be used as a basis for client choice, professional sanctions, or political pressure. If understandable information can be made available to those exploring training options, the clients themselves, by the choices they make, could exert a great influence on the improvement of quality in the training system. Those exploring options would benefit greatly from information about the rewards of entering certain occupations, the costs of obtaining the necessary skills from various providers, the relative success of providers in imparting the skills, and the ability of providers to place those whom they serve in jobs and at what wages.

This indirect approach contrasts with a more direct-effect model that uses standards as the basis for the administration of formal rewards and sanctions. The indirect-effect model works best when the agency administering the standards has limited direct control over the implementing agency but relatively open access to professional and public channels in order to publicize the performance of the implementing agency.

Capacity Building

Finally, a federal strategy for quality improvement in postsecondary training should focus on capacity building. Standards can promote continuous improvement when people and institutions know how to produce results consistent with the standards. This truism is routinely violated in the design of regulatory systems and performance standards. The JTPA uses performance standards, for example, but it does not attempt to identify what sort of practices distinguish more- and less-effective employment-training programs, except for such general practices as classroom instruction, work experience, on-the-job training, and so on. Systems of performance standards, especially those heavily oriented toward outcomes, tend to rely on a definition of program success that is based on a kind of "natural selection." As long as some organizations succeed by the standards that are set, according to the natural selection view, someone must know what to do. Efforts to improve performance then become a matter of ratcheting up the standards, thereby selecting the fittest and driving out the unfit, rather than attempting to identify the practices that work best.

Whatever the utility of this approach, it is not consistent with introducing the philosophy of continuous improvement into education and training organizations. To engage in continuous improvement, an organization must be able to diagnose its shortcomings; it must have access to the knowledge and skills required to remedy whatever shortcomings it finds; and it must have the capacity to do these things distributed throughout the organization in a way that allows for broadly based participation.

For the most part, the postsecondary training system is relatively poorly equipped to engage in this sort of continuous improvement activity. People who work in training institutions, with some notable exceptions, occupy relatively low-status roles characterized by working conditions that do not favor continuous learning. The internal structure and management of postsecondary education and training institutions, again with notable exceptions, are not conducive to the diagnosis of shortcomings or to creative solutions. Teaching loads are high, pedagogy is relatively primitive, materials and technology are often not advanced. Most institutions that operate training programs are toward the bottom of the educational hierarchy in the state and local structures.

If policy makers want to introduce continuous improvement as part of a system for ensuring quality in postsecondary training, the constraints on continuous improvement have to be removed or relaxed. A number of possible measures might signal a serious commitment to change. One measure, as we have already seen, is to encourage the development of voluntary, jointly developed skills standards in which employers, trainers, and public officials all have an important stake. Another is serious investment in developing the competence and enhancing the status of practitioners who train postsecondary students and in identifying and disseminating information on proven effective training practices. Still another measure would be support for the development of the institutional structures that are needed to undergird systemic approaches to training.

For several reasons, we favor an emphasis on continuous improvement, rather than top-down regulatory compliance, in the federal government's approach to quality assurance. We noted the compatibility of the indirect model of accountability with the diffuse authority exercised by the federal government in many parts of the postsecondary training world. An emphasis on improvement rather than compliance will also help to avoid the risk that standard-setting for postsecondary training will degrade into a minimum standards approach. Leading-edge (or world-class) standards, which we believe should be the benchmarks, run the risk of devolving toward minimum standards if compliance is too heavily stressed. We reiterate that it is important to avoid an emphasis on short-term compliance and prefer a quality assurance strategy that focuses on long-term changes in performance.

NOTES

1. See, for example, Barzelay (1992); Behn (1988); Golden (1990); Nathan (1993); National Commission on the State and Local Public Service (1993); Osborne and Gaebler (1992); and Wilson (1989). In September 1993, President Clinton announced the findings of a 6-month "national performance review," designed to reform federal agencies and programs.

2. Parts of the remainder of this chapter are from a paper prepared for the committee by Richard F. Elmore.

3. For example, the National Council of Teachers of Mathematics has developed curriculum and evaluation standards for school mathematics. The effort involved creating "a coherent vision of what it means to be mathematically literate both in a world that relies on calculators and computers to carry out mathematical procedures and in a world where mathematics is rapidly growing and is extensively being applied in diverse fields" and creating "a set of standards to guide the revision of the school mathematics curriculum and its associated evaluation toward this vision" (National Council of Teachers of Mathematics, 1989:1). The standards are meant to be used as criteria against which local and state curriculum and evaluation ideas can be judged.

4. The report also acknowledges that the skills, knowledge, and personal attributes that schools should be developing in young people are not even broadly demanded by existing firms; it says only that they should be demanded if firms are to be successful in the future. Thus, the report puts part of the onus on private firms for developing high-performance workplaces that will be compatible with the competencies of students who emerge from new educational programs.

7

Improving Federal Programs

Before returning to our analysis of how the federal government can encourage systemic reform, it is important to stress that the federal government must make sure that its own programs work as well as possible. The current array of programs supporting postsecondary training reflects the different training needs identified in this report, as well as the diversity of financing mechanisms available to the federal government to meet those needs. In Chapter 5 we argued that there is no "one size fits all" approach to matching federal policy instruments and program designs to the needs of postsecondary training's clientele. This chapter explores the reasons behind that conclusion more fully and analyzes the kinds of changes that might make existing programs work better.

POLICY INSTRUMENTS FOR PUBLIC PURPOSES

Economists and political scientists have identified a number of ways that government can provide or spur the provision of services the public needs (Savas, 1987; Weimer and Vining, 1989). Several of these figure prominently in education and training policy: vouchers, contracts, grants, direct provision, and tax expenditures.[1]

Vouchers

Federal student aid is provided in the form of a voucher. A voucher is a certificate issued by a government that can be used by the recipient to pay for some service or commodity. Although institutional details vary, in essence the voucher is a certificate that can be redeemed by the supplier of the service for cash. Postsecondary education vouchers may also be used to compensate students for part of their living costs, as well as to meet direct education expenses.

The primary appeal of vouchers is their reliance on the private marketplace for the delivery of goods and services. They can be a means of providing public financing while avoiding the alleged failings of government delivery (bureaucratization; inflexibility; inefficient production; overregulation) and preserving the presumed advantages of markets (competition among suppliers; efficient production; consumer choice). It is worth noting, however, that vouchers always require the identification and definition of a qualifying commodity or service, such as *food* in the case of food stamps or *education* in the case of educational vouchers. Thus, some minimal regulation to ensure that the provided good or service meets the definition is always implicit. In that sense, vouchers are not a pure alternative to regulation.

Two kinds of vouchers play an important role in postsecondary education and training. Pell grants subsidize education and training expenses up to the full face value of the grant. Federally subsidized guaranteed loans are also, in effect, vouchers, although the subsidy they provide is less than their face value, because students must repay them. We consider these loans a type of voucher because they, along with student aid grants, can be used at a wide range of approved educational institutions.

We usually think of vouchers as *entitlements*: any candidate who meets certain standards will automatically be entitled to voucher support.[2] In some cases, however, vouchers may be allocated by some mechanism among potential recipients.

Contracts

Governments can also ensure the provision of services by contracting directly with private suppliers. The government must establish a mechanism (often competitive bidding) to select among candidate suppliers for the service. Thus, government is more directly involved in weighing the quality of alternative suppliers than in the case of voucher support, and programs delivered through contracts typically restrict consumer choice much more. This usually requires government to establish some system for allocating potential recipients among available programs. Contracting is widespread in the Job Training Partnership Act (JTPA) and Job Opportunities and Basic Skills (JOBS) programs.

Grants

Governments may provide grants directly to other levels of government or to private or nonprofit agencies that supply services. Unlike vouchers, such grants are not tied to individual recipients; unlike contracts, grants are not tied to the performance of specified services by recipient agencies or institutions.

In education, grants that are given to colleges and schools are often referred to as *institutional aid.* (For examples of grant programs, see the discussion of Supplemental Educational Opportunity Grants, work-study programs, Perkins loans, and the Carl D. Perkins Vocational and Applied Technology Education Act in Chapter 2.)

Direct Provision

Governments can choose to provide services directly. All states, for example, own and operate postsecondary education institutions. With the exception of military academies, however, this is not a major part of the federal government's education effort.

In the education and training arena, direct service delivery is primarily found at the state and local rather than federal level. State governments play a major part in work-related training by creating and subsidizing colleges and area vocational-technical training schools.

Tax Expenditures

Tax policy represents another means at governments' disposal to influence the supply of and demand for education and training services. Tax preferences can be directed at individuals (students and their parents; employees) by making educational expenditures or the interest on educational debt tax deductible. Alternatively, tax preferences can be directed at the suppliers of educational services; for example, by making the income of colleges and universities tax exempt. Still a third option is to provide tax preferences for employer investments in the training of their workers.

Tax exemption for nonprofit colleges and universities is a significant form of federal institutional subsidy, similar in many ways to a grant. The federal government has in the past provided a major form of support for skills improvement training by not including employer reimbursements for employee training expenses in the taxable income of the employees.

CHOOSING AMONG POLICY INSTRUMENTS

Deciding whether student aid should continue to play such an important role in federal policy on postsecondary training depends in part on how good an instrument vouchers are. Questions have been raised about the utility of student aid vouchers for all the people who are currently eligible for them. In addition, proposals are sometimes made to "voucherize" second-chance and other federal programs that currently deliver services through contracts and grants. Conversely, it is sometimes suggested that student aid vouchers should be bundled with other kinds of federal support for education and training and given as block grants to states.

In comparing the advantages of various policy instruments, it is again useful to recognize that distinctions among them are not hard and fast and that the differences may be more in degree than in kind.[3] Our discussion will focus on the two most prominent mechanisms for federal subsidy of postsecondary training, vouchers and contracts. Both the voucher model and the contracting model work best if certain underlying assumptions are satisfied. For vouchers, three seem especially important.

Availability of a straightforward definition of the qualifying commodity or service. Vouchers carve out an arena within which consumers' own judgments about program quality are sovereign. This works best if there are clear and easily administered criteria for determining which products or services qualify for voucher support.

Confidence in consumer knowledge and judgment. This is surely the central assumption in the voucher approach.

The consumer has a strong stake in the outcome. Even well-informed consumers may not make good choices with public dollars unless their decisions carry a significant opportunity cost for themselves. Thus, in areas like medical care or housing, consumers themselves largely bear the costs of poor choices of providers. They will seek out the best housing or medical care their scarce resources will provide. In the case of education vouchers for disadvantaged populations, the opportunity cost to clients of spending time in a training program may be quite low, especially if the voucher helps support living costs. Given the difficulty of judging the worth of alternative investments of their time, recipients may have little incentive to avoid enrolling in unpromising programs.

The contracting model has its own ideal assumptions:

Clear criteria for governmental award of the contract.
Strong ability of government to assess the performance of contractors.
Strong ability of government or its agents to place clients in a suitable program.

The obvious conclusion is that, in the context of postsecondary training, neither contracting nor vouchers is the best all-purpose approach.

In light of the ideal conditions just discussed, the best case for vouchers is likely to be found in the following circumstances:

Relatively long-term training, which increases the consumer's stake and consumer investment in the program. A further advantage of longer-term programs is that the revenues of suppliers depend on repeat business, so there is a direct market test of consumer satisfaction.

Relatively well-qualified recipients, where there is more reason for confidence in their knowledge and judgment. Moreover, more qualified recipients will generally have higher opportunity costs of their time, which increases their incentive to invest only in effective training programs.

Traditional educational programs. A clear and easily administered criterion for defining eligible programs for vouchers is probably best met by educational programs offering academic degrees. Academic degrees are relatively well-defined entities, with a long tradition behind them. Moreover, degree programs serve a number of purposes beyond those of the federal aid system, and therefore are not responsive exclusively or primarily to the incentives generated by that system.

It is striking that these indicators of voucher effectiveness fit fairly well the original target population and target programs of federal student aid.

The best circumstances in which to use contracts are probably the following:

Intense programs that promise far-reaching effects. It should be relatively easy in such programs both to evaluate contract proposals and to monitor contractor effectiveness.

Programs targeted at students whose needs are readily identified. Perhaps the clearest example here would be in programs for persons with disabilities.

Programs targeted at recipients who are already closely connected to case workers or placement officers.

Within the general area of education and training, this suggests that the contracting approach should work best in programs to deal with physical disabilities and in highly intensive programs for highly disadvantaged recipients. The clearest example of the latter is probably the Job Corps.

The unfortunate but indisputable fact is that not much postsecondary training for the workplace falls clearly into either of the ideal areas for using contracts or vouchers. Thus, much of the vocational training that is currently supported by grant and loan vouchers is relatively short term, serves a population that is probably not well informed about training alternatives and does not face large opportunity costs for making poor choices about training alternatives, and is provided by institutions whose product is often hard to define and is not standard. Much of the training provided through contractors via JTPA and JOBS is low intensity and hard to evaluate. It also involves dealing with clients whose ideal placement is not obvious. Yet neither is it clear that the clients currently served by voucher programs are ideally suited to being served through contractors, nor is the reverse the case. This suggests that simple solutions, such as "voucherizing" all support for postsecondary training or converting all programs to contracts with service providers, are unlikely to prove satisfactory. It also suggests that policy makers should be open to considering the advantages of hybrid forms of support.[4]

The absence of strong arguments for design changes in training programs dovetails with our findings about how little is known about the effects of many current efforts and with our conclusion that many proposals for major changes in training fall into the "justification-by-faith" category. For these reasons, we do not recommend a radical restructuring of federal postsecondary training programs. As in Chapter 6, we instead argue for continuous improvement and propose a variety of first steps.

QUALIFYING TRAINING

As discussed in Chapter 2, the student financial aid programs authorized by Title IV of the Higher Education Act represent the largest source of federal funds for postsecondary training. We examine them first and then ask what else the federal government ought to do in support of qualifying training.[5]

Student Financial Aid

Through Pell grants and guaranteed student loans, the federal government provides roughly $20 billion annually to students in postsecondary training. (The other Title IV programs provide a comparatively small amount of aid to postsecondary training students, and we do not consider them further here.) While a variety of issues are currently being debated about the future of these programs, we concentrate on three that have significant consequences for training policy: student eligibility, institutional eligibility, and the problem of low-return programs of study.

Student Eligibility

The summary of federal programs in Chapter 2 makes it clear that student aid programs have evolved considerably since their inception. In particular, the growing use of federal student aid by nontraditional students and institutions has raised several new issues and problems; in recent years, it has also made the programs controversial. Funding for the programs has never expanded to reflect the broadened eligibility that has occurred over time. As a result, the inflation-adjusted value of grants and loans to individual students has tended to shrink and is likely to shrink further.

In this regard, we believe that it was a mistake to extend Pell grant eligibility to less than half-time students in the 1992 reauthorization of the Higher Education Act. Pell grants are a remarkably cumbersome and inappropriate way to assist such students. The administrative burden of providing what will often be relatively small awards will be substantial. Moreover, without increases in funding, this extension of eligibility will reduce funding available for other students. Built into the structure of student aid programs is the assumption that students are progressing toward completion of some program, but this will often not be true for this group of students. Chapter 3 cites evidence that individuals do not appear to receive significant benefits (at least economically) from limited courses. A much more reasonable way to provide support might be through permitting some funding from the campus-based programs for less than half-time students, at the discretion of an institution's financial aid officers.

Constraints on awards due to funding limits have also created tensions when administrators of other programs (such as JTPA) are perceived as utilizing student-aid-eligible training programs as a way of conserving their own resources.[6] Our own judgment is that opposition to such cost-shifting is misplaced, so long as federal law makes postsecondary training programs eligible for student assistance (see below). Student aid, especially Pell grants, were in fact created to be a foundation of support for students in postsecondary programs. Any increased use of student-aid-eligible training programs by JTPA or other administrators worsens the competition for limited resources if student aid funds are not increased accordingly. But this per se is no reason to apply a different set of rules about who qualifies for student aid to someone who happens to be a participant in another federal program.

A concern that has troubled some federal officials is that federal aid delivered for training in the form of student aid vouchers may result in significant duplication of services among various federal programs, which might be inefficient. This concern appears to have grown as the nontraditional population in student aid has grown. The limited data (see Chapter 3), coupled with the evident differences in services provided in student-aid-eligible programs versus second-chance programs, suggest that the amount of program overlap is not large. Moreover, the virtual absence of cost data made it impossible to assess whether individuals assisted through student aid receive more or less subsidy than those in similar programs of study funded through federally supported contracts or direct provision of federally funded services.

Institutional Eligibility

Another troublesome result of the spread of student aid to nontraditional settings, and the one that has caused major controversy, can be explained in terms of the policy instruments argument (see discussion above). Over the years, student aid grants and loans have been increasingly utilized by students enrolling in programs and institutions for which the assumptions of the voucher approach discussed in the previous section fit poorly. The student aid programs at their inception relied principally on an existing accrediting system for academic institutions that had a long history and considerable independence from the whole student aid process. The rapid growth of a largely new sector of profit-oriented institutions that lacked this history and were much more dependent on student aid funds has changed this picture markedly; it has also led to serious regulatory difficulties for the student aid programs.

The federal programs have not stood still in the face of these important changes. In particular, the 1992 reauthorization of the Higher Education Act introduced a number of ambitious and, for the most part, promising changes to the operation of the student aid programs. These include an effort to involve states more fully in overseeing institutions receiving federal student aid, a greater emphasis on making institutional performance a criterion in determining aid eligibility, and a new willingness to recognize that different types of institutions, with different financing structures and missions, may require different regulation. The new rules also embody a flexibility that is consistent with the arguments made about public management in Chapter 6: institutional failure to meet specified criteria will trigger state review of the institution, not an automatic determination of ineligibility for federal funds.

These new efforts deserve a chance to work and will bear close scrutiny in the years ahead.

Under the new rules, states will be required to establish or designate a single agency responsible for assessing the eligibility of institutions for participation in the federal student aid programs. The legislation establishes a number of criteria, which will trigger scrutiny of an institution (see Table 7-1), and spells out a number of dimensions of institutional activities that must be assessed (Table 7-2). Potentially, these initiatives may increase considerably the level of accountability of states in overseeing aid-eligible institutions. It seems to us that this is a desirable direction in which to move. It is hard to imagine the federal government overseeing thousands of institutions directly, and there seems little doubt that the oversight of institutions through the existing accreditation mechanism is inadequate.

Two major questions must be kept in mind in judging the future effectiveness of this effort. First, do the new requirements give the states a

TABLE 7-1   Criteria Triggering State Review of Higher Education Institutions

- Institution has a cohort default rate equal to or greater than 25 percent.

- Institution has a cohort default rate equal to or greater than 20 percent and either (1) more than two-thirds of the institution's total undergraduates receive federal student assistance or (2) two-thirds of the institution's educational and general expenditures are derived from federal aid provided to students.

- A limitation, suspension, or termination action has been taken by the Secretary of Education against the institution during the preceding 5 years.

- There has been an audit finding during the two most recent audits resulting in the institution being required to repay amounts greater than 5 percent of the student aid funds it received.

- The institution has been cited by the Secretary of Education for failing to submit audits in a timely fashion.

- The institution experiences year-to-year fluctuations of more than 25 percent in the amount of Pell grant or student loans received by its students.

- The institution fails to meet certain financial responsibility standards specified in the Higher Education Act.

- Ownership of the school changes hands.

- The institution is not affiliated with a public system of higher education and has participated in specified student aid programs for less than 5 years.

- The institution is the subject of student complaints sufficient in the judgment of the Secretary of Education to justify an institutional review.

SOURCE: Higher Education Amendments of 1992, Section 494C(b).

sufficient incentive to oversee these institutions effectively? In effect, the federal government is requiring the states to oversee the use of federal dollars. Experience will undoubtedly vary among states, and we recommend learning from that variation. Second, most of the standards against which the states must review institutions are procedural in nature rather than related to program quality. Will increased attention be given to quality? This is discussed in the next section.

The 1992 legislation does not require the states to take on this new oversight role unless federal funds are appropriated. In the months following passage of the law, it was uncertain whether Congress and the U.S. Department of Education would find funds for this effort. We strongly urge that the necessary monies be made available, because this new approach to oversight of institutional eligibility is worth a serious effort.

TABLE 7-2   Review Standards to Be Used by States Conducting
Institutional Reviews

- Availability of catalogs, admissions requirements, course outlines, schedules of tuition and fees and other rules and regulations of the institution.
- Assurance that the institution has a method to assess a student's ability successfully to complete the course of study for which he or she has applied.
- Assurance that the institution maintains and enforces standards relating to academic progress and maintains adequate student records.
- Compliance by the institution with fire and health standards.
- The financial and administrative capacity of the institution.
- For institutions financially at risk, the adequacy of provisions to protect students in the event of closure.
- For institutions whose stated purpose is to prepare students for employment, the relationship of tuition and fees to the remuneration that can reasonably be expected by students and the relationship of the course of study to providing the student with quality training and useful employment.
- The availability to students of information regarding such things as market and job availability for students in employment-oriented programs and the relationship of courses to standards for state licensure.
- The appropriateness of the number of credit or clock hours required for the completion of programs or of the length of 600-hour courses.
- Assessing the actions of owners, shareholders, or persons exercising control over the educational institution that may adversely affect eligibility for student aid programs.
- The adequacy of procedures for investigating and resolving student complaints.
- The appropriateness of advertising and promotion and student recruitment practices.
- The presence of a fair and equitable tuition refund policy.
- The success of the program as measured by graduation rates, withdrawal rates, placement rates and the rates at which graduates pass licensure exams (for vocationally oriented programs), and the achievement of other student goals such as transfer, full-time employment in the field of study, and military service.

SOURCE: Higher Education Amendments of 1992, Section 494C(d).

We also recommend that the progress of this effort be monitored and evaluated, because its success is by no means ensured. Aside from the question of funding, the new requirements raise a host of unanswered questions. They call for states to create standards, subject to disapproval by the Secretary of Education, for performance in the areas described in Table 7-2. As stated in Chapter 6, standard setting is not an easy task in postsecondary education. Moreover, the fact that the new federal requirements apply only to schools that "trip" one or more of a designated set of "triggers" means that whatever standards are used in the review process may be different than those applied by states to other postsecondary institutions. Furthermore, since the standards are to be state-based, there will almost certainly be differences in the performance requirements that schools will be expected to meet, depending on where they are located. Overall, we see a series of feasibility, equity, political, and possibly legal questions, the outcomes of which we cannot predict. On the other hand, successful implementation of the new oversight provisions for schools that "trip the triggers" may have interesting and important implications for broader quality assurance efforts of the sort discussed in Chapter 6.

The 1992 Higher Education Act reauthorization also introduced or tightened a number of federal rules. For example, the ceiling on permissible default rates has been lowered, and correspondence schools were eliminated from the loan program. An interesting set of initiatives has introduced the notion that the diversity of an institution's funding sources should affect how it is regulated. Schools that receive more than two-thirds of their funding from federal student aid, or that have more than two-thirds of their undergraduates enrolled half-time or more supported by federal student aid programs, are subject to a higher level of scrutiny than other schools. This seems to us a sensible principle, and one that might be developed further. There is also language in the reauthorization act that made programs lasting less than 6 months ineligible for student loans, unless such programs meet new quality standards to be determined by the Secretary of Education. At a minimum, these programs will have to have verified rates of completion of at least 70 percent and verified placement rates of 70 percent.[7] This too seems a worthwhile initiative.

It is important to appreciate that these new initiatives may go a long way toward eliminating some of the worst and most visible abuses of the student aid system. In fact, initiatives of the last few years are already having some of this effect. Given the demonstrated political barriers to more radical solutions that have sometimes been proposed (such as dropping proprietary schools from student aid programs entirely or developing a separate set of programs for them), the federal government should fund and otherwise fully support these new approaches and carefully gauge their effects.

Low-Return Programs

While much of the concern about student aid programs has focused on fraud and abuse, we are deeply troubled by a different problem; that is, the role of student aid in financing work-related training that appears to provide little or no economic return. This is in part an issue of the best use of scarce federal dollars. But there is another important aspect of the problem. When students invest loan dollars in ineffective training, the investment not only wastes federal resources but also leaves the students in debt.[8] Whether they succeed in paying back the loans or not, the result violates the principle that we suggested should apply to training policy as well as to medicine: do no harm.

There was strong agreement within our committee that student aid programs should increase the likelihood that subsidized training will yield positive economic returns to those trained. We also agreed that judging which mechanisms might do so requires, in part, a knowledge of local labor markets that federal and perhaps even state officials are unlikely to have. As we have found before, such uncertainty suggests that experimentation is needed.

We recommend, therefore, that the "institutional integrity" provisions established by the recent Higher Education Act amendments be modified to link the student loan eligibility of *all* students in postsecondary training programs (not just those in schools who trip the triggers for state review or who are enrolled in very short programs) to the job placement and wage performance of program graduates. We recommend requiring states to use employment and wage records (from the unemployment insurance program or other data sources) to estimate employment and earnings rates for the graduates of any training programs eligible for Title IV where a specified percentage (say 25 percent) of enrollees borrow.[11]

We further propose that each state decide on average levels of performance with regard to placement and wages that training programs would have to meet. If the graduates from a particular work-related program fail to meet these performance standards, concern would be raised about the ability of students to repay loans and the program should be subjected to scrutiny by the state review agency described above. Unless state officials found mitigating circumstances, the program (not the institution as a whole) would lose student loan eligibility.

We also recommend that the U.S. Department of Education conduct a demonstration project that would permit one or more states to determine training program eligibility for student aid funds based on criteria proposed by the states. The criteria would have to be developed in consultation with business and would have to involve determination at the local level, by entities with strong business representation, as to whether training programs were needed and whether jobs for graduates of the program were likely to be available. Whatever criteria were developed would have to be applied to all training programs. For example, if a local labor market board or Private Industry Council determined that there was little demand for cosmetologists, it could not refuse eligibility to a proprietary school program while approving the local community college unless it could demonstrate better training outcomes at the latter. It could, however, use probable earnings levels to determine whether loans should be allowed in addition to grants.

We expect that the states most likely to be able to participate in such an experiment would be those furthest along in developing a systemic approach to work force development and vigorous local planning and delivery structures. We think that the state and local officials, educators, and business and labor representatives who have cared enough to mount major systemic reforms to improve the quality of their states' work forces will also care enough about guiding students into economically beneficial programs to participate in this experiment even though their own funds may not be at stake.

Work-Based Training and School-to-Work Transitions

At several places in this volume we have noted that the United States, in contrast to many other nations, depends almost exclusively on a school-based approach for preparing people in a formal way to enter the workplace. Furthermore, whatever training those new entrants get from school is likely to be all they get for a while, since employers do not often provide extensive formal training for their new workers. We have also seen evidence that Germany, which uses a work-based approach to qualifying training for a large proportion of its young people, has results that have impressed many observers both here and in other parts of Europe. The apparent success of the German dual system approach to qualifying training, coupled with widespread dissatisfaction with the American treatment of students not bound for the baccalaureate degree, has spurred interest in so-called youth apprenticeship programs and other strategies for improving the connection between training and work and for easing the transition of young people from school to work.

Given the panel's charge, we did not focus on programs that involve only the transition from high school to the job market. However, it is not possible to separate the worlds of secondary and postsecondary education entirely, especially since several new programs, including youth apprenticeship models, provide more structured pathways from school to careers explicitly linking high schools and postsecondary training institutions.

These initiatives are part of an increasing emphasis on career-oriented schooling. The 4-year Tech-Prep programs and secondary-level career academies share with youth apprenticeship the approach in which students see directly the relationship between what they learn, how well they perform, and their ability to pursue a rewarding career. The federal government has provided financial support for both small youth apprenticeship demonstrations and the expansion of Tech-Prep programs. However, serious questions remain about the potential effectiveness of these new approaches: Will workplaces prove effective as learning sites in apprenticeship programs? Will employers be willing to offer significant numbers of apprenticeships for people at the secondary or immediate postsecondary levels? Who will perform the training at worksites, and will they require certification? What kind of school-based learning will best complement work-based apprenticeships? Which occupations in the United States will lend themselves most readily to an apprenticeship method of training? (See the discussion of these and other issues in Rosenbaum et al., 1992.)

As indicated in Chapter 5, the federal government should encourage experimentation. In particular, we believe the time is right for large-scale demonstrations of the youth apprenticeship model.

Current demonstrations involve only about 40-100 apprentices per site and a relatively small number of employers. They are too small to resolve the considerable uncertainty as to what proportion of occupations can utilize youth apprenticeship effectively in recruitment and training. None of the existing demonstrations have the capacity to document the net effects of apprenticeships on workers in comparison with what would have taken place without this form of training. Most important, current sites cover too small a proportion of youth to provide a realistic test of what would happen if youth apprenticeship were part of the standard secondary-postsecondary system. Youth apprenticeship must involve a significant part of a local community before most employers, students, parents, and teachers learn about the system and how it can affect their futures.

A city in which a large segment of a cohort (perhaps 20-25 percent) enters youth apprenticeships might well experience improvements not only for the apprentices but for others as well. For example, the overall milieu of a school could become more academically positive, if students who were formerly bored and disruptive become apprentices interested in obtaining skills immediately relevant to their success at the workplace. That could change the school atmosphere so that student peers no longer discourage good students from succeeding academically. As word filters down about promising career options that students can begin in late high school, 8th and 9th grade students may see new incentives to learn and raise their academic skills. Engaging large numbers of inner-city youth with natural mentors at the worksite may prove especially significant, since many lack a close, informal contact with adults holding good jobs.

Scale may also be important from a purely operational standpoint. For example, having too few students engaged in apprenticeships might limit a school system's ability to create special courses related to the workplace training. The ability of the system to deal effectively with issues of liability, contracting, certification, and the training of trainers may well depend on the scale of the programs.

We recommend, therefore, that the federal government fund a set of large-scale demonstration projects, rather than distribute smaller amounts of money to many school districts. To mount the demonstrations, the federal government can draw on its experience with a previous large-scale youth demonstration, the Youth Incentive Entitlement Pilot Projects (YIEPP). The U.S. Department of Labor held a competition for the awarding of large resources to selected sites. This process proved effective in concentrating funds so that the country could learn about the feasibility of providing job guarantees to poor high school-age youth in an entire community and about the effect of such jobs on high school graduation rates, employment levels, and the earnings of poor youth.

The federal government could adopt a similar approach to choose sites for large-scale youth apprenticeship demonstrations. As a by-product, the very offer of federal sponsorship could mobilize communities and states in the competitive process to establish agreements among employers, schools, students, and labor organizations. If so, even communities that did not win large grants would have begun developing closer and probably more effective linkages between employers and schools.

While experimenting with youth apprenticeship, however, the federal and state governments, along with localities and businesses, should also continue to develop other promising career-oriented approaches to preparing young people for work. An important part of the task is learning how to meld youth apprenticeship, Tech-Prep, career academies, cooperative education, and other strategies into a coherent set of options that will give young people a clear map of structured pathways to follow in moving from school to the workplace.

SKILLS IMPROVEMENT TRAINING AND
WORKER RETRAINING

Despite widespread agreement that skills improvement training in the United States is available to too few workers, especially front-line workers, we do not find consensus among the experts on whether this calls for major federal intervention. Clearly, though, the federal government can help foster new employer attitudes and practices. On the question of retraining workers who are displaced from their jobs by changing economic conditions, there is far more agreement that federal action is appropriate, though no unanimity about whether enough is known to design effective federal

interventions. At minimum, though, the federal government should consolidate its raft of existing worker retraining activities, as discussed below.

Developing public policy aimed at improving the skills of the current
work force is beset by several dilemmas. It was noted in Chapter 1 that
firm decisions about training are influenced in complex ways by the labor
market system in which they operate. There and in Chapter 3 we identified
a series of reasons why many U.S. firms appear reluctant to invest in their
employees. But, as Osterman (1990:273-274) points out, it is difficult to
decide whether these reasons justify public intervention.

> If there is a problem, and the problem impedes the firm's productivity,
> then we should expect the firm to remedy the situation. If the firm does
> not act, then the reasonable inference is that the problem is not serious
> enough to justify additional resources, either financial or organizational.

To the extent that underlying labor market institutions and policies affect
firm calculations about the benefits of training, there are likely to be complex tradeoffs inherent in any proposals for change. Osterman goes on to
point out the absence of good models that indicate how government can
best influence private decisions about employment practices, a major shortcoming in designing public policy, even if there was an agreement that such
policy is warranted.

Even where the case for public policy is conceptually strongest, the
underlying evidence about the seriousness of the problem is often weak.
For example, government intervention is often an appropriate remedy in
situations where economic externalities exist, such as in the case of the firm
that trains an employee, only to have that employee leave the firm. We saw
in Chapter 1 that labor mobility is higher in the United States than abroad.
We do not know, however, how much of their investment in trained workers
employers actually lose because of higher mobility levels or the extent to
which this mobility really deters employers from providing training.

For all of these reasons, we are not prepared to endorse a major federal
effort to require increased training by firms. Certainly, the federal government should encourage further investigation into the need for and the likely
effects of such a policy. One of the issues that needs to be pursued is
whether a stronger case can be made that market failures exist that inhibit
firms from providing optimal amounts of training from a societal point of
view, and if more robust models for effective public intervention can be
found. Also needed is continuing analyses of how the implementation of
training taxes and subsidies to firms for training is proceeding at the state
level and in other nations and about the lessons that could guide the design
of federal policies should they become warranted.

Meanwhile, the federal government should take steps to awaken firms
to the competitive advantages of new forms of workplace organization and

to make them aware of training options and how best to utilize them. Such a role can be carried out through such mechanisms as awards for exemplary firms (modeled after the U.S. Commerce Department's Malcolm Baldrige Award, for example), evaluation and dissemination, and assistance for system- and capacity-building initiatives. The federal government should develop a strategic plan for implementing such a program and exploiting to full advantage related federal activities scattered around the various agencies.[10] We propose a mechanism for doing this in Chapter 8.

The federal government should also sponsor experiments and demonstration projects with new labor-market structures that might help overcome the sluggishness of American firms in adopting a transformed or high-performance model of workplace organization. Kochan and Osterman (1991:51-52) and Rogers and Streeck (1993) suggest existing joint union-management training programs (such as those in the auto and communications industries) and some kind of American variant of the works councils found overseas as models that could be developed. Such models offer another advantage as well: by giving employees a significant voice in firm human resource policies, they could serve as a counterweight to the tendency of employers to offer firm-specific training rather than training that increases the general skills and mobility of their employees. (For evidence that joint training programs are more concerned with the broad career needs of workers than are company training programs, see Ferman et al., 1990.) Bassi (1992:48-49) provides evidence that small firms would be encouraged to undertake workplace education programs (emphasizing basic skills) if there were a greater availability of networks or forums among businesses to discuss training, employer-sponsored education, and training consortia.

In addition, the federal government could take steps to encourage workers to undertake training on their own. There are several reasons why this would be desirable, in addition to the obvious one that too many workers fail to receive formal training from their employers. We have just mentioned the fact that firm-sponsored training tends to be narrowly focused on the needs of the business, while employees have an interest in broader training that will enhance their mobility in the labor market beyond the firm. Society, too, has an interest in fostering labor mobility, since it lessens the shocks of economic change. Furthermore, the American labor force is characterized by a growing number of so-called contingent workers (Belous, 1989) who are not eligible for employer-sponsored benefits. These workers cannot expect to have their training needs met by the companies for whom they work.

There are various ways in which the federal government could encourage individual workers to pursue training. They could involve significant spending, however. We did not analyze them in depth and so are not in a position to recommend them, but further investigation might suggest that they would provide benefits that justify the costs. Two options relate to income taxes. An individual now can deduct education expenses only insofar as they relate to his or her current work; even then, expenses are not deductible if the education is needed to meet the minimal requirements for the job or would prepare the individual for a new line of work. This provision might be changed. The second tax-related option involves the exclusion from income (for employees) of employer-paid educational expenses, such as tuition reimbursements. This exclusion has repeatedly been extended on a temporary basis but is currently scheduled to lapse at the end of 1994. Workers might have more inducement to take advantage of employer-paid benefits if the deduction were certain. It could be limited to lower-income earners to limit the costs to the federal government. Finally, proposals have been made at various times for individual training accounts to which government would contribute or for programs that would guarantee everyone a certain number of years of training after high school, to be used whenever the individual chose (e.g., Hovey, 1985). Before such a system could be justified, however, we believe that much needs to be done, as this report documents, to develop the kind of quality training system that would make such an enormous investment worthwhile.

While the arguments for federal investment in skills improvement training for the general work force are mixed, a stronger case can be made for so-called dislocated workers. These are unemployed workers who lack the necessary basic and occupational skills for reemployment or are workers displaced from their jobs by factory closings or large-scale job cutbacks. Firms obviously will not have the same self-interest in workers they are about to let go as they might be expected to have in their continuing work force, so it is not feasible to expect them to be the primary sponsors of retraining. Furthermore, worker dislocation is sometimes the direct result of federal actions. Reductions in defense activities affect many communities, for example, and new trade agreements like the pending North American Free Trade Agreement can also lead to job dislocation as economic activity lessens in some sectors and increases in others.

We did not have enough evidence available to make a comprehensive set of recommendations about federal policy on worker retraining. There are complex issues involved, including the relative effectiveness of job placement versus retraining efforts, the interaction of dislocated worker programs and provisions, and how relatively new federal legislation requiring early warning of plant closings affects the implementation of strategies to help the workers who will be displaced.

We do believe, however, that two clear problems are apparent from the evidence reviewed and the principles laid out in Chapter 5. First, federal dislocated worker programs need to be reduced in number and consolidated.[11] Second, as pointed out in Chapter 3, experience with the Trade

Adjustment Assistance Act shows that meaningful access to reemployment training is impeded by requirements that such training can be provided only to workers dislocated by a particular cause. Not only is training for such workers delayed by the time it takes to demonstrate that unemployment resulted from the appropriate cause, but other dislocated workers living in the same community and having equivalent needs cannot receive training because they cannot demonstrate that their unemployment was directly due to that cause. While we cannot make specific recommendations for remedial action based on our analyses, we suggest that this would be a good topic for the federal government to take up in the near future.

SECOND-CHANCE TRAINING

Our belief in the importance of experimentation and evaluation is nowhere stronger than in our recommendations on federal support for second-chance training. Figuring out what works is both extremely important and exceedingly difficult. Through JTPA and JOBS, we have learned much over the past decade, but we need to learn much more before we can confidently prescribe wholesale changes.

Fortunately, as we saw in Chapter 3, over the last 20 years there has been a serious federal-, state-, and foundation-funded effort to raise the quality of evaluations. However, as it relates to postsecondary education and training for the workplace, the evidence is still very partial. Many of the welfare-to-work programs of the 1980s, for example, did not emphasize education and training services, and several relevant studies are still under way.

Nonetheless, available findings are already affecting policy by enabling programs to be improved continuously. This has been particularly striking in welfare employment programs, where lessons from studies of state initiatives in the 1980s were actively used in the development of state and federal legislation (e.g., in California's Greater Avenues for Independence, or GAIN, program and in Congressional debate preceding the passage of the Family Support Act of 1988, containing the JOBS program) (Baum, 1991; Haskins, 1991). In particular, the evidence that low-cost services were not effective for the most disadvantaged welfare recipients contributed to the push for more intensive education and training in JOBS. More generally, the relatively consistent evidence that welfare-to-work programs had positive effects and were cost effective for single parents (mostly women), prompted Congress to increase the funding available for JOBS, compared to the resources provided for the predecessor WIN program of the 1980s (Wiseman et al., 1991).

At this time, there is only partial evidence on the success of JOBS (Friedlander et al., 1993). While these results are encouraging, it is too soon to know whether JOBS' emphasis on education and training will in fact have higher payoffs and succeed with more disadvantaged, long-term welfare recipients. However, one problem is currently clearly affecting the potential payoff from JOBS: the less-than-full participation by the states. Unfortunately, JOBS implementation began just as the economy went into a decline and budgetary pressures on state governments became intense. At least partly for this reason, federal funds are not being fully utilized. (Only 65.5 percent of funds were spent in fiscal 1992 [U.S. Congress, 1992].) Given the available record of success, we believe that the incentives and matching rates in JOBS should be altered to increase the federal contribution and encourage more state activity.

While we conclude that there is very reliable and relatively encouraging evidence on the effectiveness of programs for adult women, and a weaker record for adult men, the evidence is much less positive for second-chance programs for out-of-school youth. Here, many approaches have been tried, few rigorously studied, and fewer still found to have positive results. The case for a major federal response is strong. With the exception of the Job Corps, most programs that have been seriously studied have been found wanting.

We draw several conclusions from this discouraging record, along with the evidence in Chapter 3 that we do not know how to fix youth programs. First, the most critical challenge is to make the first-chance system work better for the young people it now fails. Second, it is time for the federal government to dedicate resources to testing more innovative and far-reaching second-chance strategies and to do this on several fronts at the same time.

We make the second recommendation based on our conviction that society cannot walk away from these young people or from the challenge of building a system that serves them better. We do not expect first-chance, qualifying training programs at least in the short run to succeed with all young people; we must have a second-chance system that effectively picks up where first chance programs leave off.

But the evidence to date suggests that the answer is not to expand the existing services or earmark a growing proportion of JTPA funds to at-risk youth until it is clearer that programs are worthwhile. First of all, because of the magnitude of changes to services for youth required by the 1992 amendments to JTPA, we should determine whether the design elements contained in the new JTPA youth program are more effective than the program designs that were in effect in 1987-1989 and were evaluated by the National JTPA Study.[12]

In addition, the federal government should launch a major effort to implement and research more innovative programs for young people. Eight years ago, the National Research Council published a report on youth programs and studies (Betsey et al., 1985) pointing to the limited knowledge on effective programs and calling for tests of new ideas coupled with random assignment evaluations to determine their impacts.

We reiterate this plea and urge that some JTPA youth program resources be redirected to finance tests of a variety of new approaches to second-chance programming for youth. We note that, too often, such studies have been conducted serially. At this time, we urge that the government not await the final outcome of one study to launch another, nor await the completion of all studies to act on improving the system.

A number of radically different strategies warrant systematic testing. Such approaches include:

Long-term, holistic, developmental programs. The intention would be to build young people's self-esteem, cognitive abilities, social responsibility, and leadership skills, and promote their involvement in their communities. In addition to providing academic remediation and job training, such programs would focus heavily on providing youth with opportunities to engage in community service, develop one-on-one relationships with responsible adults, and participate in regular, positive, structured, and supervised, peer-centered activities. Ideally, such programs would be part of a continuum of services starting in the early school years. This would be difficult to put into effect. However, many of the concepts are implemented in interventions for young dropouts, such as YouthBuild,[13] a project for 16- to 24-year-olds currently operating in eleven sites.

Post-placement follow-up. JTPA services normally end when a participant finds a job. However, many studies have shown that, once working, young people often encounter problems—for example, child care, housing, transportation; inappropriate work behavior or attitudes—that result in them returning to the streets or going on welfare (Olson et al., 1990; Pavetti, 1992).

Residential programs. A comparison of the findings on the Job Corps (a residential program) and JOBSTART (a nonresidential and less intensive version of the Job Corps) points to the potential importance of the residential factor.

Concurrent and integrated versus sequential education and training. The findings on JOBSTART and the Minority Female Single Parent Demonstration raise important issues about the relative effectiveness of these two ways of organizing education and training services.

Work experience linked to other services. The JTPA and JOBSTART studies pointed to the high opportunity cost, in terms of lost earnings, that youth faced by participating in these programs. Combining paid work experience with education and training could address this issue and make those services more relevant through their extension to a real-world setting.

Variants could include the conservation or service corps, a combination of training and work experience, or the YouthBuild model.

Variation in the intensity and duration of service. JTPA provides relatively short-term services, which are often also not very intensive. It would be important to identify whether there is a threshold of intensity after which larger impacts appear.

Family-centered strategies. These programs could seek to build on the positive experience with family literacy programs and other intergenerational programs targeted to reach younger children. Such programs would be designed to help young parents fulfill their responsibilities by fostering community-based partnerships with families. Services might include life skills, parenting education, education and employability services, recreation, primary health services, counseling, case management, peer tutoring, mental health services, and referrals to other services, such as substance abuse treatment.

Self-help strategies. These programs would actively involve young people in solving their own problems through individual and communal action. Youth would be involved in designing the program and would play a central role in its governance. Such an approach might involve the use of vouchers and other strategies for individualizing or customizing services.

Small programs with high-quality services. In testing any of the above approaches, a special emphasis could be placed on smaller programs that create a family environment and make special efforts to provide intensive, high-quality services.

We believe that the commitment to research, evaluation, and continuous improvement that is evident in JTPA and JOBS needs to be extended to the second-chance remediation programs for adult education. It was noted earlier how little is known about these programs.[14] Two recent studies (Grubb et al., 1991; Chisman, 1989) both decried the paucity of available research and evaluation. According to these studies, too little evidence exists against which to judge current programs or to provide a foundation upon which to base future efforts. Both reports place a high priority on increased allocation of resources for research and evaluation of adult basic education, and both call on the federal government to take the lead in providing these resources (Grubb et al., 1991:102-103; Chisman, 1989:24). In 1991, Congress created the National Institute for Literacy to provide a national focal point for research, technical assistance and research dissemination, policy analysis and program evaluation across the various programs and research efforts concerned with adult literacy. Though it is too early to evaluate the work of the institute, we consider its creation to have been a step in the right direction. We are not aware, however, of any existing evaluations of adult education that involve random-assignment experimental research beyond those being carried out as part of the JOBS evaluation. We recommend that the federal government undertake such research to learn about the impacts of adult education programs and to provide information on effective practices that can be used to spur program improvement.

In addition to the need for improved research and evaluation, both Chisman and Grubb et al. point to program fragmentation as a serious problem. Chisman (1989:6-7) finds that, at an institutional level, the diversity of agencies and programs involved with providing basic skills education has meant "a pattern of institutional fragmentation in which basic skills are a low-level priority for almost everyone." According to Chisman, this pattern holds at the federal, state, and local levels. Grubb et al. (1991:55-56) discovered that individuals frequently are referred from job training and vocational education programs to the adult education system, with little cohesiveness between the programs, a general disregard for the quality of program to which an individual may be referred, and little or no tracking of individuals. The result is that individuals in job-training and vocational education programs are often referred to low-quality programs and frequently drop out or become lost to the system.

Chisman and Grubb et al. call for improved coordination among adult education programs to fix what Chisman (1989:9) calls the "jumbled system of funding, service delivery, and responsibility." Whether this coordination could be accomplished by adopting improved policies within the current structure (Grubb et al., 1991:100) or whether new federal oversight structures are needed (Chisman, 1989:20) is a subject we did not have time to investigate. This would be an appropriate issue for early consideration by the federal government.

NOTES

1. There are few, if any, pure examples of policy instruments. Actual programs often represent hybrids that draw features from more than one category. Nonetheless, the general categories can be useful in sorting things out.

2. Pell grants are not an entitlement in a budgetary sense, since funding for Pell is subject to annual appropriations. Pell legislation ensures that all qualifying applicants will receive funding, however, by adjusting the size of grants to accommodate budgetary limits.

3. Vouchers, grants, contracts, and tax expenditures all share, for example, a reliance on the private market (including private, nonprofit organizations) for service delivery. Vouchers, which are usually thought of as being comparatively free of governmental regulation, always have some restrictions on qualifying forms of training or education. As these restrictions become tighter, the range of qualifying suppliers becomes more narrowly defined. In the extreme, there may be little difference to an institution between being awarded a federal contract to perform services and being on a short list of qualified recipients of vouchers. At the same time, a system of contracting may be operated in a way that gives students some latitude about which contracted supplier to work with; their range of choice could sometimes approach that which vouchers would provide. Similarly, a targeted tax preference for indi-

viduals may appear to have the effect of a voucher; a tax preference for suppliers may be similar to a grant; and so on.

4. It may, for example, be more feasible to improve the effectiveness of voucher-supported programs by providing more standardized information about the products and performance of institutions eligible for voucher use than by wholesale replacement of vouchers with other forms of support. Or it may be possible to make contracting mechanisms work more effectively by introducing better methods of monitoring and quality control than by voucherizing them.

5. We chose not to examine the Perkins Vocational and Applied Technology Education Act in depth, because the funds it provides to postsecondary training are small compared to the student aid programs and to the funds provided from other sources (e.g., states) for postsecondary training; and a major evaluation of the act is currently under way, with a final report due in 1994. Though the principal purpose of the Perkins Act is program improvement, a goal consistent with our emphasis on the importance of enhancing quality, we note that Perkins has historically focused more on secondary vocational education and has not been a strong force for improvement of postsecondary training programs. This may change with the new emphases on Tech-Prep programs and performance measures and standards built into the 1990 Perkins legislation. We hope that the Perkins evaluation will give attention to what program improvement might mean for postsecondary institutions and to the effects of the 1990 changes.

6. The U.S. Department of Labor received a number of letters from higher education representatives opposed to a 1991 set of proposed rules (*Federal Register* 56(2):296-300) that encouraged JTPA administrators to make maximum use of student aid before allocating JTPA funds for postsecondary schooling expenses.

7. As the committee finished its report, the regulations needed to implement these new rules had not been issued; and schools offering programs of study of between 300 and 600 clock hours in length (roughly 3 to 6 months) remained eligible to participate in student loan programs regardless of their completion and placement rates.

8. Ineffective training means several things. Training may not result in economic benefits to individuals if the quality is poor or if the trainee drops out before completing the program. Even good training will not pay off, however, if there are no jobs available for which that training is suitable, or if the available jobs pay poorly. We believe these factors are part of the reason for high default rates among students enrolled in postsecondary training.

9. Unemployment insurance (UI) wage-record data are increasingly used in the JTPA performance management system (National Commission for Employment Policy, 1992); some states are beginning to explore the usefulness of UI data in vocational education as well (Amico, 1993). We believe that many states would therefore find it comparatively easy to extend the use of UI to the student aid arena. We prefer not to mandate the use of these particular data, however; some states might have their own information systems that would accomplish similar purposes or would prefer to use other wage records, such as those from Social Security.

10. One such related activity is the network of manufacturing technology centers supported by the National Institute of Standards and Technology. A report of the National Research Council (1993) addresses, among other things, how these centers can assist smaller manufacturers meet their training needs.

11. The National Governors' Association (NGA) has identified eighteen different federal dislocated worker programs, each with different eligible grantees, administrative structures, eligible participants, allowable services, and performance goals. NGA reports that a state that recently sought to address worker dislocation due to reductions in defense spending found itself applying to and receiving funding from eight federal programs administered by three federal agencies.

12. The amendments were intended to address many of the criticisms of JTPA youth programs. They established a separate youth program, stipulated that 50 percent of the youth

served must be out of school, targeted services toward those with multiple employment barriers (including drop-outs, pregnant and parenting youth, ex-offenders, and youth with low basic skills), required comprehensive assessments and individualized service strategies, reformed on-the-job training practices, mandated that service delivery areas address the full range of young people's needs, encouraged long-term services, and authorized work experience, community service, and mentoring.

13. YouthBuild offers education, skills training, paid work, leadership development, and counseling. Programs are small, with the emphasis on high-quality services, support staff, and structuring activities in ways that respect and empower the young people in the program.

14. This is a situation that will be partially remedied by a 44-month study to evaluate existing adult education programs, now under way under the auspices of the U.S. Department of Education. For the interim report of the National Evaluation of Adult Education Programs, see U.S. Department of Education (1992); the final report is due to be completed in the spring of 1994 and should begin to fill a research vacuum in the field of adult basic education. Because of the focus of the JOBS program on improving the basic education of welfare recipients, the evaluation of the JOBS and California's Greater Avenues for Independence programs will also provide relevant information.

8

Becoming an Agent of Change

As noted in Chapter 5, the committee has strong reservations about the federal government trying to micromanage programs for training for the workplace. We believe that the states should be the primary source of managerial leadership and policy coherence in this field.

Nevertheless, we envision the federal government playing an important new role vis-à-vis postsecondary training: as a catalyst or an agent of change in encouraging systemic reform. In this chapter, we examine how the federal government could become an agent of change, in terms of both its functions and institutional structures through which these functions could be carried out.

FUNCTIONS CONTRIBUTING TO SYSTEM-BUILDING

In our deliberations about what the federal government should do to encourage the building of a postsecondary training system, we identified six functions to be performed. The first three would support the system-building that, we argued in Chapter 5, offers the best hope of creating coherent, readily accessible, articulated, effective, and high-quality postsecondary training for the workplace. The second three would develop the federal leadership role through activities we believe the federal government is best positioned to carry out.

Making Grants

States may have difficulty finding the start-up resources needed to pull their disparate postsecondary training systems together. New, consolidated information systems may need to be developed, initial comprehensive planning undertaken, new umbrella organizations set up, and so forth. Therefore, we believe the federal government should make grants to state governments (and to general-purpose local governments, where appropriate, after consultation with the states in which they are located) for systems development, program integration, the design of new data systems, and other aspects of managerial capacity-building for work force preparation. These activities could include establishing and testing new managerial arrangements, such as coordinated service delivery, training managers for new challenges, and developing data systems for linking employment and training institutions and developing client-tracking systems at the local level.

Rationalizing Federal Requirements

In Chapter 3 we described how conflicting and contradictory federal requirements complicate the task of systemic reform at the state and local levels. The federal government needs to develop common or compatible program definitions; procedures for determining eligibility; and fiscal, administrative, and planning requirements in its programs that support postsecondary training.

Granting Waivers

States that are making good progress in developing integrated work-force development systems should be able to seek waivers from provisions of federal laws and regulations that impede reform efforts. Waivers would allow states to use resources authorized under various federal work-force development programs in a coherent manner that meets employer and client needs. Waivers would give states a way to improve the coherence of their training systems right away, until the federal government rationalizes its own fragmented array of programs and requirements.

Waivers should be available only on application and granted only to states who meet *readiness conditions*. These would identify states that are making significant progress toward developing systemic approaches to work force development. These conditions would presumably change over time (for example, to include more emphasis on performance and outcome information as better tools for creating this information become available). Readiness conditions might include the following:

• The state has a systemic approach to training that includes both public- and private-sector activities and a clear commitment to involvement on the part of the private sector.
• The state has a system for integrated planning by education, labor, and the private sector at the state and local levels.

• The state has taken steps to simplify access to programs by clients and employers and to improve accountability, by, among other things, moving to develop integrated information systems and performance data.

• The state has taken steps to eliminate barriers to effective service delivery created by state rules and regulations.

• There is a clear commitment from the governor and state legislature to building a work force development system.

States would decide which federal programs they wish to include in their initiatives and would have the flexibility to decide how to meet the readiness conditions. One result of this approach is that, over time, a number of natural experiments would develop from which to learn how work force development systems can best be created.

Developing National Skills Standards

In Chapter 6 we argued that existing federal efforts to encourage the development of skills standards lack an adequate framework. We believe that the federal government needs to take responsibility for resolving the numerous design issues identified in that chapter and for creating a national framework within which individual skills-standards boards could operate.

Supplying Research and Development

The subjects for attention could include management research, studies related to setting and implementing skills standards, the development of methods for setting up management and data systems, and research on training methods. We have a special concern about research issues and information needs that cross program and departmental lines, since these tend to be neglected at present. For example, the federal government should support the development of broad-based longitudinal studies that cut across program lines but that can be matched with data collected by specific programs. Far too little is currently known about how the various training programs interact to affect individual trainees. It is also important to improve the ability of information systems to meet guidance and counseling needs at the local level as well as administrative and research requirements. The National Center for Education Statistics, the Bureau of Labor Statistics, and the National Occupation Information Coordinating Committee all need to be involved in the establishment of a common national framework to improve client access to information. Common definitions, connections between databases, and usefulness of management information systems for direct service providers are all areas requiring attention. Finally, the federal government should also sponsor research on such issues as the effects of incentives in performance management systems, which affect multiple training programs.

Reporting

In Chapter 5 we argued that the federal government is uniquely well-situated to articulate the goals and evaluate the progress of the nation in improving postsecondary training for the workplace. One way to do this would be through an annual report on the state of the American work force. In proposing this, we mean to restore and enhance a practice that existed for 20 years, from 1963 to 1982, when the U.S. Department of Labor (sometimes in cooperation with other departments) prepared an annual "Employment and Training Report of the President" on employment and training needs, issues, and programs.[1] The report we envision should be broader in coverage than those reports, however, and should emphasize training more heavily. It should highlight institutional capacity-building and linkages among institutions and program participants in the field of work force development.

MEANS OF BECOMING AN AGENT OF CHANGE

We believe that the United States is in the middle of an important period of innovation and system-building in postsecondary (and other) training. Much of it is occurring at the state and local levels, as it should. As we have said, the federal government should act as an agent of change to encourage these developments. To do so, the federal government needs to take a lesson from the states that have restructured themselves to improve their ability to take a systemic approach to work force development issues. With dozens of programs scattered among various executive branch departments (most notably, Education, Health and Human Services, and Labor), what options does the federal government have for taking a more comprehensive view? We see a number of ways the functions described in the preceding section could be carried out; not all have to be accomplished in the same way.

The most straightforward approach would be to assign the responsibility for these functions to one of the existing departments. However, most of our committee members find this approach problematic. We doubt that any one department will have or will be perceived to have an evenhanded, comprehensive interest in all of the important pieces comprising the postsecondary training puzzle. We fear existing departments would instead continue to emphasize their traditional areas of interest and expertise. While we are concerned about relying solely on existing departments to perform the system-building functions we envision, however, we recognize that some of the functions or subfunctions might well be assigned to them.

Another approach would be to restructure the executive branch the way some states (and, recently, Australia) have done by bringing training programs together in a single department.[2] We did not seriously consider this option, however, nor the related one of moving programs from one existing department to another to achieve more apparent rationality. Besides probably exceeding our charge, such reorganizations fly in the face of our sense of the politically feasible. As the National Commission for Employment Policy (1991b:12) described coordination options for employment and training programs:

> There appears to be little enthusiasm in either the Executive or Legislative Branches for combining either all federal assistance programs or all employment and training programs under a more logical organization structure. The time and costs involved in Executive Branch reorganization are great . . . . In addition, the jurisdictional issues associated with congressional committees and Executive Departments, historical reasons, and the problems of responding to different special interest groups present formidable obstacles to reorganization.

Nevertheless, without such formal organizational consolidation, the problem remains of how the federal government can develop an integrated view of national training needs and the ability to encourage changes consistent with that view. Two other conventional approaches to coordination are legislative mandates and administrative action. Legislative mandates require government agencies to coordinate their actions with other agencies. One example is a requirement under the Family Support Act that the Secretary of Health and Human Services coordinate JOBS education and training services with the Secretaries of Education and Labor. Another is the requirement under the Carl D. Perkins Vocational and Applied Technology Education Act that state vocational education plans be reviewed by state JTPA Job Training Coordinating Councils. Administrative action involves steps like the interagency agreement established in November 1989 among the U.S. Departments of Health and Human Services, Education, and Labor to provide jointly technical assistance to states in implementing the JOBS program. Legislative mandates and administrative action sometimes improve coordination among programs (National Commission for Employment Policy, 1991b:9-12) and probably reduce the turf struggles among departments and agencies. They fail, however, to provide the strong systemic perspective that is a major problem with current federal policy, nor are they sturdy vehicles for carrying out the leadership role that we have recommended the federal government assume.

We investigated two earlier federal efforts (the Joint Funding Simplification Act of 1974 and the Low Income Opportunity Board [LIOB] that was created in the White House in 1987) to help states and localities coordinate services by coordinating federal funding from several agencies and waiving some federal rules. These efforts were more limited in scope than the vehicle we are seeking; they also had only mixed success.

Only 56 projects were funded under the Joint Funding Simplification Act from 1972 to 1984. States and localities found that lengthy and costly preapplication procedures, individual federal agency add-on requirements, and processing delays under the coordinated agency review procedure outweighed the theoretical benefits of better-integrated projects and improved program coordination (U.S. Office of Management and Budget, 1984). The act was terminated in 1985.

LIOB, which encouraged states to adopt innovative and systemic approaches to welfare by creating a single point of contact for those wishing to obtain waivers from federal statutes and regulations, more closely resembles the waiver function we wish to create. It still required sign-off by the program agencies, however. We favor some mechanism for providing a central waiver-granting authority that would avoid the difficulties of seeking individual departmental approvals.

Most of our committee members believe that a new mechanism is needed if the federal government is to be the influential agent of change that we think is needed. A single federal entity, whose range of interests spans the disparate aspects of postsecondary training (and of other parts of the employment and training system that are beyond our charge) can bring the necessary breadth and integrated perspective to federal policy. Creating such an entity is preferable to assigning lead responsibility to one or another department because training issues cross departmental boundaries, and we want all parties to feel equal ownership of the effort.

The option we analyzed most carefully was the creation of an Office of Work Force Development, which would be established with high visibility and significant powers. The model we have in mind is the National Science Foundation (NSF). Like NSF, the office we discussed would be independent, not located in the Executive Office of the President or under the aegis of an existing federal agency, and not structured as an interagency board. The director of the office would have a fixed term and be subject to Senate confirmation. The office would be governed by a policy-making board, the equivalent of NSF's National Science Board. New board members would be appointed by the president, with the advice of the current board and be subject to Senate confirmation as well.

Such an office could be the leading edge of the federal effort to spark improvement and reform in postsecondary training, by carrying out most or all of the functions identified in the preceding section. In its grant-making activities, it could focus more broadly than existing departments do, emphasizing support of state and local efforts that enhance system building. It could take the lead in pulling together the necessary federal departments to work out ways of rationalizing requirements and calendars as well as providing (through waivers) a way for states to overcome the barriers that conflicting federal rules now construct. We believe that the office could also be the umbrella organization under which a national skills-standards board could work out the design issues and create the framework we found is needed (see Chapter 6) to build a national (not federal) skills standards system. Furthermore, the office could take responsibility for the kind of cross-program and cross-departmental research and information system needs that have not been adequately addressed to date.

We think that it is crucial to involve the important constituencies in the activities of the office, but different groups and structures are needed for different functions. The governing board should include nonfederal officials, employers, training providers, and leading scholars on work force development issues. The skills-standards board mentioned above should be led by employers but should include training providers and state and local officials. A waiver panel, composed of representatives of the federal agencies who provide significant support for postsecondary training, should advise the office on the establishment of general standards that would be applied to individual applications for waivers.

We further believe that nonfederal representatives should be involved in the review of both grant applications and waiver requests; we believe this could be accomplished through a peer-review process. Peer review, involving federal, state, local, and private-sector representatives, would help insulate the grant and waiver processes from political pressures. We believe that a degree of political insulation for the office is important in enabling the office to pick winners quite consciously, rather than operating in an automatic and formulaic way. Peer review would also help evaluate the feasibility of state proposals and would help all the partners develop a feeling of ownership in the system approach.

All of our committee members agree on the need for the federal government to become an agent of change in the task of building a strong postsecondary training system in the United States. We differ somewhat on the best vehicle for carrying out this role. We all believe, however, that the federal government should take on the functions we have identified and, with them, a new and critically needed role as catalyst in encouraging the development of a training system equal to the world's best.

NOTES

1. The report was called the "Manpower Report of the President" from 1963 to 1975. As best we can determine, no report was issued in 1981.

2. In 1987, Australia consolidated its federal education and employment departments into a new Department of Employment, Education, and Training.

References

Adelman, C.
  1992   *The Way We Were: The Community College as American Thermometer.*
          Washington, D.C.: U.S. Department of Education.
Advisory Commission on Intergovernmental Relations
  1992   *Characteristics of Federal Grant-in-Aid Programs to State and Local
          Governments: Grants Funded FY 1991.* Report No. M-182. Washing-
          ton, D.C.: Advisory Commission on Intergovernmental Relations.
Amico, L.
  1993   *State Capacity to Use UI Wage Records: The Vocational Education
          Experience.* Washington, D.C.: National Governors' Association, Na-
          tional Occupational Information Coordinating Committee, and U.S. De-
          partment of Education.
Angrist, J., and A. Krueger
  1991   Does compulsory school attendance affect schooling and earnings? *Quarterly
          Journal of Economics* 106:979-1014.
Apling, R.N., and S.R. Aleman
  1990   *Proprietary Schools: A Description of Institutions and Students.* Con-
          gressional Research Service. Washington, D.C.: U.S. Government Print-
          ing Office.
Ashenfelter, O.
  1987   The case for evaluating training programs with randomized trials. *Eco-
          nomics of Education Review* 6(4):333-338.
Australian Education Council
  1990   *National Report on Schooling in Australia, 1990. Statistical Annexe.*
          Carlton, Australia: The Curriculum Corporation.

177

Bailey, T.R.
  1987   Employment and training programs. Pp. 163-196 in C. Brecher and
          R.D. Horton, eds., *Setting Municipal Priorities, 1988*. New York: New
          York University Press.
  1989   *Changes in the Nature and Structure of the Workforce: Implications for
          Skill Requirements and Skill Formation*. New York: National Center on
          Education and Employment, Teachers College, Columbia University.
Bailis, L.N.
  1984   *What's Happening to CBO's Under JTPA and Where Do We Go From
          Here?* Highlights of the NYEC Survey. Washington, D.C.: National
          Youth Employment Commission.
  1987   *Community-Based Organizations and Vocational Education: The Path
          to Partnership*. Columbus, Ohio: National Center for Research on Vo-
          cational Education.
Banerjee, N., Y. Zhou, and C. Caruso
  1989   *Unfair at Any Price: Welfare Recipients at New York Proprietary Schools*.
          New York: INTERFACE, 666 Broadway, Suite 800, New York, N.Y.
          10012.
Bardach, E., and R. Kagan
  1982   *Going by the Book: The Problem of Regulatory Unreasonableness*. New
          York: Twentieth Century Fund.
Barnow, B.S.
  1987   The impact of CETA programs on earnings: a review of the literature.
          Journal of Human Resources 22(2):157-193.
  1992   Performance standards in state and local programs. Pp. 277-309 in C.F.
          Manski and I. Garfinkel, eds., *Evaluating Welfare and Training Pro-
          grams*. Cambridge, Mass.: Harvard University Press.
Bartel, A.
  1992   *Productivity Gains from the Implementation of Employee Training Pro-
          grams*. NBER Working Paper #3893. Cambridge, Mass.: National
          Bureau of Economic Research.
Barzelay, M.
  1992   *Breaking Through Bureaucracy: A New Vision for Managing in Gov-
          ernment*. Berkeley, Calif.: University of California Press.
Bassi, L.
  1992   *Smart Workers, Smart Work: A Survey of Small Businesses on Work-
          place Education and Reorganization of Work*. Washington, D.C.: Southport
          Institute for Policy Analysis.
  In   Workplace education for hourly workers. *Journal of Policy Analysis
  press   and Management*.
Batt, R., and P. Osterman
  1993   *Public Policy and Workplace-Centered Training: National Lessons from
          Local Experience*. Washington, D.C.: Economic Policy Institute.
Baum, E.B.
  1991   When the witch doctors agree: the Family Support Act and social sci-
          ence research. *Journal of Policy Analysis and Management* 10(4):603-
          615.

Becker, G.S.
1964   *Human Capital: A Theoretical and Empirical Analysis, with Special Reference to Education.* New York: National Bureau of Economic Research.

Behn, R.D.
1988   Management by groping along. *Journal of Policy Analysis and Management* 7(4):643-663.

Bell, S.H., N.R. Burstein, and L.L. Orr
1987   *Overview of Evaluation Results: Evaluation of the AFDC Homemaker-Home Health Aide Demonstrations.* Cambridge, Mass.: Abt Associates Inc.

Belous, R.S.
1989   How human resource systems adjust to the shift toward contingent workers. *Monthly Labor Review* 112(3):7-12.

Bendick, M., Jr.
1989   Matching workers and job opportunities: what role for the federal-state employment service. Pp. 81-108 in D.L. Bawden and F. Skidmore, eds., *Rethinking Employment Policy.* Washington, D.C.: The Urban Institute Press.

Berman, E., J. Bound, and Z. Griliches
1993   *Changes in the Demand for Skilled Labor within U.S. Manufacturing Industries: Evidence from the Annual Survey of Manufacturing.* NBER Working Paper No. 4255. Cambridge, Mass.: National Bureau of Economic Research.

Berryman, S.E., and T.R. Bailey
1992   *The Double Helix of Education and the Economy.* New York: Institute on Education and the Economy, Teachers College, Columbia University.

Berryman, S.E., and J.E. Rosenbaum
1992   Certification of work competencies. Pp. 51-59 in J.E. Rosenbaum et al., *Youth Apprenticeship in America: Guidelines for Building an Effective System.* Washington, D.C.: William T. Grant Foundation Commission on Youth and America's Future.

Betsey, C.L., R.G. Hollister, and M.R. Papageorgiou, eds.
1985   *Youth Employment and Training Programs: The YEDPA Years.* Committee on Youth Employment Programs, National Research Council. Washington, D.C.: National Academy Press.

Bishop, J.H.
1990   Incentives to study: can we find them? *ILR Report* 28(1):24-29.
1994   Formal training and its impact on productivity, wages, and innovation. In L. Lynch, ed., *Training and the Private Sector: International Comparisons.* Chicago: University of Chicago Press.

Blanchflower, D., and L.M. Lynch
1994   Training at work: a comparison of U.S. and British youths. In L. Lynch, ed., *Training and the Private Sector: International Comparisons.* Chicago: University of Chicago Press.

Bloom, H.S., L.L. Orr, G. Cave, S.H. Bell, and F. Doolittle
    1993   *The National JTPA Study: Title II-A Impacts on Earnings and Employment at 18 Months.* Bethesda, Md.: Abt Associates Inc.

Bradburn, N., and D. Gilford, eds.
    1990   *A Framework and Principles for International Comparative Studies in Education.* Board on International Comparative Studies in Education, National Research Council. Washington D.C.: National Academy Press.

Breneman, D.W., and S.C. Nelson
    1981   *Financing Community Colleges: An Economic Perspective.* Washington, D.C.: The Brookings Institution.

Bureau of the Census
    1990   *What's It Worth? Educational Background and Economic Status, Spring 1987.* Current Population Reports, Series P-70, No. 21. Washington, D.C.: U.S. Department of Commerce.
    1992a   *Educational Attainment in the United States: March 1991 and 1990.* Current Population Reports, Series P-20, No. 462. Washington, D.C.: U.S. Department of Commerce.
    1992b   *Money Income of Households, Families, and Persons in the United States, 1991.* Current Population Reports, Series P-60, No. 180. Washington, D.C.: U.S. Department of Commerce.

Bureau of Labor Statistics
    1985   *How Workers Get Their Training.* Washington, D.C.: U.S. Department of Labor.
    1992   *How Workers Get Their Training: A 1991 Update.* Washington, D.C.: U.S. Department of Labor.

Burghardt, J., A. Rengarajan, A. Gordon, and E. Kisker
    1992   *Evaluation of the Minority Female Single Parent Demonstration.* New York: Rockefeller Foundation.

Burtless, G., and L. Orr
    1986   Are classical experiments needed for manpower policy? *Journal of Human Resources* 21(4):606-639.

Carnevale, A.P.
    1992   Skills for the new world order. *The American School Board Journal* 179(5):28-30.

Carnevale, A., L. Gainer, and J. Villet
    1990   *Training in America: The Organization and Strategic Role of Training.* San Francisco, Calif.: Jossey-Bass.

Carroll, D., and S. Peng
    1989   *Enrollment, Completion, Attrition, and Vocational Course-Taking Patterns in Postsecondary Education: A Comparison of 1972 and 1980 High School Graduates Entering Two-Year Institutions.* National Center for Education Statistics Survey Report CS 89-360. Washington, D.C.: U.S. Department of Education.

Casey, B.
    1991   Recent developments in the German apprenticeship system. *British Journal of Industrial Relations* 29(2):205-222.

Cave, G., and F. Doolittle
  1991   *Assessing JOBSTART*. New York: Manpower Demonstration Research Corporation.
Cave, G., F. Doolittle, and C. Toussaint
  1993   *JOBSTART: Final Report on a Program for School Dropouts*. New York: Manpower Demonstration Research Corporation.
Chisman, F.P.
  1989   *Jump Start: The Federal Role in Adult Literacy*. Southport, Conn.: Southport Institute for Policy Analysis.
Clark, C.S.
  1992   Youth apprenticeships. *The CQ Researcher* 2(39): 907-920, 922-923.
Cohen, M.S., and D.W. Stevens
  1989   The role of the employment service. In Commission on Workforce Quality and Labor Market Efficiency, *Investing in People*. Washington, D.C.: U.S. Department of Labor.
College Board
  1993   *Trends in Student Aid: 1983 to 1993*. Washington, D.C.: College Board.
Commission on the Skills of the American Workforce
  1990   *America's Choice: High Skills or Low Wages!* Washington, D.C.: National Center on Education and the Economy.
Connolly, S.J.
  1992a International Comparisons of Workforce Preparation Programs and Policies. Paper prepared for the Committee on Postsecondary Education and Training for the Workplace, Commission on Behavioral and Social Sciences and Education. St. Hilda's College, Oxford University.
  1992b Young People's Pathways from Education into the Workplace in the UK. Paper prepared for the Committee on Postsecondary Education and Training for the Workplace, Commission on Behavioral and Social Sciences and Education. St. Hilda's College, Oxford University.
Corson, W., P. Decker, P. Gleason, and W. Nicholson
  1993   *International Trade and Worker Dislocation: Evaluation of the Trade Adjustment Assistance Program*. Princeton, N.J.: Mathematica Policy Research, Inc.
Creticos, P.A., and R.G. Sheets
  1990   *Evaluating State-Financed, Workplace-Based Retraining Programs: A Report on the Feasibility of a Business Screening and Performance Outcome Evaluation System*. Research report 89-08. Washington, D.C.: National Commission for Employment Policy and National Governors' Association.
Dertouzos, M.L., R.K. Lester, R.M. Solow, and The MIT Commission on Industrial Productivity
  1989   *Made in America: Regaining the Productive Edge*. New York: Harper Collins.
Dougherty, K.
  1987   The effects of community colleges: aid or hindrance to socioeconomic attainment? *Sociology of Education* 60(2):86-103.

Eisner, R.
   1989   Employer approaches to reducing unemployment. Pp. 59-80 in D.L.
           Bawden and F. Skidmore, eds., *Rethinking Employment Policy*. Wash-
           ington, D.C.: The Urban Institute Press.
Elias, P., E. Hernaes, and M. Baker
   1994   Vocational education and training in Britain and Norway. In L. Lynch,
           ed., *Training and the Private Sector: International Comparisons*. Chi-
           cago: University of Chicago Press.
Ferman, L.A., M. Hoyman, and J. Cutcher-Gershenfeld
   1990   Joint union-management training programs: a synthesis in the evolution
           of jointism and training. Pp. 157-189 in L.A. Ferman, M. Hoyman, J.
           Cutcher-Gershenfeld, and E.J. Savoie, eds., *New Developments in Worker
           Training: A Legacy for the 1990s*. Madison, Wis.: Industrial Relations
           Research Association.
Fraas, C.J.
   1990   *Proprietary Schools and Student Financial Aid Programs: Background
           and Policy Issues*. Washington, D.C.: Congressional Research Service.
Freeman, R.B.
   1994   *Working Under Different Rules*. New York: Russell Sage Foundation.
Friedlander, D.
   1988   *Sub-Group Impacts and Performance Indicators for Selected Welfare
           Employment Programs*. New York: Manpower Demonstration and Re-
           search Corporation.
Friedlander, D., and J.M. Gueron
   1992   Are high-cost services more effective than low-cost services? Pp. 143-
           198 in C.F. Manski and I. Garfinkel, eds. *Evaluating Welfare and Training
           Programs*. Cambridge, Mass.: Harvard University Press.
Friedlander, D., J. Riccio, and S. Freedman
   1993   *GAIN: Two-year Impacts in Six Counties*. New York: Manpower
           Demonstration Research Corporation.
Fuhrman, S.H.
   1993   The politics of coherence. In S.H. Fuhrman, ed., *Designing Coherent
           Education Policy: Improving the System*. San Francisco, Calif.: Jossey-
           Bass.
Galladay, M., and R.M. Wulfsberg
   1981   *Condition of Vocational Education*. Washington, D.C.: U.S. Depart-
           ment of Education.
Gallinelli, J.
   1979   Vocational education at the secondary level: a review of development
           and purpose. In T. Abramson et al., eds., *Handbook of Vocational Edu-
           cation Evaluation*. Beverly Hills, Calif.: Sage Publications.
Gitter, R.J.
   1992   Foreign labor developments. *Monthly Labor Review* 115(4):25-29.
Golden, O.
   1990   Innovation in public sector human services programs: the implications
           of innovation by groping along. *Journal of Policy Analysis and Man-
           agement* 9(2):219-248.

Greenberg, M.
1992   *Welfare Reform on a Budget: What's Happening in JOBS.* Washington, D.C.: Center for Law and Social Policy.

Gregory, R.
1992   Young People's Pathways into Work: the Australian Experience. Paper prepared for the Committee on Postsecondary Education and Training for the Workplace, Commission on Behavioral and Social Science and Education. Center for Economic Policy Research, The Australian National University.

Groot, W., J. Hartog, and H. Oosterbeed
1994   Returns to within company schooling of employees: the case of the Netherlands. In L. Lynch, ed., *Training and the Private Sector: International Comparisons.* Chicago: University of Chicago Press.

Grubb, W.N.
1989   Access, Achievement, Completion, and "Milling Around" in Postsecondary Vocational Education. Paper from MPR Associates, Inc. (1995 University Avenue, Suite 225, Berkeley, Calif. 94704) for the National Assessment of Vocational Education.

1990   The Economic Returns to Postsecondary Education: New Evidence from the National Longitudinal Study of the Class of 1972. Unpublished paper, School of Education, University of California, Berkeley.

1991   The Effects of Postsecondary Education on Access to Occupations. Unpublished paper, School of Education, University of California, Berkeley.

1992   Postsecondary vocational education and the sub-baccalaureate labor market: new evidence on economic returns. *Economics of Education Review* 11(3):225-248.

1993a   Further tests of screening on education and observed ability. *Economics of Education Review* 12(2), in press

1993b   The long-run effects of proprietary schools on wages and earnings: implications for federal policy. *Educational Evaluation and Policy Analysis* 15(1):17-33.

1993c   The varied economic returns to postsecondary education: new evidence from the class of 1972. *Journal of Human Resources* 28(2):365-382.

Grubb, W.N., and L.M. McDonnell
1991   *Local Systems of Vocational Education and Job Training.* Berkeley, Calif.: National Center for Research on Vocational Education, University of California.

Grubb, W.N., and R.H. Wilson
1992   Trends in wage and salary inequality, 1967-88. *Monthly Labor Review* 115(6):23-39.

Grubb, W.N., J. Kalman, M. Castellano, C. Brown, and D. Bradby
1991   *Readin', Writin', and 'Rithmetic One More Time: The Role of Remediation in Vocational Education and Job Training Programs.* Berkeley, Calif.: National Center for Research in Vocational Education, University of California.

Grubb, W.N., T. Dickinson, L. Giordano, and G. Kaplan
1992   *Betwixt and Between: Education, Skills, and Employment in Sub-Bacca-*

laureate Labor Markets. Berkeley, Calif.: National Center for Research on Vocational Education, University of California.

Gueron, J.M., and E. Pauly
1991   *From Welfare to Work.* New York: Russell Sage Foundation.

Haggstrom, G., T. Blaschke, and R. Shavelson
1991   *After High School, Then What? A Look at the Postsecondary Sorting Out Process for American Youth.* Santa Monica, Calif.: The RAND Corporation.

Hamilton, S.F., and M.A. Hamilton
1992   Learning at work. Pp. 17-23 in J.E. Rosenbaum et al., eds., *Youth Apprenticeship in America: Guidelines for Building an Effective System.* Washington, D.C.: William T. Grant Foundation Commission on Youth and America's Future.

Hansen, J.S.
1991   The roots of federal student aid policy. Pp. 3-19 in J.P. Merisotis, ed., *The Changing Dimensions of Student Aid.* San Francisco, Calif.: Jossey-Bass, Inc.

Haskins, R.
1991   Congress writes a law: research and welfare reform. *Journal of Policy Analysis and Management* 10(4):616-632.

Heckman, J.J.
1992   Randomization and social policy evaluation. Pp. 201-230 in C.F. Manski and I. Garfinkel, eds., *Evaluating Welfare and Training Programs.* Cambridge, Mass.: Harvard University Press.

Hill, P.T., J. Harvey, and A. Praskac
1993   *Pandora's Box: Accountability and Performance Standards in Vocational Education.* Santa Monica, Calif.: The RAND Corporation.

Hollenbeck, K.
1992   Postsecondary Education as Triage: The Consequences of Postsecondary Education Tracks on Wages, Earnings, and Wage Growth. Paper presented at the Western Economics Association meeting, San Francisco.

Hollister, R.G., Jr., P. Kemper, and R.A. Maynard, eds.
1984   *The National Supported Work Demonstration.* Madison: University of Wisconsin Press.

Holzer, H., R. Black, M. Cheatham, and J. Knott
In   Are training subsidies for firms effective? The Michigan experience.
press   *Industrial and Labor Relations Review.*

Honeyman, D., M.L. Williamson, and J.L. Wattenbarger
1991   *Community College Financing 1990: Challenges for a New Decade.* Washington, D.C.: American Association of Community and Junior Colleges.

Hovey, H.A.
1985   *The Role of Federal Tax Policy in Employment Policy.* Washington, D.C.: National Governors' Association.

Irwin, P.M., and R.N. Apling
1991   *Vocational Education: Major Provisions of the Amendments (P.L. 101-392).* Washington, D.C.: Congressional Research Service.

Job Training Longitudinal Survey Research Advisory Panel
    1985   *Recommendations of the Job Training Longitudinal Survey Research Advisory Panel*. Report prepared for the Office of Strategic Planning and Policy Development, Employment and Training Administration. Washington, DC: U.S. Department of Labor.

Kane, T.J., and C.E. Rouse
    1993   Labor Market Returns to Community College. Unpublished paper, John F. Kennedy School of Government, Harvard University.

Katz, L.F., and K. Murphy
    1992   Changes in relative wages, 1963-1987: supply and demand factors. *Quarterly Journal of Economics* 107(1):35-78.

Kochan, T., and P. Osterman
    1991   Human Resource Development and Utilization: Is There Too Little in the U.S.? Unpublished paper, Sloan School of Management, Massachusetts Institute of Technology.

Kolberg, W.H., and F.C. Smith
    1992   *Rebuilding America's Workforce: Business Strategies to Close the Competitive Gap.* Homewood, Ill.: Business One Irwin.

Lad, L.J.
    1992   *Current Principles and Practices in Association Self-Regulation.* Washington, D.C.: American Society for Association Executives.

Lalonde, R., and R. Maynard
    1987   How precise are evaluations of employment and training programs: evidence from a field experiment. *Evaluation Review* 11(4):428-451.

Lane, J.
    1992a   Summary of Workforce Preparation Program and Policies International Comparison. Paper prepared for the Committee on Postsecondary Education and Training for the Workplace, Commission on Behavioral and Social Sciences and Education. Department of Economics, American University.
    1992b   Summary of Young People's Pathways into Work: International Comparison. Paper prepared for the Committee on Postsecondary Education and Training for the Workplace, Commission on Behavioral and Social Sciences and Education. Department of Economics, American University.

Lee, J., and J.P. Merisotis
    1990   *Proprietary Schools: Programs, Policies, and Prospects.* ASHE-ERIC Higher Education Report 5. Washington, D.C.: George Washington University.

Levitan, S.A., and F. Gallo
    1988   *A Second Chance: Training for Jobs.* Kalamazoo, Mich.: W.E. Upjohn Institute for Employment Research.

Levy, F., and R. Michel
    1991   *The Economic Future of American Families: Income and Wealth Trends.* Washington, D.C.: The Urban Institute Press.

Levy, F., and R. Murnane
    1992   U.S. earnings levels and earnings inequality: a review of recent trends

and proposed explanations. *Journal of Economic Literature* 30(3):1333-1381.

Lyke, R., T. Gabe, and S.R. Aleman
   1991   *Early Labor Market Experiences of Proprietary School Students.* Congressional Research Service. Washington, D.C.: U.S. Government Printing Office.

Lynch, L.M.
   1991   Private sector training and skill formation in the United States. Pp. 117-145 in G. Libecap, ed., *Advances in the Study of Entrepreneurship, Innovation, and Economic Growth*, Vol. 5. Greenwich, Conn: JAI Press.
   1992   Private-sector training and the earnings of young workers. *American Economic Review* 82(1):299-313.
   1993   Payoffs to Alternative Training Strategies at Work. Paper prepared for the Working Under Different Rules Conference sponsored by the National Bureau of Economic Research, Inc. Washington, D.C., May 7.
   1994   *Training and the Private Sector: International Comparisons.* Chicago: University of Chicago Press.

Mangum, S.L., and D.E. Ball
   1987   Military skill training: some evidence of transferability. *Armed Forces and Society* 13 (3):425-441.

Mangum, S., G. Mangum, and G. Hansen
   1990   Assessing the returns to training. Pp. 55-89 in L.A. Ferman, M. Hoyman, J. Cutcher-Gershenfeld, and E.J. Savoie, eds., *New Developments in Worker Training: A Legacy for the 1990s*. Madison, Wis.: Industrial Relations Research Association.

Manpower Demonstration Research Corporation
   1980   *Summary and Findings of the National Supported Work Demonstration.* Cambridge, Mass.: Ballinger Publishing.

Manski, C.F.
   1989   Schooling as experimentation: a reappraisal of the postsecondary dropout phenomenon. *Economics of Education Review* 8(4):305-312.

Manski, C.F., and I. Garfinkel, eds.
   1992   *Evaluating Welfare and Training Programs.* Cambridge, Mass.: Harvard University Press.

Marshall, R., and M. Tucker
   1992   *Thinking for a Living: Work, Skills, and the Future of the American Economy.* New York: Basic Books.

McDonnell, L., and R. Elmore
   1987   Getting the job done: alternative policy instruments. *Education Evaluation and Policy Analysis* 9(2):133-152.

McKean, R.
   1980   Enforcement costs in environmental and safety regulation. *Policy Analysis* 6(3):269-287.

McPherson, M.S., and M.O. Schapiro
   1991   *Keeping College Affordable: Government and Educational Opportunity.* Washington, D.C.: The Brookings Institution.

Mikulecky, L.
   1989   Second chance basic skills education. Pp. 215-258 in Commission on Workforce Quality and Labor Market Efficiency, *Investing in People: A Strategy to Address America's Workforce Crisis*, Vol. 1. Washington, D.C.: U.S. Department of Labor.

Mishel, L., and R. Teixeira
   1991   *The Myth of the Coming Labor Shortage: Jobs, Skills, and Incomes of America's Workforce 2000*. Washington, D.C.: Economic Policy Institute.

Murnane, R.J., and F. Levy
   1992   Education and training. Pp. 185-222 in H.J. Aaron and C.L. Schultze, eds., *Setting Domestic Priorities: What Can Government Do?* Washington, D.C.: The Brookings Institution.

Murphy, K., and F. Welch
   1993   Occupational change and the demand for skill: 1940-1990. Pp. 122-126 in Papers and Proceedings of the Hundred and Fifth Annual Meeting of the American Economic Association. *American Economic Review* 83(2):122-126.

Nathan, R.P.
   1990   Federalism—the great "composition." Pp. 231-332 in A. King, ed., *The New American Political System*, 2nd ed. Washington, D.C.: American Enterprise Institute.
   1993   *Turning Promises into Performance: The Management Challenge of Implementing Workfare*. New York: Columbia University Press.

National Academy of Engineering
   1993   *Mastering a New Role: Shaping Technology Policy for National Economic Performance*. Washington, D.C.: National Academy Press.

National Alliance of Business
   1992   *Building a Workforce Investment System for America*. Washington, D.C.: National Alliance of Business.

National Assessment of Vocational Education
   1989a   *Summary of Findings and Recommendations*, Final report, Vol. I. Washington, D.C.: U.S. Department of Education.
   1989b   *Postsecondary Vocational Education*. Final Report, Vol. IV. Washington, D.C.: U.S. Department of Education.

National Board of Employment, Education and Training
   1991   *Progress and Prospects in Improved Skills Recognition*. Canberra: Australian Government Publishing Service.

National Center for Education Statistics
   1992a   *Methodology Report for the 1990 National Postsecondary Student Aid Study*. Washington, D.C.: U.S. Department of Education.
   1992b   *National Postsecondary Statistics, Collegiate and Noncollegiate: Fall 1991*. Washington, D.C.: U.S. Department of Education.
   1992c   *Digest of Education Statistics 1992*. Washington, D.C.: U.S. Department of Education.
   1992d   *Current Funds Revenues and Expenditures of Institutions of Higher Education:*

Fiscal Years 1982-1990. Washington, D.C.: U.S. Department of Education.

National Commission for Employment Policy

1991a   *Assisting Dislocated Workers.* Washington, D.C.: National Commission for Employment Policy.

1991b   *Coordinating Federal Assistance Programs for the Economically Disadvantaged: Recommendations and Background Materials.* Special Report No. 31, October, Washington, D.C.: National Commission for Employment Policy.

1992   *Using Unemployment Insurance Wage-Record Data for JTPA Performance Management.* Washington, D.C.: National Commission for Employment Policy.

National Commission on Excellence in Education

1983   *A Nation at Risk: The Imperative for Educational Reform.* Washington, D.C.: U.S. Government Printing Office.

National Commission on the State and Local Public Service

1993   *Hard Truths/Tough Choices: An Agenda for State and Local Reform.* Albany, N.Y.: Rockefeller Institute of Government.

National Council for Vocational Qualifications

1993   General National Vocational Qualifications, April 1993. NCVQ Information Note. London, England.

National Council of Teachers of Mathematics

1989   *Curriculum and Evaluation Standards for School Mathematics.* Reston, Va.: National Council of Teachers of Mathematics.

National Governors' Association

n.d.   *Human Resource Investment Councils.* Washington, D.C.: National Governors' Association, Center for Policy Research and Analysis.

1991   *Streamlining and Integrating Human Resource Development Services for Adults.* Washington, D.C.: National Governors' Association, Center for Policy Research and Analysis.

1992   *Enhancing Skills for a Competitive World.* Report of the Action Team on Lifelong Learning. Washington, D.C.: National Governors' Association.

National Research Council

1993   *Losing Generations: Adolescents in High-Risk Settings.* Panel on High Risk Youth, Commission on Behavioral and Social Sciences and Education, National Research Council. Washington, D.C.: National Academy Press.

1993   *Learning to Change: Opportunities to Improve the Performance of Smaller Manufacturers.* Committee to Assess Barriers and Opportunities to Improve Manufacturing at Small and Medium-Sized Companies, Manufacturing Studies Board, Commission on Engineering and Technical Systems. Washington, D.C.: National Academy Press.

Office of Vocational and Adult Education

1991   *Adult Education Act: 1966-1991.* Washington, D.C.: U.S. Department of Education.

Olson, K.W.
  1974   *The G.I. Bill, the Veterans, and the Colleges.* Lexington: The University Press of Kentucky.
Olson, L., L. Berg, and A. Conrad
  1990   High Job Turnover Among the Urban Poor: The Project Match Experience. Unpublished paper, Center for Urban Affairs and Policy Research, Northwestern University.
Organisation for Economic Co-operation and Development
  1989   *Pathways for Learning: Education and Training from 16 to 19.* Paris: Organisation for Economic Co-operation and Development.
  1993   *Employment Outlook.* Paris: Organisation for Economic Co-operation and Development.
Osborne, D.
  1990   *Laboratories of Democracy.* Boston: Harvard Business School Press.
Osborne, D., and T. Gaebler
  1992   *Reinventing Government: How the Entrepreneurial Spirit is Transforming the Public Sector.* Reading, Mass.: Addison-Wesley.
Osterman, P.
  1988   *Employment Futures: Reorganization, Dislocation, and Public Policy.* New York: Oxford University Press.
  1990   Elements of a national training policy. Pp. 257-281 in L.A. Ferman, M. Hoyman, J. Cutcher-Gershenfeld, and E.J. Savoie, eds., *New Developments in Worker Training: A Legacy for the 1990s.* Madison, Wis.: Industrial Relations Research Association.
  1993   How Common is Workplace Transformation and How Can We Explain Who Adopts It? Unpublished paper, Sloan School, Massachusetts Institute of Technology.
Pavetti, L.
  1992   The Dynamics of Welfare and Work: Exploring the Process by Which Young Women Work Their Way Off Welfare. Paper presented at the Annual Research Conference of the Association for Public Policy Analysis and Management, Denver, October 29.
Pines, M.
  1992   The devil is in the details. Pp. 30-31 in National Youth Employment Coalition, *Making Sense of Federal Job Training Policy.* Washington, D.C.: National Youth Employment Coalition and William T. Grant Foundation Commission on Youth and America's Future.
Porter, M.E.
  1990   *The Competitive Advantage of Nations.* New York: The Free Press.
Puma, M., N.R. Burstein, K. Merrill, and G. Silverstein
  1990   *Evaluation of the Food Stamp Employment and Training Program.* Bethesda, Md.: Abt Associates Inc.
Quigley, J., and E. Smolensky
  1989   The tax treatment of training and educational expenses. Pp. 803-850 in Commission on Workforce Quality and Labor Market Efficiency, *Investing in People: A Strategy to Address America's Workforce Crisis*, Vol. 1. Washington, D.C.: U.S. Department of Labor.

Rauberger, T.K.
   1992a   International Comparison of Workforce Preparation Programs and Poli-
           cies. Paper prepared for the Committee on Postsecondary Education and
           Training for the Workplace, Commission on Behavioral and Social Sci-
           ences and Education. Universitat Luneburg, Germany.
   1992b   Young People's Pathway into Work: International Comparison. Paper
           prepared for the Committee on Postsecondary Education and Training
           for the Workplace, Commission on Behavioral and Social Sciences and
           Education. Universitat Luneburg, Germany.
Riccio, J., B. Goldman, G. Hamilton, K. Martinson, and A. Orenstein
   1989   *GAIN: Early Implementation Experiences and Lessons.* New York:
           Manpower Demonstration Research Corporation.
Rivlin, A.M.
   1992   *Reviving the American Dream: The Economy, the States, and the Fed-
           eral Government.* Washington, D.C.: The Brookings Institution.
Rogers, J., and W. Streeck
   1993   Workplace Representation Overseas: The Works Councils Story. Paper
           prepared for the Working Under Different Rules Conference sponsored
           by the National Bureau of Economic Research, Inc. Washington, D.C.,
           May 7.
Rosenbaum, J., and T. Kariya
   1989   From high school to work: market and institutional mechanisms in Ja-
           pan. *American Journal of Sociology* 94(6):1334-1365.
   1992a   International Comparison: Postsecondary Education and Pathways to
           Work in Japan. Paper prepared for the Committee on Postsecondary
           Education and Training for the Workplace, Commission on Behavioral
           and Social Sciences and Education. Northwestern University.
   1992b   Youths' Pathways into Work in Japan. Paper prepared for the Commit-
           tee on Postsecondary Education and Training for the Workplace, Com-
           mission on Behavioral and Social Sciences and Education. Northwest-
           ern University.
Rosenbaum, J.E., D. Stern, M.A., S.F. Hamilton, S.E. Berryman, and R. Kazis
   1992   *Youth Apprenticeship in America: Guidelines for Building an Effective
           System.* Washington, D.C.: William T. Grant Foundation Commission
           on Youth and America's Future.
Sandell, S.H., and K. Rupp
   1988   *Who Is Served in JTPA Programs: Patterns of Participation and Inter-
           group Equity.* Washington, D.C.: National Commission for Employ-
           ment Policy.
Savas, E.S.
   1987   *Privatization: The Key to Better Government.* Chatham, N.J.: Chatham
           House Publishers, Inc.
Scribner, S., and P. Sachs
   1990   *A Study of On-The-Job Training.* New York: Institute on Education and
           the Economy, Teachers College, Columbia University.

1991 *Knowledge Acquisition at Work.* New York: Institute on Education and the Economy, Teachers College, Columbia University.
Secretary's Commission on Achieving Necessary Skills (SCANS)
1991 *What Work Requires of Schools.* Washington, D.C.: U.S. Department of Labor.
Shannon, J., and J.E. Kee
1989 The rise of competitive federalism. *Public Budgeting and Finance* 9(4):5-20.
Soskice, D.
1994 Reconciling markets and institutions: the German apprenticeship system. In L. Lynch, ed., *Training and the Private Sector: International Comparisons.* Chicago: University of Chicago Press.
State Higher Education Executive Officers
1991 *The Methods and Effectiveness of State Licensing of Proprietary Institutions.* Denver, Colorado: State Higher Education Executive Officers.
Stern, D., and J. Ritzen, eds.
1991 *Market Failure in Training? New Economic Analysis and Evidence on Training of Adult Employees.* Berlin: Springer-Verlag.
Stevenson, H.
1992 Learning from Asian schools. *Scientific American* 9(4):5-20.
Stigler, G.
1971 The theory of economic regulation. *Bell Journal of Economics and Management Science* 2(1):1-21.
Topel, R.H., and M.P. Ward
1992 Job mobility and the careers of young men. *Quarterly Journal of Economics* 107(2):439-79.
Tuma, J.
1992 Patterns of Enrollment in Postsecondary Vocational and Academic Education. Unpublished draft paper prepared for the National Assessment of Vocational Education, Washington, D.C.
U.S. Congress
1992 *1992 Green Book.* Committee on Ways and Means, House of Representatives. Washington, D.C.: U.S. Government Printing Office.
U.S. Department of Defense
1991 *Military Manpower Training Report for FY 1992.* Washington, D.C.: U.S. Department of Defense.
U.S. Department of Education
1988 IPEDS History and Background. September. U.S. Department of Education, Washington, D.C.
1990a *Guaranteed Student Loan Programs Data Book.* Washington, D.C.: U.S. Department of Education.
1990b *Annual Evaluation Report.* Washington, D.C.: U.S. Department of Education.
1991 *Annual Report to the President and to the Congress Fiscal Year 1991 on the Federal Activities Related to the Rehabilitation Act of 1973 as Amended.* Washington, D.C.: U.S. Department of Education.

1992 *National Evaluation of Adult Education Programs: First Interim Report.* Office of Policy and Planning. Washington, D.C.: U.S. Department of Education.

U.S. Department of Labor

1992 Classroom training providers FY 1990. Pp. 4-10 in *JTPA Program Highlights: Data from the Job Training Quarterly Survey.* Washington, D.C.: U.S. Department of Labor.

1993 JTPA Title IIA and III enrollments and terminations during program year 1991 (July 1991-June 1992) *Job Training Quarterly Survey.* Division of Performance Management and Evaluation. Washington, D.C.: U.S. Department of Labor.

U.S. General Accounting Office

1988 *Defaulted Student Loans: Preliminary Analysis of Student Loan Borrowers and Defaulters.* Washington, D.C.: U.S. Government Printing Office.

1990a *Defaulted Student Loans: Analysis of Defaulted Borrowers at Schools Accredited by Seven Agencies.* Washington, D.C.: U.S. Government Printing Office.

1990b *Training Strategies: Preparing Noncollege Youth for Employment in the U.S. and Foreign Countries.* GAO/HRD-90-88. Washington, D.C.: U.S. Government Printing Office.

1991 *Transition from School to Work: Linking Education and Worksite Training.* GAO/HRD-91-105. Washington, D.C.: U.S. Government Printing Office.

1992a *Apprenticeship Training: Administration, Use, and Equal Opportunity.* GAO/HRD-92-43. Washington, D.C.: U.S. Government Printing Office.

1992b *Dislocated Workers: Comparison of Assistance Programs.* GAO/HRD-92- 153BR. Washington, D.C.: U.S. Government Printing Office.

1992c *Dislocated Workers: Improvements Needed in Trade Adjustment Assistance Certification Process.* GAO/HRD-93-36. Washington, D.C.: U.S. Government Printing Office.

1992d Multiple Employment Programs. BAO/HRD-92R. Letter Report to Senator Edward M. Kennedy, July 24, 1992.

1992e *Welfare to Work: States Serve Least Job-Ready While Meeting JOBS Participation Rates.* GAO/HRD-93-2. Washington, D.C.: U.S. Government Printing Office.

U.S. Office of Management and Budget

1984 *Report to Congress: Joint Funding Simplification Act.* Report accompanying February 8, 1984 letter from OMB Director David Stockman to the Honorable Theodore S. Weiss, chairman of the Subcommittee on Intergovernmental Relations and Human Resources, Committee on Government Operations, U.S. House of Representatives. Washington, D.C.: U.S. Government Printing Office.

U.S. Office of Technology Assessment

1990 *Worker Training: Competing in the New International Economy.* OTA-ITE-457. Washington, D.C.: U.S. Government Printing Office.

U.S. President
  1992   *Economic Report of the President.* Washington, D.C.: U.S. Government Printing Office.
U.S. Senate, Committee on Governmental Affairs
  1991   *Abuses in Federal Student Aid Programs.* Report prepared by the Permanent Subcommittee on Investigations. Washington, D.C.: U.S. Government Printing Office.
Venn, G.
  1964   *Man, Education, and Work: Postsecondary Vocational and Technical Education.* Washington, D.C.: American Council on Education.
Vickers, M.
  1991   *Building a National System for School-to-Work Transition: Lessons from Britain and Australia.* Somerville, Mass.: Jobs for the Future.
  1992   Workforce Preparation Programs and Policies in Australia. Paper prepared for the Committee on Postsecondary Education and Training for the Workplace, Commission on Behavioral and Social Sciences and Education. Graduate School of Education, Harvard University.
Weimer, D.L., and A.R. Vining
  1989   *Policy Analysis: Concepts and Practice.* Englewood Cliffs, N.J.: Prentice Hall.
Weiss, A.
  1994   Productivity changes associated with learning by doing. In L. Lynch, ed., *Training and the Private Sector: International Comparisons.* Chicago: University of Chicago Press.
Wilson, J.Q.
  1989   *Bureaucracy: What Government Agencies Do and Why They Do It.* New York: Basic Books, Inc.
Wiseman, M., P.L. Szanton, E.B. Baum, R. Haskins, D.H. Greenberg, and M.B. Mandell
  1991   Research and policy: a symposium on the Family Support Act of 1988. *Journal of Policy Analysis and Management* 10(4):588-666.
Zeckhauser, R., and W.K. Viscusi
  1979   Optimal standards with incomplete enforcement. *Public Policy* 27(4):437-456.

APPENDIX

Biographical Sketches of Committee Members and Staff

RICHARD P. NATHAN is professor of political science and public policy and serves as director of the Nelson A. Rockefeller Institute of Government and provost of the Rockefeller College of Public Affairs and Policy, State University of New York in Albany. His previous positions include professor of public and international affairs at Princeton University and senior fellow at The Brookings Institution. His government service includes associate director for the National Commission on Civil Disorders (Kerner Commission), assistant director for the U.S. Office of Management and Budget, and Deputy Undersecretary for Welfare Reform of the U.S. Department of Health, Education, and Welfare. His publications include *Turning Promises Into Performance* (Columbia University Press, 1993); *The Administrative Presidency* (MacMillan, 1983); *Reagan and the States* (Princeton University Press, 1987); and *Social Sciences in Government* (Basic Books, 1988).

SUE E. BERRYMAN is an education specialist with The World Bank in Washington, D.C., where she provides technical expertise for the Bank's human capital work in the Middle East, North Africa, Eastern Europe, and the former countries of the Soviet Union. Her most recent publication, co-authored with Thomas R. Bailey, is *The Double Helix of Education and the Economy*. Previously she directed the Institute on Education and the Economy at Teachers College, Columbia University; was a behavioral scientist with The RAND Corporation; was a faculty member at the University of Minnesota; worked as a research associate in the director's division of the Oak Ridge National Laboratory; and taught at the Harvard Business School. She received a magna cum laude B.A. degree from Pomona College, undertook graduate training in anthropology at the University of Pennsylvania, and received a Ph.D. degree from the Social Relations Department at Johns Hopkins University.

BERNARD L. CHARLES is a senior executive with The McKenzie Group. Formerly, he was senior vice president of Quality Education for Minorities (QEM) Network. Prior to that position, he served as senior program officer for the Carnegie Corporation of New York, where he directed a multimillion dollar national program to increase the representation of African Americans, Hispanics, Native Americans, women, and persons with disabilities in science, mathematics, and engineering fields. He was formerly dean of Academic Affairs and professor and chair of the Department of Urban Teacher Education for Livingston College, Rutgers University, and was also coordinator of the master plan for City University of New York. He has taught and lectured at numerous universities, including the University of Cape Town in South Africa, and the University of Cape Coast in Ghana. He received a B.S. degree from Fisk University and an M.S. degree from Yeshiva University in New York City.

ROBERT C. FORNEY is a retired executive vice president, member of the board of directors, and member of the executive committee of E.I. du Pont de Nemours & Company. During his almost 40-year career with du Pont, he held a wide variety of research, manufacturing, engineering, marketing, and general management positions. He is a member of the National Academy of Engineering and serves on the board of several for-profit and not-for-profit organizations. Dr. Forney received B.S. and Ph.D. degrees in chemical engineering and an M.S. degree in industrial engineering from Purdue University.

RICHARD B. FREEMAN is program director of the National Bureau of Economic Research's Program in Labor Studies, professor of economics at Harvard University, and executive program director of the Comparative Labor Market Institutions Program at the London School of Economics' Centre for Economic Performance. He is currently a member of The Secretaries of Labor and Commerce Commission on The Future of Worker Management Relations. He is also serving as chair of the International Experts's Commission on the Social Costs of Transition in Eastern Europe, a program organized by the Institute for Human Sciences in Austria. Previously, he taught at the University of Chicago and Yale University. His research interests include youth labor market problems, higher education, trade unionism, high-skilled labor markets, economic discrimination, social mobility, income distribution, and equity in the marketplace. He received a Ph.D. degree from Harvard University.

EVELYN GANZGLASS is policy studies director for employment and social services at the National Governors' Association. She has more than 25
years' experience in developing and implementing new ideas in the fields of
work force development, youth, adult literacy, and welfare reform policy.
The focus of much of this activity has been on strengthening connections
among employment and training, education, economic development, and
social service policies and programs. She formerly worked at the U.S.
Department of Labor.

W. NORTON GRUBB is professor at the School of Education, University
of California, Berkeley. His research interests include the role of schooling
in labor markets, the flows of students into and through postsecondary education, the interactions among education and training programs, community
colleges, and social policy toward children and youth. He is also a site
director for the National Center for Research in Vocational Education, which
has supported some of his research on education and job training programs.
He received a Ph.D. degree in economics from Harvard University.

JUDITH M. GUERON is president of the Manpower Demonstration Research Corporation (MDRC). Since the creation of MDRC, she has worked
to provide policy makers and practioners with reliable evidence on the effectiveness of alternative public policies aimed at improving the well-being
of disadvantaged adults and youths. To do this, she has pioneered the use
of social experiments to field-test welfare reform and employment and training
programs. She was awarded the 1988 Myrdal Prize for Evaluation Practice
from the American Evaluation Association. She received a Ph.D. degree in
economics from Harvard University.

G. PHILLIPS HANNA retired in 1987 from the position of chief of the
Labor Branch in the U.S. Office of Management and Budget, where he
directed the staff responsible for analyzing and presenting recommendations
on the design, operation, management, budget, accomplishment, and effectiveness of government labor programs, including employment and training.
While in that position, he received the Rogers W. Jones Award for executive
leadership by the American University and the rank of distinguished executive in the Senior Executive Service by the President of the United States.
He received an M.A. degree in political science from Princeton University.

JANET S. HANSEN became the study director for the Committee on
Postsecondary Education and Training for the Workplace after serving for a
year as a committee member. Previously, she was a policy analyst at the
College Board, focusing on issues relating to higher education finance, federal and state student assistance programs, and how families pay for col-

lege, and she served as the Board's director for policy analysis from 1984 to 1991. She also served as Director for Continuing Education and Associate Provost at the Claremont Colleges and as Assistant Dean of the College at Princeton University. She received a Ph.D. degree in public and international affairs from Princeton.

MARY ALLEN JOLLEY is director of the Office of Economic and Community Affairs and assistant to the president of the University of Alabama. She formerly worked as a staff member for the Committee on Education and Labor, U.S. House of Representatives, developing education policy. She also worked as public affairs director for two national associations and served as vice president for development of a community college in Charleston, South Carolina. In her current position she links the resources of the University of Alabama to economic growth and development guided by the university's strategic plan that has been developed cooperatively with the state and local communities. She received a B.S. degree from the University of Alabama.

ROBERT I. LERMAN is professor of economics and chair of the Department of Economics at the American University. He has written widely on poverty and welfare programs, child support issues, youth employment programs and patterns, family formation patterns of young people, young unwed fathers, and on the case for youth apprenticeship programs. He has also worked directly on welfare and employment policy issues for the Congressional Joint Economic Committee and the U.S. Department of Labor. Dr. Lerman received an A.B. degree from Brandeis University and a Ph.D. degree from Massachusetts Institute of Technology.

DAVID A. LONGANECKER, who resigned from the committee on May 10, 1993, when he became Assistant Secretary for Postsecondary Education, U.S. Department of Education, was until then the executive director of the Colorado Commission on Higher Education. In that capacity he also served as executive director of the Department of Higher Education and as an officer of the Governor's cabinet. Prior to his position in Colorado, he was at the Minnesota Higher Education Coordinating Board, first as deputy executive director, then as executive director. His prior positions also include adjunct faculty member of the University of Minnesota College of Education and principal analyst for postsecondary education and chief of the education and employment unit within the Human Resources Policy Unit of the Congressional Budget Office. He received a Ph.D. degree in administration and policy analysis in higher education from Stanford University.

MICHAEL McPHERSON is professor of economics and chair of the Department of Economics at Williams College. His research interests include economics of higher education, policy formation and implementation, and economics and moral philosophy. He is coeditor of the book *Economics and Philosophy*. He received a Ph.D. degree in economics from the University of Chicago.

LARRY L. ORR, a senior economist with Abt Associates, Inc., is the project director for the National JTPA Study and is on the editorial board for the report *Evaluation and Program Planning*. He was formerly director, Office of Income Security Policy Research, U.S. Department of Health, Education, and Welfare, and director, Office of Technical Analysis, U.S. Department of Labor. His research interests include analysis of public policy issues using experimental methods and effects of employment and training programs. He received a Ph.D. degree from Massachusetts Institute of Technology.

FRANKLIN D. RAINES is vice chairman of Federal National Mortgage Association (Fannie Mae). In that capacity he is in charge of Fannie Mae's legal, credit policy, finance, and corporate development functions. Prior to joining Fannie Mae he was a general partner in municipal finance at the investment banking firm of Lazard Freres. He received a B.A. degree in government from Harvard College and a J.D. degree from Oxford University as a Rhodes Scholar.

JOAN L. WILLS is director, Center for Workforce Development, Institute for Educational Leadership in Washington, D.C. She has served on several boards and commissions, including a presidential appointment to the Commission for Employment and Unemployment Statistics. She has been a member of the American Council on Education's Commission on Education Credit and Credentials, the Development Training Institute, the National Job Training Partnership, Youthwork, Inc. and National Child Labor Committee. She is a board member of the Corporation for Enterprise Development and several advisory panels, including the Council of Chief State School Officers, Aspen Institute, the U.S. Office of Technology Assessment, and the Organisation for Economic Co-operation and Development. She serves as a senior scholar for the National Center on the Educational Quality of the Workforce funded by the U.S. Department of Education, housed at the University of Pennsylvania. She received an M.S.W. degree from the Ohio State University.

Index